WHAT A BLOODY
AWFUL COUNTRY

KEVIN MEAGHER

WHAT A BLOODY AWFUL COUNTRY

NORTHERN IRELAND'S CENTURY OF DIVISION

Biteback Publishing

First published in Great Britain in 2021 by
Biteback Publishing Ltd, London
Copyright © Kevin Meagher 2021

Kevin Meagher has asserted his right under the Copyright, Designs and Patents Act 1988
to be identified as the author of this work.

ISBN 978-1-78590-666-4

10 9 8 7 6 5 4 3 2 1

A CIP catalogue record for this book is available from the British Library.

Set in Adobe Caslon Pro and Trade Gothic

Printed and bound in Great Britain by
CPI Group (UK) Ltd, Croydon CR0 4YY

MIX
Paper from
responsible sources
FSC
www.fsc.org
FSC® C020471

To the people of Northern Ireland.
In the full expectation that a better century awaits.

CONTENTS

LIST OF ABBREVIATIONS

B-Specials – Ulster Special Constabulary

INLA – Irish National Liberation Army

IRA – Irish Republican Army

NICRA – Northern Ireland Civil Rights Association

NILP – Northern Ireland Labour Party

RHI – Renewable Heating Incentive

RUC – Royal Ulster Constabulary

SDLP – Social Democratic and Labour Party

UDA – Ulster Defence Association

UDR – Ulster Defence Regiment

UFF – Ulster Freedom Fighters

UUP – Ulster Unionist Party

UVF – Ulster Volunteer Force

INTRODUCTION

There are already lots of books about Northern Ireland and, I dare say, a few more will be published about its centenary to add to the groaning bookshelves. Historians, political scientists, journalists, activists and even participants in the country's thirty-year 'Troubles' have all had their say. For a place where political dialogue has often been lacking, there is no shortage of brilliant and insightful writing already out there, covering every twist and turn of the past century. Rather than re-tread the footsteps of so many eminent chroniclers of Northern Ireland's past, what I have attempted to do in this book is highlight some of the significant events as I see them, particularly from the British point of view. I will explore the missed signals, the turning points, the principled decisions that, at various stages, should have been taken, as well as the raw realpolitik of how Northern Ireland was governed over the past 100 years.

As I see it, there are three key viewpoints that are worthy of examination. First, the Unionists. They oversaw Northern Ireland, uninterrupted, for fifty years, from 1921 until 1972; at which point, Northern Ireland's idiosyncratic experiment with devolution was curtailed. The place was created in their image to lock in a Protestant–Unionist hegemony. They circled the waggons early on and froze the Catholic minority out. But what might they have done differently, in, say, responding more imaginatively to the civil rights movement of the mid- to late 1960s, which was trying to get a fair deal for Catholics? Why have Unionists failed time after time to initiate a dialogue – to stretch out the hand to Catholic–Nationalists – and by doing so, try to create a level playing field that might have helped head off demands for Irish unity and thus secure the long-term future of the Union? What more could mainstream Unionism have done in facing down the threat from within – namely the rank sectarianism of Loyalists – whipped up by Ian Paisley during that time?

I am also interested in the tactics used by Nationalists and Republicans. How might they have played their cards differently? Could they have been more adept at navigating Unionist politics in the 1960s, better utilising the window of opportunity represented by Prime Minister Terence O'Neill and his attempt to steer the Unionist state in a more moderate direction? Might peaceful, direct action have ultimately been more fruitful than armed resistance and shortened the Troubles, or avoided them altogether? Could Nationalists have channelled their initial advantage, in terms of occupying the moral high ground in the face of Stormont's aggression towards them, into real political influence, rather than allowing the civil rights effort to dissipate, superseded, as it was, by violence?

Ultimately, however, I am concerned with the approach taken

by successive British governments, particularly during the three decades of conflict from the late 1960s until the signing of the Good Friday Agreement in 1998. History did not end there, but it is a useful bookmark in approaching British policy, as it represented a clear switch of emphasis away from majoring on security considerations, in favour of developing a lasting political settlement. As a student of British policy in Northern Ireland, I remain frustrated and even appalled at many of the decisions taken by ministers over the years. Indeed, it is an area of politics that has escaped forensic examination by British journalists and academics. Why was Westminster content to allow Northern Ireland to be run 'off the books' for half a century, facilitating majority Unionist rule and the creation of a manifestly unfair and discriminatory society? Why did the British government not react faster and more decisively in supporting the demand for civil rights and ensuring Stormont acceded to them? Why did ministers allow themselves to be dragged into political quicksand by trying to defeat Irish Republicanism by military means? How did they end up sponsoring Loyalist terror gangs as they waged a relentless campaign of sectarian murder against Catholic civilians? Governments always bear culpability – both for what they do and for what they fail to do.

There are sins of commission and omission in later chapters of the country's story that bear far greater public debate than they have so far received. The affairs of Northern Ireland, visceral though they are, largely remain poorly understood and have barely registered in British politics. The Troubles may have stretched across nine parliaments and six premierships, encompassing twenty-two Secretaries of State for Northern Ireland, along with innumerable junior ministers and their shadows (not to mention the 300,000 British servicemen and women who served there), but, throughout, the country remained a place apart, remote both in proximity to the rest of the United Kingdom and the affections of the British public.

There was a long period after partition had bedded in when little happened, only for dramatic events to suddenly flash across front pages from the mid-1960s onwards. Irish history abides by Lenin's maxim that in politics there can be decades where nothing happens and then weeks where decades happen. Between 1798 and 1803, for instance, there were two attempts at ending British rule in Ireland by force. First, by the United Irishmen, and five years later by a young nobleman, Robert Emmet. The leaders of both rebellions were executed for their trouble (what makes these events doubly significant is that they were led by Protestants). Again, between 1916 and 1921 Ireland went from the Easter Rising, through the War of Independence, to a point which saw Britain forced to retreat from twenty-six of Ireland's thirty-two counties and eventually negotiate a deal which created the Irish Free State and Northern Ireland.

History just seems to matter more to the Irish than the British (perhaps this is a result of the subjugated having a keener recollection than that of the subjugator). Both Nationalists and Unionists draw strength from the tales of their forebears. The memory of sacrifice and suffering bleeds into the present day as a warning for contemporary politicians on both sides of the political divide not to sell out their principles. All this is poorly understood in Westminster and helps explain many of the missed signals. When Martin McGuinness first visited Downing Street for a meeting with Tony Blair, he was shown into the Cabinet Room, remarking: 'So this is where all the damage was done.' Blair's chief of staff, Jonathan Powell, the key British negotiator of the Good Friday Agreement, assumed McGuinness was referring to the Irish Republican Army (IRA) mortar attack on John Major's Cabinet in 1991, which blew out the windows and forced ministers to duck under the table. Of course, McGuinness was referring to events seventy years earlier when Michael Collins and the Irish plenipotentiaries negotiated the deal that led to the creation of the Irish Free State and the partition of the country.

The period between 1964 and 1969 set the seal on the Troubles. It saw the birth of the civil rights movement, infused, as it was, with the optimism of non-violent direct action, imported wholesale from the United States. Those fresh-faced students singing 'We Shall Overcome' would find out the hard way about Stormont's unyielding nature when they were bludgeoned off the streets during a protest march in Derry in October 1968, courtesy of the Royal Ulster Constabulary's (RUC's) part-time reservists, the Ulster Special Constabulary (the notorious 'B-Specials'). Footage of the assault was broadcast around the world, although much, much worse was to come over the next five years.

In August 1969, British soldiers were sent in at Stormont's request following a wave of Loyalist violence against Catholics. In hindsight, it is plain to see that this deployment exacerbated the conflict, but, from the perspective of the time, the move was initially welcomed by besieged Catholic communities who were facing an onslaught from Loyalist mobs that were furious at moderate concessions being forced upon Northern Ireland by Westminster. Ian Paisley was instrumental in whipping up the frenzy. At the time he was just a rabble-rousing evangelical minister, but his later impact during the 1970s and 1980s would help define the Troubles. And by 'define' I mean intensify. The period between 1969 and 1974 was critical. Any hope of retrieving the situation and finding a durable political settlement was lost in those initial five years of the Troubles.

In 1970, the Social Democratic and Labour Party (SDLP) was formed, drawing together leading lights of the civil rights movement to represent moderate Nationalist opinion. A year later, Paisley launched the Democratic Unionist Party as a bulwark against what he regarded as the sell-outs of mainstream Unionism. For the next thirty years he would act as a ratchet, pulling Unionist politics sharply rightwards with the sheer brute force of his rhetoric and personality. In August 1971, internment without trial was introduced. Applied in a partisan way, it saw hundreds of innocent Catholics dragged from their homes and jailed in a Second World War-era prisoner-of-war camp and an old prison ship docked in Belfast Harbour. To Nationalists, the British Army was now simply an adjunct to the Stormont regime. In the immediate aftermath of internment, seventeen people were killed by the British Army, including a Catholic priest who was giving the last rites to a dying man in the Ballymurphy area of Belfast.

Things then deteriorated further. A protest march against internment in Derry in January 1972 saw twenty-seven people shot when British paratroopers opened fire. Thirteen were killed outright and a fourteenth later died of their injuries. 'Bloody Sunday' would turbo-charge the Troubles, swelling the IRA's ranks and showing the world that Britain had completely lost control. 'Unjustified and unjustifiable' was how Conservative Prime Minister David Cameron would sum up the killings four decades later. That year, 1972, was the single bloodiest year of the Troubles. The sky fell in and any hope of political normality was lost amid the smoke and tear gas. Edward Heath's Conservative government closed Stormont and introduced direct rule from Whitehall. Amid the carnage of the early 1970s, serious attempts were made to divine a political path. The Sunningdale Accord of 1973 promised much, guaranteeing cross-community devolved government for the first time. It collapsed following a wave of strikes by Loyalist workers, who brought Northern Ireland to a standstill and earned a fierce rebuke from British Prime Minister Harold Wilson, who accused Loyalists of being 'spongers on British democracy'.

The period from 1974 until the end of the decade saw a security crackdown and the attempted 'normalisation' of Northern Ireland. The amiable Merlyn Rees, Wilson's Secretary of State, tried to resuscitate power-sharing, but the prospects were now stone-cold dead. Wilson gave way to James Callaghan in 1976 and he appointed the abrasive Roy Mason to the Northern Ireland job. His hard-line approach involved treating Republicans as ordinary criminals, and this led to an escalating campaign of non-compliance that started with them refusing to wear prison uniforms, shivering in their cells during Belfast's cold winters under just their blankets. This escalated into 'dirty protests' where they refused to 'slop out' and smeared excrement on their cell walls. The crackdown was severe, earning Mason the permanent enmity of the IRA, who, he boasted in 1979, were 'weeks away' from defeat. Of course, this was not even the halfway mark in the conflict.

Enter Margaret Thatcher, infamously promising to 'bring harmony where there is discord' on the steps of Downing Street after becoming Prime Minister. Little of the former applied to Northern Ireland. Weeks before she won the general election in May 1979, her close confidant and shadow Northern Ireland Secretary, Airey Neave, was assassinated by a car bomb as he was driving out of Parliament's underground car park. The Irish National Liberation Army (INLA) claimed responsibility; however, mystery has long surrounded Neave's death given his entanglements with the intelligence community. Lurid rumours persist. In August 1979, the IRA murdered Lord Louis Mountbatten and three others (including two children) by blowing up his boat as he holidayed in County Sligo in the Irish Republic. On the very same day, they also killed eighteen British soldiers at Warrenpoint in County Down in a bomb attack. Sixteen of the victims were from the Parachute Regiment, and this was its biggest loss of life since the Second World War.

Thatcher's political inheritance was challenging, to say the least, but the Iron Lady made matters immeasurably worse when it came to handling the Republican hunger strike in 1981. Ten men starved to death for standing up for the principle of not being treated as common criminals in a final escalation of the blanket and dirty protests that had started under the previous Labour government. Thatcher traded on her reputation for steely defiance, and let ten men go to their deaths, but almost immediately relented on their key demands afterwards. As we will see, the hunger strike proved to be a turning point. It demonstrated to Thatcher and Westminster more generally just what 'steely defiance' really meant. It also resulted in Sinn Féin inching the Republican movement towards a twin-track strategy – 'ballot box and Armalite' – capitalising on the outpouring of Nationalist public support for the dead men.

There were further attempts at instituting cross-community devolution by Thatcher's Northern Ireland Secretary, James Prior, but, yet again, these proved fruitless. Bombing and atrocities came and went, with Thatcher herself narrowly surviving assassination in October 1984 during the Conservative Party conference, when a bomb with a long timer, which had previously been left in the Grand Hotel where she and most of her Cabinet were staying, exploded in the early hours. Thirty-four people were injured and five were killed. In the background, Thatcher had been negotiating with the Irish government – partly to improve their joint security response – and out of it sprang the Anglo-Irish Agreement. The treaty's most significant effect was to give the Irish state consultee status in the affairs of Northern Ireland. Unionists were livid and denounced Thatcher for capitulating to a Republican agenda (which was odd given that Sinn Féin opposed the agreement believing it made Irish unity *less* likely). Unionist Members of Parliament resigned en masse and a series of by-elections were triggered. This augmented their grass-roots campaign, which saw tens of thousands take to the streets in opposition to the agreement. As is so often the case, Westminster was largely unmoved, particularly as the Unionists' tactic backfired when they lost one of the by-elections.

Again, the Anglo-Irish Agreement was a turning point that would eventually lead to the Good Friday Agreement. The remainder of the 1980s were brooding and bloody, with a steady stream of murder and destruction on all sides. Buoyed from weapon shipments from Libya, the IRA stepped up its campaign. Loyalists did the same with arms smuggled from South Africa. Meanwhile, the British government's 'dirty war' was in full swing. The SAS were deployed. Allegations then followed of a 'shoot to kill' policy and the use of torture methods against Republicans. And then, darkest of all, came collusion between the security forces and Loyalist paramilitaries.

The measures taken by British ministers to maintain security opened a new front in legal activism as due process became a secondary concern. A Belfast human rights lawyer, Pat Finucane, had successfully appealed several flawed prosecutions, mainly on behalf of Republicans, but his practice had also represented Loyalists. This did not deter Loyalist gunmen, who were working on intelligence provided by a British double agent, from smashing down his front door while he was eating Sunday dinner with his wife and young children and shooting him fourteen times right in front of them. A police investigation and two judge-led reviews agreed that collusion had taken place, making his death a state-sponsored assassination.

By the late 1980s, a secret dialogue began between John Hume, the leader of the Nationalist Social Democratic and Labour Party, and Sinn Féin's president, Gerry Adams. This slow-burning, rolling conversation would eventually lead to the Republican movement embracing an exclusively political track, but not for a few more years. Further proof would be needed that the cause of Irish unity could be delivered without the leverage of armed struggle. Such an indication came in November 1990, when Thatcher's final Northern Ireland Secretary, Peter Brooke, famously remarked that Britain had 'no selfish, strategic or economic interest' in maintaining Northern Ireland and would only do so to safeguard the principle of consent (which stipulated that Northern Ireland would endure if the majority of people living there wished to remain part of the UK).

The early 1990s continued a grim pattern, with both the IRA and the British government recognising that outright military victory over the other was an impossibility, and either side content to test and retest this hypothesis. John Major, who had replaced Margaret Thatcher, began a perfunctory round of talks about establishing a devolved assembly between the four main parties: the Ulster Unionists, the SDLP, the Democratic Unionists and Alliance, but it led nowhere. The real action was taking place elsewhere. Gerry Adams and John Hume resumed their private dialogue, seeking a basis upon which the Republican movement would end its armed campaign and enter the political mainstream. By December 1993, the so-called Hume–Adams Dialogue helped spur the Irish and British governments into issuing a joint concordat that would lay the foundation for an

IRA ceasefire and the beginning, in earnest, of the peace process. Just twelve clauses long, the Downing Street Declaration was nevertheless a milestone and promised to respect the various traditions on the island of Ireland and 'over a period' to build the trust necessary 'to end past divisions, leading to an agreed and peaceful future'.

An IRA ceasefire was announced in August 1994, followed by a similar move by Loyalists in October. By December, Sinn Féin was meeting with the Northern Ireland Office, although British ministers insisted on acts of disarmament before substantive talks could begin. Such a precondition was too much for the IRA and the ceasefire collapsed. Matters were not helped when Major's weakened position in the House of Commons (after losing a series of by-elections) saw him turn to the Ulster Unionists for support. Even during this interregnum, with the IRA launching 'spectacular' bombing attacks on Canary Wharf in London and Manchester City Centre, there was a palpable sense that political moves had advanced too far for the moment to be squandered. The 1997 general election provided the perfect opportunity to reboot the peace process aided by a new British Prime Minister in Labour's Tony Blair – an arch-pragmatist with a huge parliamentary majority. A second IRA ceasefire was called. Blair injected new pace and enthusiasm into proceedings and a series of intense negotiations followed in April 1998 which ran right up to the Easter holidays, culminating in the Belfast Agreement – or, as it is invariably known, the Good Friday Agreement.

The remainder of the tale becomes a bit more familiar. The cast of characters changes. The SDLP's John Hume, together with the Ulster Unionist leader, David Trimble, both won the Nobel Peace Prize for their efforts in bridging the political and sectarian divide and sealing a deal on the Good Friday Agreement. In a few short years, both their parties were eclipsed by Sinn Féin and the Democratic Unionists. Theoretically, this was bad news as Paisley actively opposed the Good Friday Agreement, noisily protesting outside the negotiations, and there seemed little chance of him sitting down with the 'men of violence' that he had spent so long denouncing. Whether out of personal ambition or a sense of greater calling, the old man seized the moment and entered into coalition with Martin McGuinness, a former IRA commander, in 2007. Yet this oddest of odd couples found a rapport – a bonhomie, even – earning themselves an unlikely nickname. The 'Chuckle Brothers' nevertheless moved the agenda forward and, against all the odds, made good the potential of the Good Friday Agreement, at least for a while. Peace (of sorts) and progress (of sorts) became possible. However, the Good Friday Agreement settlement remains fragile, for ever a work in progress.

This brisk canter through Northern Ireland's dismal, blood-drenched history (which is much worse in fine detail) is difficult for people in Britain to fully comprehend. For people like me growing up in Britain during the 1980s and early 1990s, I dare say one atrocity simply melted into another. The appearance of the BBC's then Ireland editor, Denis Murray, pensive and sombre and usually wearing a funereal expression as he stared into the camera on the evening news, was enough of a cue to tell you something dreadful had happened that day, much as it had the day or week before. Bodies covered over, laying prostrate in the street. Debris-strewn roads following yet another bomb explosion. Ambulances. The mangled wreckage of a burnt-out car. Those curious armoured Land Rovers. Gun-toting soldiers and police at the scene of the latest atrocity. Yet, all this happened in a part of the UK, and all the time our political leaders were desperate to maintain the fiction that we were not in the throes of a low-fi civil war.

'For God's sake, bring me a large Scotch,' Reginald Maudling, Edward Heath's Home Secretary, demanded of an official as he returned to Belfast airport after his first visit to Northern Ireland in 1970.[1] 'What a bloody awful country!' he exclaimed. In that respect, W. B. Yeats's poem 'The Fascination of What's Difficult' could have been written for the British ministers who followed Maudling. Dealing with Northern Ireland's affairs

> Has dried the sap out of my veins, and rent
> Spontaneous joy and natural content
> Out of my heart.

Northern Ireland was not built to last, which is why Unionists went to excessive lengths to slope the pitch in their favour in its founding years. Although Protestants initially outnumbered Catholics two to one, the temptation to fortify their position further by rigging the electoral system to control local government and housing allocations, while encouraging open discrimination against Catholics in the workplace, was too much for them to resist. Westminster (and, to some degree, Dublin) observed a policy of simply ignoring Northern Ireland, whenever possible, for decades. But when pressure for change had built up by the mid-1960s and that tactic was no longer possible, British ministers moved with insufficient haste to take the side of the civil rights movement and redress the legitimate grievances of the beleaguered Catholic minority – which they should have – and thus head off a downward spiral. Had they done so, perhaps we would have been spared the Troubles. If Westminster had helped to face down Unionist hardliners and buttress the reform-minded Unionist Prime Minister, Terence O'Neill, then perhaps the worst of what was to follow might never have occurred. But it was not to be. To paraphrase a different Yeats poem, things fell apart and the centre did not hold. Mere anarchy was loosed.

By the time the government realised all this, events had over-taken them. Troops were on the ground and had quickly been pulled into the conflict, siding with the atrophying Stormont administration. Bombs were going off and in a splicing of met-aphors, the hatches were battened down and the can had been kicked down the road. Periodic attempts at restoring devolution foundered; mainly due to Unionist belligerence about giving Catholics a say in running the place. That was how low the bar was. But rather than face down such blatant sectarianism – saving Unionists from themselves in the process – British min-isters acquiesced, time and time again. In the same breath, they sanctioned counter-insurgency tactics that were honed during other post-colonial conflicts and used them on the streets of what were, ultimately, British cities. Internment. The shooting

of protestors. Interrogation centres. Juryless trials. Agents pro-
vocateurs. Supergrass hearings. Loyalist death squads used as
proxies. A failure to take control of matters in the 1960s had
led to British ministers plunging headlong into a miasma. There
will be no legacy process for the Troubles in an attempt to establish, for the record at least, what went on and who did what
to whom. A willingness to engage with such a process is one of
the few things that unites Loyalist and Republican paramilitaries; scandalously, it is the British state with the most to lose if
the unexpurgated truth is revealed.

The centenary of Northern Ireland will divide along political
and communal lines and three things are clear. The first is that
Nationalists and Republicans will rue the day that the partition
of Ireland occurred. It reduced them to second-class citizens in
their own land. For them, Northern Ireland has been an unmit-
igated disaster. They were never offered a stake in the place and,
with the growing prospect of Irish unity in the next few years,
are looking beyond its narrow confines with greater confidence
than ever.

The second is that Unionists and Loyalists will celebrate the
pluck of 'their wee country'. Here they are, 100 years on, still
hanging on having overcome, as they see it, Republican insur-
rectionists bent on destroying the place. They will sense the half-
smiles from their fair-weather friends in Westminster as they
celebrate the creation of 'their' state. They know that, given the
choreography, the British government – *any* British government
– would abandon them without a second glance. After all, it was
the Conservative *and Unionist* Party that shut down Stormont

under Edward Heath. It was Margaret Thatcher who brought the Irish government into the equation with the signing of the Anglo-Irish Agreement, and it is Boris Johnson who has agreed a Brexit deal that leaves Northern Ireland partly inside the European Union.

The third point relates to the second. There will be no subsequent commemorations about the founding of Northern Ireland. No more anniversaries or release of specially minted coins. The British now have all the choreography they need. The Good Friday Agreement contains a provision for a 'border poll' – the colloquial term for a constitutional referendum – when it seems likely that there is a majority for change. It is now a question of timing. Over the next few years, a combination of demographic, electoral, economic and constitutional pressures will conspire to activate the clause. Without the numbers left to automatically confect a majority, the likelihood is that Northern Ireland will be voted into oblivion by its own inhabitants. For now, that argument is for another day. As far as this book is concerned, Northern Ireland is a masterclass in failed statecraft – an abiding testament to the dangers of political paralysis and the temptation to avoid taking hard decisions in a timely manner. A century on and we are still living with the consequences.

Finally, just a word on my intended audience. Northern Ireland has been, for 100 years, part of the United Kingdom, but it has often not felt like that, certainly to Catholic–Nationalists who faced marginalisation and discrimination, but also to Protestant–Unionists, who know in their marrow that there is precious little loyalty shown by Westminster in return for the fealty they show.

But my main preoccupation in the succeeding pages is to try to engage a British audience with some of the key issues. This may be a tall order, as Northern Ireland barely flickers on the British public's consciousness. Much of what follows will be unfamiliar and lost amid the simplicities of broadcast news coverage of the Troubles and the far more nuanced reality on the ground. And while I am at it, just a word on descriptions and acronyms. For the uninitiated, Northern Irish politics has its own periodic table of terms. How do we even describe the main participants? 'Catholics' and 'Protestants'? This is partly accurate in terms of groupings, but not in terms of their motivations (Catholics were not trying to convert Protestants and vice versa). 'Nationalists' and 'Unionists'? This is how we describe the 'respectable' political actors and main communities in secular terms. 'Republicans' and 'Loyalists' are generally reserved for the paramilitaries, but in a post-conflict scenario where religious affiliation is weakening and an increasing percentage of Northern Irish people reject all of the above, what then? Nowadays, someone can be a Protestant Republican or a Catholic Unionist. The imperfect solution for the writer is to employ Protestant–Unionist–Loyalist and Catholic–Nationalist–Republican classifications in a bespoke way, depending on the context.

Understanding Northern Ireland and its century of division matters, not least because it has cost so much blood and treasure; the price of Britain's failed statecraft. As a result, the 'Irish question', posed in the mid-1800s, continues to cast a menacing shadow over British politics. The creation of Northern Ireland – splitting the difference between Nationalist and Unionist demands – merely led to a brooding stalemate that exploded back into life from the late 1960s until the advent of the Good Friday Agreement. But this is not the end of the issue. People in Britain are relieved to see an end to the killing and bombing, and memories of those dark decades have, for many, faded over time. Over coming years, however, we will need to decide, fully and finally, how, and when, to make good on that provision in the Good Friday Agreement for a poll on whether Ireland should be unified. We need to understand Northern Ireland because we will need to engage with its future, or lack thereof, in a few short years. Content to tread water for the past twenty-two years since its signing and put off the day when hard decisions need to be made, it is becoming more and more obvious that we are running out of road. To again mix metaphors, it feels like the final act is upon us. Northern Ireland will again move centre stage and demand our attention. In preparing for this endgame, Westminster and Whitehall should break the habit of a lifetime and fully appreciate the context in which MPs will have to make momentous decisions. This book is a small contribution to that effort.

Kevin Meagher
March 2021

CHAPTER 1

BUILT TO FAIL

Can you picture the Scottish Parliament? I am not sure that I can. Its actual name is the 'Scottish Parliament Building', which gets translated to 'Holyrood' in the same way the Palace of Westminster simply becomes 'Westminster'. The Welsh Assembly – *Senedd Cymru* for Welsh speakers – is similarly absent from my mind's eye. The point I am making is that there is something anonymous about our devolved seats of government. I cannot visualise them without referring to the internet. Even then they are a bit underwhelming. Glass and concrete. Functional but hardly iconic. The Scottish and Welsh seats of power could be mistaken for being modern concert halls, or provincial branches of one of the big five accountancy firms. In the same way, you would walk past the European Parliament in Brussels without knowing what it was (resembling, as it does, a modern university). Perhaps this is a reflection on our political age. You cannot very well commission grandeur when public regard for politics is so low. Architecture takes the hit, and so we have unremarkable buildings – soulless and anonymous – to match our unremarkable politicians. A bit like when a football club moves from its old stadium, invariably ramshackle and too small but with lots of character and history, to a purpose-built alternative.

I expect, however, that many more people are familiar with 'Stormont'. They might not understand the finer details, but they will recognise it as Northern Ireland's seat of government, a land they would otherwise spend little time concerning themselves about. They may, in fact, be able to visualise it too. An imposing classical-style building made from white Portland stone. It is the grounds, though, that set it apart, with that famous mile-long avenue leading up to it providing a perfect backdrop for television reporters down the years as they chronicle the toing and froing of political life in Northern Ireland. The impressive vista reflects the reality that, for half a century, between 1921 and 1972, Northern Ireland enjoyed near total autonomy. It had its own 'Parliament Buildings' because it made its own laws. It had its own government, too, complete with a Prime Minister and Cabinet. It was the British state's earliest and most ambitious experiment in political devolution.

Arnold Thornely, the architect of Parliament Buildings, was also responsible for designing the Mersey Docks and Harbour Board Building, one of the 'Three Graces' on the UNESCO-designated Liverpool waterfront (if anything, it is far grander than Parliament Buildings; it is built in the Edwardian baroque style with an imposing central dome and additional stone cupola at each corner). It speaks to a different age. For Liverpool, like Belfast, these were boom years. Imperial pomp matched by commercial success. Their civic buildings were manifestations of this strength and confidence. If anything, Thornely's imprint on Liverpool is even more pronounced than it is on Belfast.

Architecture aside, it is what went on inside Stormont that forms the focus of this book. The decisions that were made there shaped Northern Ireland and gave us a century of division. Newly hewn in 1921 and without historical or cultural legitimacy before that point, Northern Ireland should have been pregnant with opportunity. Granted, the manner of its emergence, following decades of strife as Irish Nationalists and Republicans vied to liberate their country from British rule, was challenging, to put it mildly. But what quickly emerged set the tone for subsequent decades. In summary, Northern Ireland went bad from the start. If the intention of partitioning Ireland was the hope that it provided a least-worst option in avoiding a sectarian bloodbath by pushing through Irish Home Rule, then the reality is that it simply created two conflicts. The first was the bitter Irish Civil War between pro- and anti-treaty forces on the terms of partitioning Ireland between 1922 and 1923, and the second was the Troubles, five decades later, which, as we will see, was a bloody internecine conflict that lasted for thirty years.

But let me begin by rolling back a few years. There were two British general elections in 1910 – which provides a flavour of the general tumult in Westminster at the time – in the first of which the Liberals lost the 124-seat majority they had won in the 1906 landslide, with Prime Minister Herbert Asquith scraping back in with just two more seats than Arthur Balfour's Conservatives. Asquith was able to form a government with support of the Irish Parliamentary Party's seventy-one MPs, led by John Redmond. At the time there was an ongoing row about the House of Lords stymieing the Liberals' 'People's Budget' in 1909, including, as it did, higher tax rates for the wealthy (there was also a levy on whiskey, which the Irish Parliamentary Party did not like). This would lead to the 1911 Parliament Act, which enshrined the primacy of the Commons over the Lords for evermore. A second election was called in December to try to break the deadlock from the first, but the result was a virtual carbon copy, with the Liberals nudging ahead of the Conservatives by just a single seat, 272 to 271 (although the Conservatives won the popular vote in both elections). The Irish Parliamentary Party were kingmakers once again and looked forward to the prospect of Asquith bringing forth a third and final attempt at Home Rule for Ireland after previous attempts by William Gladstone in 1886 and 1893. The issue represented a forty-year fault line in British politics which had led to a major schism in his party, with Liberal Unionists breaking away to join with the Conservatives in opposing the policy. Nevertheless, with Redmond's support, Asquith now had the parliamentary numbers necessary to proceed. To be sure, it was a transactional arrangement. Gladstone was a committed proponent of Irish Home Rule but many Liberals were not, even those that did not break away as Liberal Unionists. 'Their non-conformist roots hardly sat easily with the policy of coercing Ulster Protestants for the benefit of Irish Roman Catholics,' as the historian D. G. Boyce noted.[1]

Unionist opposition to Home Rule, led by Sir Edward Carson, leader of the Irish Unionist Party since 1910, and Sir

James Craig, the Unionist MP for East Down, was swift and predictable, and had two strands. The first came in Parliament with an attempt to block the progress of the Home Rule Bill. This tactic had clearly proven sufficient in halting the two previous attempts at Home Rule; however, the passage of the Parliament Act would not allow the Lords to indefinitely obstruct government legislation this time around. They calculated that stirring opposition in the north of the country ('Northern Ireland' was not yet common parlance) and the prospect of partition might be enough to dissuade Redmond from accepting a reduced Home Rule option that only included the south. They were aided by Andrew Bonar Law, the Conversative Leader of the Opposition, who was a staunch Unionist, albeit more bothered about Ulster, his ancestral home, than he was about the rest of Ireland. The second strand of their effort came outside Parliament. Carson and Craig would show the strength of grass-roots opposition against Home Rule by rallying Irish Protestants against it. In September 1912, they published 'Ulster's Solemn League and Covenant' – a 189-word petition, which rejected Home Rule in characteristically strident prose:

> Being convinced in our consciences that Home Rule would be disastrous to the material well-being of Ulster as well as of the whole of Ireland, subversive of our civil and religious freedom, destructive of our citizenship, and perilous to the unity of the Empire, we, whose names are underwritten, men of Ulster, loyal subjects of His Gracious Majesty King George V, humbly relying on the God whom our fathers in days of stress and trial

confidently trusted, do hereby pledge ourselves in solemn covenant, throughout this our time of threatened calamity to stand by one another in defending for ourselves and our children our cherished position of equal citizenship in the United Kingdom, and in using all means which may be found necessary to defeat the present conspiracy to set up a Home Rule Parliament in Ireland. And in the event of such a Parliament being forced upon us we further solemnly and mutually pledge ourselves to refuse to recognise its authority. In sure confidence that God will defend the right we hereto subscribe our names. And further, we individually declare that we have not already signed this Covenant. God Save the King.

Nearly half a million people signed the covenant, with women offered a shorter, less dramatic version (although more women than men signed it). Some signatories were so enraptured that they were said to have written their names in blood. The description of the Home Rule Bill as a 'present conspiracy' was plainly ridiculous. The issue was hidden in plain sight and had been wending its way around Parliament for forty years at this stage. In that respect the threatening tone of the covenant was an affront to parliamentary sovereignty. The message was crystal clear: legislate for Home Rule and there will be trouble. In 1913, Carson and Craig went much further, forming the Ulster Volunteer Force (UVF) – a 100,000-strong militia – to increase pressure on the British government. To underline their intent, 24,000 German rifles and millions of rounds of ammunition were smuggled into Northern Ireland via Larne port, with the authorities apparently oblivious (to put this in context, the 1913 UVF had more men than the British Army did in 2020). Any move towards Home Rule would be met with violent resistance. In April 1914, fifty-eight British Army officers based at the Curragh Camp in County Kildare let it be known that they would refuse to obey any order to move against the UVF following murmurings from the government that they might have to bring them into line. The 'Curragh Mutiny' would loom large in the thoughts of subsequent governments when the prospect of facing down Loyalist hardliners arose. In July, Bonar Law spoke at a mass meeting of supporters at Blenheim Palace:

> I said so to [the Liberals] and I say so now, with the full sense of the responsibility which attaches to my position, that if the attempt be made under present conditions, I can imagine no length of resistance to which Ulster will go, in which I shall not be ready to support them, and in which they will not be supported by the overwhelming majority of the British people.

In the modern world we would look harshly on any movement threatening violence against the decision of a sovereign Parliament. For the Leader of Her Majesty's *Loyal* Opposition to do so against the elected government of the United Kingdom seems utterly unconscionable to a contemporary audience. Fortunately, parliamentary authority prevailed and the Bill passed its various stages, and after three attempts, a major schism in the Liberal Party and a huge backlash from its opponents, Home Rule for Ireland now seemed assured. There was, then, a pivot in twentieth-century British–Irish relations – a *Sliding Doors* moment when things might have worked out differently. The passage of the 1914 Home Rule Act would give Ireland dominion status, but, crucially, keep the country intact. It might have been seen by some as a meagre construct alongside the aspiration of a full-blown Irish Republic, but there is a tendency to overlook this critical moment, and it remains the closest Ireland – all thirty-two counties of it – came to being a unified state.

There was, however, a significant complication. The outbreak of the First World War in autumn 1914 saw the Act suspended until the conflict was concluded. Instead, Irishmen of both traditions were inveighed upon to take up arms for Britain. More than 200,000 did so. Carson's Ulster Volunteers weighed in enthusiastically with many going on to form the 36th Ulster Division (which would fight bravely and take catastrophic casualties at the Battle of the Somme). Many members of the Irish Volunteers – a similar armed militia but founded in response to Carson's UVF and with the opposite aim of protecting the cause of Home Rule – did likewise, at the behest of Redmond, who entreated them to fight 'for the rights of small nations', comparing Ireland with the plight of Catholic Belgium which was also facing down the yoke of an imperial oppressor. Many joined the 36th Ulster Division, under the command of an Irish-born British officer, Major-General Sir William Hickie – a strong supporter of Home Rule who would later sit in the Irish Senate as a Nationalist representative. Others joined the 10th (Irish) Division, which suffered heavy losses at the 1915 landing at Suvla Bay on the Gallipoli Peninsula. Among the mud, carnage and death the Irish Protestants of the 36th Ulster Division, made up of the Ulster Volunteers, stood side by side with Irish Volunteers in the 16th (Irish) Division at the Battle of Messines in June 1917 in what would be a rare moment of common cause. By the end of the war, 35,000 Irishmen, from both green and orange traditions, had perished, with tens of thousands more injured. As war raged in France, revolutionary Ireland saw a moment to strike under the principle that 'England's difficulty is Ireland's opportunity'. At Easter in 1916, the Irish Republican Brotherhood, backed by those Irish Volunteers who did not enlist for the war, made their move. The week-long Easter Rising and the declaration of an Irish Republic on the steps of the General Post Office in Dublin served as a rebuke both to British authority and also to the kind of minimalist Nationalism that Redmond stood for.

The harsh treatment of the leaders of the Easter Rising – courts martial and execution for sixteen of the commanders and signatories of the Declaration of Independence – turned the tide of Irish public opinion. Once agnostic about the Rising, they quickly stirred against British rule. Redmond's blundering response – agreeing that the leaders should face execution even though he called for clemency for other rebels – sealed his reputation as a sell-out. Sinn Féin scored a series of electoral breakthroughs in parliamentary by-elections that followed, and in the 1918 general election the party won seventy-three out of 105 parliamentary seats across Ireland and immediately declared an Irish Republic. The War of Independence that followed saw the nascent IRA wage a guerrilla campaign against British rule, undermining it to such an extent that the government of David Lloyd George – Asquith's successor in 1916 – sought a negotiated settlement. But he still had the Unionists to contend with and created Northern Ireland in the 1920 Government of Ireland Act as Britain was effectively driven from the rest of the country. The partition of Ireland, first mooted a decade earlier, was eventually agreed to during the referendum on accepting the terms of the 1922 truce between Britain and Irish plenipotentiaries. The threat of not agreeing to the deal was the prospect of an 'immediate and terrible war', as Lloyd George coldly described it. Agreeing to partition was the price that the rest of Ireland had to pay for the establishment of an Irish Free State and the avoidance of a much larger conflict that the IRA was simply not equipped to fight. Putting his best spin on it, Michael Collins, one of the delegates that signed the agreement with Britain and the organising genius behind the IRA's guerrilla campaign against the British presence in Ireland, memorably described the deal as the 'freedom to achieve freedom'. Many of his countrymen and erstwhile colleagues disagreed, and Ireland was plunged into a bitter civil war that would cost Collins his life just nine months later.

So, Ireland was partitioned. The six counties of Ulster were carefully chosen to maximise the Protestant–Unionist majority. Before his death in 1918 John Redmond had regarded partition of the country as 'an unnatural abomination and a blasphemy'. James Connolly – a socialist theoretician and trade unionist who was one of the chief organisers of the Easter Rising and a signatory of the Declaration of Independence – decried the 'carnival

of reaction' that partition would let loose. He was later executed by a British firing squad while he sat strapped to a chair as
he was unable to stand due to his injuries. Still, hope persisted
that a better future might still be possible. This was certainly the
message conveyed by King George V when he opened Northern Ireland's new Parliament in June 1921. In a quite remarkable
speech, lacking any of the bellicosity of the Unionist luminaries
who affected loyalty to him, George began thus:

> For all who love Ireland, as I do with all my heart, this is a pro-
> foundly moving occasion in Irish history. My memories of the
> Irish people date back to the time when I spent many happy days
> in Ireland as a midshipman. My affection for the Irish people has
> been deepened by the successive visits since that time, and I have
> watched with constant sympathy the course of their affairs.
>
> I could not have allowed myself to give Ireland by deputy alone.
> My earnest prayers and good wishes in the new era which opens
> with this ceremony, and I have therefore come in person, as the
> head of the Empire, to inaugurate this parliament on Irish soil. I
> inaugurate it with deep-felt hope and I feel assured that you will
> do your utmost to make it an instrument of happiness and good
> government for all parts of the community which you represent.
>
> This is a great and critical occasion in the history of the Six
> Counties – but not for the Six Counties alone, for everything which
> interests them touches Ireland, and everything which touches Ire-
> land finds an echo in the remotest parts of the Empire. Few things
> are more earnestly desired throughout the English-speaking
> world than a satisfactory solution of the age-long Irish problems,

which for generations embarrassed our forefathers, as they now weigh heavily upon us.

I appeal to all Irishmen to pause, to stretch out the hand of forbearance and conciliation, to forgive and to forget, and to join in making for the land which they love a new era of peace, contentment, and goodwill.[2]

The King finished with a fascinatingly elliptical remark: 'May this historic gathering be the prelude of a day in which the Irish people, North and South, under one parliament or two, as those parliaments may themselves decide, shall work together in common love for Ireland upon the sure foundations of mutual justice and respect.'

These generous words were an eloquent and emollient response to troubled times. Interestingly, he did not refer to 'Northern Ireland', referencing instead Ireland and the 'six counties' (a phrase later redolent of Irish Republicans). His call for 'mutual justice and respect' evidently fell on deaf ears, but his remark about the opening of the Parliament being a prelude to the day when 'North and South' might be united 'as those parliaments may themselves decide' is essentially what became known as the principle of consent – a cornerstone of the deal hammered out in the Good Friday Agreement, seventy-seven years later. Even the King was anticipating the possibility that Northern Ireland might not survive in the long haul. What did Unionists make of it? The only way of interpreting his speech was as a coded rebuke to the division and violence of the preceding decade. The King was being equidistant; there was no special praise for those loyal to the Crown. In that respect, it must have been a bittersweet moment for Edward Carson and James Craig. A battle won but a war lost. Carson had initially been offered the role of Prime Minister of Northern Ireland but turned it down. His aim was to keep the whole of Ireland in the Union. In that respect, he simply regarded partition as a defeat and refocused his attentions on his legal career.

The opening of the Northern Ireland Parliament at Belfast City Hall – it would move to the Presbyterian Church's Union Theological College from 1921 until Parliament Buildings were completed on the Stormont estate in 1932 and thereafter became 'Stormont' – was set against a backdrop of serious and sustained communal violence. Since July the previous year, Belfast had been in turmoil, with Loyalist mobs driving Catholic workers out of the shipyards and factories, burning out Catholic-owned businesses and forcing families to flee majority-Loyalist communities. It was not always so. A six-week strike at the start of 1919 saw shipyard workers – Protestants and Catholics alike – band together to demand a 44-hour working week. This quickly spread to other engineering and textiles companies across the city and formed part of a wave of industrial unrest across Britain. The strike committee, led by a Catholic shop steward, was by all accounts orderly and peaceful. The committee helped the city council and Royal Irish Constabulary to keep Belfast moving, going so far as to co-operate with the appointment of 300 special constables, who were nominated by the strike committee to help maintain law and order and avoid conflict with the police.

A book was written at the time by a Catholic priest, Fr John

Hassan, under the pseudonym 'G. B. Kenna', and chronicled those violent few years around the foundation of Northern Ireland. *Facts and Figures of the Belfast Pogrom, 1920–1922* provides a compelling account of the period.[3] Unionist leaders would not stand for working-class Protestants making common cause with working-class Catholics and plotted to stymie it:

> The result was the formation of the bogus and sectarian trade union called the Unionist Labour Party, under the direction of Sir Edward Carson, and favoured by the Tory employers. The political activities of this party were completely successful in driving a solid wedge between the Protestant and Catholic workers.

Carson made a speech on 12 July 1920 – a date known as the 'Glorious Twelfth' by Loyalists commemorating the victory of King William of Orange at the Battle of the Boyne in 1690 – whipping up the crowd and offering a not-too-coded warning of what was to come. To Kenna's ears it was 'a very bitter speech – outlandish, one would say, for any man holding such a responsible position'. He added:

> The chief theme of the harangue was that the Loyalists of Ulster were in imminent peril from Sinn Féin, that he [Carson] was losing hope of the Government's defending them, and that they must be up and doing to protect themselves. 'And those are not words,' he said; 'I am sick of words without action.'

What came next is, a century later, chilling in its design and heart-breaking in its consequences, and more than warrants the title of Kenna's book. 'Catholics in the shipyards and other places had hints that trouble was brewing,' he recorded,

> Some of their less reticent Protestant mates had told them as much, and even mentioned the day fixed upon – the 21st of July. They preferred, however, to treat such reports as bluster, and when 'the day' arrived they went as usual to the yards. Nearly 5,000 of them were employed there, efficient men in every department of those great concerns; 1,025 of them were ex-service men, many of whom had fought for Britain not in one but in several wars. Probably more than three-fourths of all these workers were at the time followers of Joseph Devlin [a Nationalist MP], and politically opposed to Sinn Féin.

There was a meeting of Loyalists at lunchtime and immediately afterwards trouble began. Loyalist mobs started attacking their Catholic co-workers and any other Protestants that stood with them. Many were beaten and kicked as the rampage ensued with some being thrown into the murky water of the docks – 25ft deep – and showered with 'Belfast confetti' – nuts, bolts and rivets. As they tried to clamber out, they were driven back in by the baying mob. One Catholic worker was said to have swum a mile out into the estuary of the river Lagan to make his escape. Of course, the effect was obvious enough. As Kenna put it: 'Since that day … no Catholic – with the exception … of one or two office hands – has been allowed to earn a living in Belfast's chief industrial concerns, the shipbuilding yards.'

'Remember the 21st' had been chalked up all over the shipyards in the weeks before the attacks began. This was a calculated move. A brutal reminder that Protestants ran this place. But this was merely the start. Shops were looted. Churches, a monastery and a convent of nuns were attacked. Catholics were driven out of majority-Protestant parts of Belfast in what we would now understand as ethnic cleansing. And the rout of Catholic workers was not confined to the shipyards. A similar purge took place in engineering companies, large factories, warehouses and shops. Some employers pleaded with Loyalists not to expel their Catholic co-workers, many of whom were highly skilled and vital to the success of the business. Visiting the shipyards a few months later, Sir James Craig spoke to the assembled workers. 'Do I approve of the action you boys have taken in the past?' he asked rhetorically. 'I say, Yes.'

Carson's call to action had been clear. That such an onslaught was deliberate, timed and emphatic in its intent is still shocking a century later. This was no accident. It was not a case of stirring up a crowd and then simply losing control of it. A reporter from the *Daily Mail* said the trouble was down to 'an organised attempt to deprive Catholic men of their work, and to drive Catholic families from their homes'. A journalist from the *Daily News* (the liberal Victorian and Edwardian newspaper first established by Charles Dickens) likened the situation in Belfast to 'Russian or Polish pogroms'. While the *Westminster Gazette* said that it was 'common knowledge in Belfast and frequently admitted by individual Unionists, that plans were matured at least two months ago to drive all Home Rule workmen in the shipyards out of their employment'.[4]

Kenna wrote about an incident in August 1920 where a griev-
ing mother, with her dead child laid out in her house ahead of
the funeral, was forced to flee a Loyalist mob: 'In the middle of
the tumult she took up the corpse from the bed and fled with it
by a back way and through the streets to a place of greater safety.'[5]
In another incident in June 1922 a young doctor's housekeeper
answered the door to a Loyalist gang, who proceeded to knock
her down, douse her in petrol and set her on fire, leaving her
with grievous injuries. Creditably, the Unionist *Belfast Telegraph*
described the attackers as 'contemptible and cruel' and called for
them to be 'hunted out of society'. Indeed, the violence in Belfast
in the early 1920s was as bad as anything that would be seen fifty
years later during the Troubles. What was the mindset that drove
Loyalists to such a course of action? Three days after Carson's
speech on 12 July, a reader's letter signed as being from an 'Observer' appeared in the staunchly Unionist *Belfast News Letter*:

Sir – I notice that in his great speech on the Twelfth, Sir Edward
Carson made one statement, which, if I may be permitted to say
so, is far from accurate. He says that the Roman Catholics make
little progress in Ulster. Now I certainly think this is a serious
error and the very worst security into which the Protestants
could be lulled. In my opinion, the progress made by the Roman
Catholics in Ulster is extraordinarily rapid and extensive. Take
the village where I live, for instance, which is one of the most
Protestant communities of Ulster. There is a population of about
1,000. Some thirty years ago it was an entirely Protestant village, without, I believe, one single Roman Catholic inhabitant.

Now nearly one-half of the inhabitants are Catholics, and they are increasing rapidly ... It seems to me that in a comparatively short number of years the majority of Ulster's inhabitants will undoubtedly be Roman Catholics, if things go on as at present. After looking facts in the face, and not ignoring them because they may be unpleasant, the next thing to do is to counter them energetically in every possible way.[6]

It is difficult to give such sentiments the benefit of the doubt. Catholics were viewed as the enemy, pure and simple. They were taking over. They needed to be stopped – by any means. A follow-up letter, published the next day, went even further:

Sir – I can heartily endorse everything your correspondent says in his letter, and I am afraid that it is only too true that our Ulster Unionism is at present suffering from 'sleeping sickness'.

We Protestants should ask ourselves how is it that Roman Catholics have made such headway in our midst? I think if we did we should not have any difficulty in finding the answer. We are up against an insidious system of 'peaceful penetration' which has, to my mind, too long taken advantage of our fear of being called bigoted. 'Observer' rightly states that it is time Unionists roused themselves to action, and I quite agree with him that unless we do so without delay we shall be left homeless and helpless very shortly.

This was not just rhetoric or the empty threats of armchair blowhards. It was an attempt to justify – to set the ground – for the violence that was shortly to come. It was part of a concerted demonisation of Catholics and contained the essential elements of the Loyalist political narrative that has endured for the past century: virulent anti-Catholicism, combining lurid conspiracies with faux victimhood. We would see the same approach time and time again over the remainder of the twentieth century.

Of course, the facts tell quite a different story from that presented by the correspondents to the *News Letter*. Between June 1920 and June 1922, 2,000 people were injured in communal violence in Belfast, with 428 people killed, and two-thirds of them were Catholics (which is equivalent, in today's UK, to around 20,000 deaths). Some estimates suggest 10,000 Catholics were driven out of their workplaces and thousands more were chased or burnt out of their homes. Sectarianism, then, as on so many other occasions during Northern Ireland's centenary of division, was the most reliable way for Unionist politicians to mobilise a Loyalist working class which might have found common cause with their working-class Catholic neighbours.

All this begs the question: if you were going to start your own state and wanted to incorporate best practice and make it a success, what are the key elements you would include? What are the key principles that you would abide by? What checks and balances would you introduce? Assuming you had any pretensions about being a democracy, and entertained even a passing regard for civil rights, you would guarantee free and fair elections. This would include universal suffrage, which would ensure that every citizen of this new country had a chance to vote for his or her elected representatives and that the government of the state reflected the outcome of the vote. You would ensure

39

equality before the law, that rights were upheld and that justice was blind. Also, that policing in this new state was equitable and civilianised. It might be a good idea to adopt the British tradition of policing by consent enunciated by Sir Robert Peel ('the police are the public and the public are the police'). Another cornerstone would be to safeguard a fair and transparent approach to allocating public spending and maintaining equal access to public services. People should not only be free to practise their religious faith, but their religion should not hinder the life chances of any of your new citizens untowardly. In making your new society a success, you would seek to transcend past grievances, learning from previous mistakes and avoid repeating them as you build your new country. You would probably want to bind your population around shared assumptions, symbols and practices; building understanding and amity among your various communities so that they held certain views and outlooks in common.

If this seems a reasonable list of attributes in building a new state, now consider how they applied to the foundation of Northern Ireland. First off, 'Ulster', certainly as many Unionists refer to Northern Ireland, is a sleight of hand. The historic province of Ulster – one of Ireland's four provinces – includes nine Irish counties: Antrim, Armagh, Cavan, Derry, Donegal, Down, Fermanagh, Monaghan and Tyrone. Northern Ireland was created by carving out six of them. Not just any six, of course; there was a deliberate ploy to lock in a Protestant–Unionist ascendancy at the time of partition ensuring a 2:1 ratio over Catholics. If the three additional Ulster counties had been included, there would have been a 56 per cent to 44 per cent composition, and Unionists might have found themselves outnumbered by Catholics after a few years. This demographic chicanery is symptomatic of how Northern Ireland, from its very inception, was a loaded deck.

At the time of partition, the lower house of Northern Ireland's new Parliament was elected by proportional representation. This was a feature of the 1920 Government of Ireland Act and designed to ensure fair representation for the Catholic minority in what was, clearly, a fundamentally divided society. One of the early moves of the new Unionist government was to abolish proportional representation in local elections and switch to Westminster's first-past-the-post system with fixed boundary constituencies. (By 1929, this change had also been made for Westminster seats.) This manipulation of the system was hardly subtle. Boundaries were skewed – gerrymandered – to return a Unionist majority. Catholic votes where corralled into larger constituencies to waste their voting power. The effect? The votes of Catholic–Nationalists simply counted for less and in a city like Derry – which had a large Catholic majority – Unionists ruled. Across Northern Ireland, Unionists controlled 85 per cent of local government with only 66 per cent of the population. But the electoral corruption was twofold. It was not enough to simply fix the boundaries in a brazenly sectarian way; the franchise itself was corrupted. The voting qualification for non-Westminster elections was based not on universal suffrage, but on property ownership. Poorer Catholics (along with the poorest Protestants) lost out given that they were disproportionately less likely to own their own homes. Moreover, there was also a business franchise which could see an additional six votes awarded to nominees of the business owners who were, disproportionately, Protestant–Unionists. To underscore just how compromised the electoral system became, there were 900,000 voters for Westminster and Stormont elections, but just 600,000 for local elections. A third of the electorate mysteriously disappeared – helping to secure Unionism's rotten boroughs. As a result of the switch away from proportional representation, Nationalists lost their majorities in thirteen of twenty-four councils they had originally controlled at the time of partition. The British government made clear its displeasure at the change as it undermined the guarantees in the 1920 Government of Ireland Act. However, James Craig, Northern Ireland's Prime Minister, along with his entire Cabinet, threatened to resign if they were forced to back down. A dangerous precedent was set. Westminster avoided getting involved in Northern Irish affairs and even observed a dubious convention that devolved matters should not be raised in the House of Commons. This partially explains why the festering problems at the heart of a deeply divided society went unheard for half a century.

So, free and fair elections in Northern Ireland were alien, which meant that there was no transfer of power either. Unionists ran the show and that, as far as they saw it, should be a permanent situation. The Ulster Unionist Party (UUP) governed Northern Ireland, without challenge, between 1922 and 1972, when Stormont was eventually prorogued by Edward Heath's government as the Troubles escalated. There is no hyperbole,

then, in stating that Northern Ireland was from the very beginning a corrupted, sectarian state; and this was by design not
accident. For Unionists, the ends justified the means. They based
their outlook on a reductive assumption that treating Catholics
equitably came at their expense. But if anything the effect was
deeper than that. As the writer Gore Vidal wryly observed about
his enemies: 'It is not enough that I succeed. Others must fail.'
It was not sufficient that Unionists had confected a majority in
this new state; Catholics must still have their noses rubbed in it.

Of course, there is no point in simply accruing power if you
are not then prepared to use it. Or misuse it. The corruption
at the heart of Northern Ireland's political system transferred
down into the way Northern Ireland was administered. The
effect was marked. A survey conducted in 1943 found there were
no Catholics in the fifty-five most senior civil service jobs and
just thirty-seven in the 600 middle-ranking posts.[7] By the late
1950s, only a single Catholic had been appointed as a permanent secretary, the highest rank in the civil service. In 1933, the
Minister for Labour, J. M. Andrews (who would later become
the second Prime Minister of Northern Ireland), responded to
complaints from Unionist MPs that too many of the porters
at Stormont were Catholics. 'I have investigated the matter,'
he said, 'and I find that there are thirty Protestants, and only
one Roman Catholic there temporarily.' So, Catholics were not
welcome at any level of the administration of Northern Ireland.
Not even fit to act as porters in a building that, at least theoretically, was meant to represent the entire population of Northern
Irish society. (In a mark of how narrowly Northern Ireland was

governed, Andrews's brother was the Lord Chief Justice, while a second brother was the managing director of the shipbuilder Harland & Wolff and died on board the *Titanic* in 1912.)

How do we explain the systematising of this abuse of power? Invariably, the motive is ascribed to Unionist fear about both the fragility of Northern Ireland and the lack of support among the Catholic–Nationalist population for its very existence. Unionists closed ranks and looked on suspiciously. A familiar excuse for what went on in the first half-century of Northern Ireland's existence was that Catholics simply did not want to be part of the new state or see Northern Ireland succeed. They adopted a sullen attitude that contributed to their lack of advancement. Unionists had the right, as they saw it, to get on with building their 'wee country', and if Catholics did not want to participate then the consequences were on them. This might wash as an explanation, but it is hardly a justification; and neither is it true. Discrimination was deliberate, pervasive, rigorously pursued and deep-seated in its effects. Even if Catholics wanted to be part of Northern Ireland, Unionism's 'group capture' of the public sector and the open sectarianism of so many workplaces simply made that impossible.

Unionist control of every aspect of Northern Ireland was aided by repressive legislation that allowed Stormont to crack down on dissent. A Special Powers Act was introduced in 1922, granting the Minister for Home Affairs sweeping control to arrest, detain and search. Although it was supposed to last for just a year, the legislation remained active until Stormont was prorogued in 1972. It was the sort of catch-all measure that, in the modern era, would have human rights campaigners raging against such disproportionate and unchecked measures. One of its Kafkaesque general provisions included the following:

> Any person who attempts to commit, or solicits or incites or endeavours to persuade another person to commit, or procures, aids or abets, or does any act preparatory to, the commission of, any act prohibited by the regulations, or any order, rules or other instrument made thereunder, or harbours any person whom he knows, or has reasonable grounds for supposing, to have acted in contravention of the regulations, or any order, rules, or other instrument made thereunder, shall be guilty of an offence against the regulations.[8]

The Act included the power of stop and search; the right to enter a building without warrants; the introduction of internment without trial; the imposition of curfews; and the ability to ban assemblies, marches and flags. There would be a shorter list of areas the Act did not impinge upon. It even had things to say about the keeping of 'motor spirit' (or petrol, presumably to prevent the production of 'Molotov cocktails'):

> Every person who uses or keeps motor spirit, whether for the purpose of supplying motive power to motor-cars or for any other purpose, shall supply such information in relation to the motor spirit used or kept by him, and the purposes for which and the manner in which it is used or kept by him, as the civil authority may by any general or special order require.

To complement these quasi-military powers came a quasi-military police force in the shape of the RUC and their notorious B-Specials. As James Craig argued at the time: 'There is no reason why every Loyalist in Ulster should not have arms in his hands legally.' As an arrangement it hardly met the Peelian principle that the police are the people and vice versa. There was no attempt at policing by consent. Unlike the British constabulary the RUC was routinely armed and served as an extension of the Stormont regime. Throughout its existence, nine out of ten RUC officers were Protestants, while the B-Specials were exclusively so (with many recruited straight from the UVF). They would go on to earn notoriety in the late 1960s for clubbing civil rights protestors, but their sectarian reputation was sealed early on. A particularly savage incident in 1922 serves as a vignette. Five men (four wearing police uniform) broke into the Belfast home of a prosperous Catholic businessman, Owen McMahon, and shot him dead before killing three of his sons and an employee. Another of his sons died shortly afterwards, while another was fortunate enough to survive his injuries. When he asked why he was being targeted, Owen McMahon was told it was because he was 'a respected papist'. This was not an isolated case.

For a population of just 1.2 million, Northern Ireland had an armed police officer or soldier for every seventeen inhabitants. The government of Northern Ireland, its civil service and its police were made up of one faction of a divided society. This had a secondary effect in that it provided a steady supply of well-paid, secure public sector jobs for the Unionist clan, a sort of 'Orange Keynesianism'. Indeed, the impact of the Orange Order

– or the Loyal Orange Institution (to give it its Sunday name) – was keenly felt in the new Northern Ireland. It is rather difficult to describe to anyone outside Northern Ireland, but its effect has been clear enough. Established in 1795 to commemorate the victory of King William of Orange over King James II at the Battle of the Boyne in 1690, the Order styles itself as a fraternal organisation dedicated to preserving reformed Christianity from the clutches of Catholicism. Yes, it has its halls and marches and regalia to which the uninitiated looking at Northern Ireland from afar might already be familiar; but the Order's political purpose is to use its grass-roots power to avert any backsliding from Unionism's political class. It is a 'trade union' for a muscular, uncompromising brand of populist Protestant–Unionist politics.

It has played a central role in Irish affairs for the past 200 years, vigorously opposing attempts at Home Rule in the late nineteenth century, and helped organise the signing of the Ulster Covenant and the formation of the Ulster Volunteers. The Order has exerted enormous influence right into the present day, not least because it helped the Ulster Unionist Party and had representation on its governing council. Indeed, between 1921 and 1969 – from partition to the start of the Troubles – only three of fifty-four Unionist Cabinet ministers were not members of the Order. The impact of a nakedly sectarian organisation on the governing class of Northern Ireland was clear. With citizens forced to endure annual marches past their homes and churches, the Orange Order was there to remind everyone in whose image and interests Northern Ireland was formed. And the answer was not Catholic–Nationalists.

To this day, Catholics are banned from the Order, as is anyone married to a Catholic, or, indeed, anyone who attends a Catholic service for any reason. While it is true that the Order endures in residual form in places like Glasgow and Liverpool – both of which have a history of sectarianism stemming from large Irish migration in the nineteenth and twentieth centuries – it is quite impossible to imagine its presence on the streets of London. The equivalent in British politics would be like having a campaign group with links to the Labour Party that openly expressed a profound distaste for Jews, or a network allied to the Conservative Party, with members on its ruling council that casually despised Muslims. Of course, no commentary on those years is complete without citing James Craig's infamous remark that Stormont was a 'Protestant Parliament and a Protestant State'.[9] Craig clearly viewed himself as a Prime Minister for Unionists only, and asserted that he was 'an Orangeman first and a politician and Member of this Parliament afterwards'. He made these remarks in 1934, which, although it was another time and world away, revealed a mindset that has been carried forwards into the modern age: the siege mentality of political Unionism: 'We hold what we have.' It is a worldview that has caused irreparable harm and lies at the heart of this century of division.

So, the apparatus of Northern Ireland's political and governing system, together with its political class, were deliberately orientated towards the advancement of one section of society over and above the interests of a significant minority of the population. Its defenders would maintain that Stormont did not make discriminatory laws. Indeed, the nature of Northern Ireland's inequality was more subtle and pervasive than that. Discrimination against the Catholic minority essentially came in two parts. The first was in public housing allocations. Northern Ireland was created as a patchwork of small local authorities; it inherited a Victorian system that saw a staggering seventy-three local authorities to administer local services for just 1.2 million people. (As few as 50,000 houses were built between the First and Second World Wars, storing up a housing shortage that would do so much to fuel the later Troubles.) One of the basic problems is that Northern Ireland's councils devised their own local policies. This ensured a delicate balance between Catholic and Protestant populations in the carefully drawn electoral boundaries which maintained electoral segregation. A familiar complaint against Unionist-controlled councils was that Catholics were considerably less likely to be rehoused than Protestants. Although Catholics were in a majority in the Fermanagh area, 82 per cent of the 1,048 council houses built between 1945 and 1967 went to local Protestants. In 1965, a batch of 194 new homes built in Dungannon were all allocated to Protestants. A particular bugbear was that the allocation of homes was not based on need, with single Protestants often taking priority over larger Catholic families. An all-too-familiar pattern emerged across Northern Ireland in which local councils used their discretionary power to blatantly discriminate against Catholics.

The second aspect of discrimination was around employment. The public sector is commonly used by contemporary politicians to ensure best practice when it comes to progressive work practices and addressing the under-representation of certain groups, but this worked in reverse in Northern Ireland. The public sector was used to reward the loyal, Protestant–Unionist workers of Northern Ireland. Civil service and policing and security jobs went to Protestants. As they did in many local councils too. In the mid-1960s, Derry Council employed 177 workers, but just thirty-two were Catholics in what was a majority Catholic city. Things were just as marked in the private sector. Here, discrimination was much easier. If your first name did not denote which tribe you came from, your surname probably would. And if these did not, which school you went to or your home address would probably give you away. Discrimination of this kind was insidious (and, to be fair to Northern Ireland, the issue lingers into the modern day elsewhere). The upshot was that as late as the 1990s, Catholics in Northern Ireland were twice as likely as Protestants to be unemployed, with Catholic redoubts in West Belfast and Derry having the highest structural unemployment in the UK.[10]

After the upheaval and carnage of Northern Ireland's founding years, a pattern gradually asserted itself. Unionist control meant Catholics were on the receiving end of systematic discrimination and became second-class citizens in the land of their birth. There were spasms of activity by the IRA throughout, particularly during their border campaign of the late 1950s and early 1960s, but this lacked popular support. What Catholic–Nationalists lacked was a compelling political figure to rally around, or sustained political momentum to change their condition. The south, meanwhile, had its own problems grappling with a moribund economy and the aftershocks of its own founding, while Westminster was content to look the other way, glad the querulous Irish were out of sight and mind. So, beaten out of the shipyards, burnt out of their homes, terrorised by the state and its sectarian police force, openly discriminated against by local government and employers, hated and despised by Unionist politicians and demonised by Protestant clergy, the Catholics of Northern Ireland were on their own.

CHAPTER 2

WE SHALL OVERCOME

Hope is a subjective term, but even set against the division and pain of Northern Ireland's birth and the long, stale decades of the mid-twentieth century, the early 1960s gave cause for hope that a brighter future was possible, with a confluence of modernising and moderating forces in play. This was the decade of John F. Kennedy's election as US President. Of British Prime Minister Harold Macmillan's landmark 'winds of change' speech heralding the start of the decolonialisation of Africa. By 1964, he had been replaced by another Harold, Harold Wilson, who was leading a new Labour government and promising to sweep away a British *ancien régime* by embracing the 'white heat' of technology and building a new, classless society. There was a new Taoiseach in the south, too, in the shape of Seán Lemass, who was determined to modernise Ireland's economy and drive the country forward. There was even a new reforming Pope, John XXIII, who was intent on bringing the Church into the modern world. Meanwhile, the European Economic Community had come into being in 1957, auguring a new era in inter-governmental co-operation between former enemies. If France and Germany could work together for their mutual benefit, then anything was possible. The peace and rising prosperity of the immediate post-war world was met with a new generation of leaders determined to learn from their predecessors' mistakes and do things differently.

Northern Ireland had its own version of a Kennedy or Wilson after a fashion. The election of Terence O'Neill as leader of the Ulster Unionists and Prime Minister of Northern Ireland in 1963 was a moment of hope, certainly when judged against events by the end of the decade. By 1969, the violence engulfing Northern Ireland would see the deployment of British troops and, from that point onwards, any prospect of constitutional politics was dashed. In that regard, the period from O'Neill's election, as only the fourth Prime Minister of Northern Ireland in the four decades since partition, to the dramatic events of 1968 to 1969 represented the last, best chance for Northern Ireland. After that, anything approaching normality was lost; engulfed by the fire and fury of what we euphemistically refer to as the Troubles.

Captain O'Neill (as he was often described) was both a predictable appointment in the dead men's shoes world of Unionist politics, but also something of a curiosity. Anglo-Irish and born in central London, he was more Knightsbridge than Banbridge. A tall, suave patrician, and 'One Nation' Tory. A splash of nobility among Ulster Unionism's grey merchant class. Educated at Eton and having served in the 6th Guards Tank Brigade during the Second World War, O'Neill was also a tragic figure. He lost two brothers in the Second World War, while his father was the first Member of Parliament to be killed fighting in the First World War. He had risen through the ossified world of Unionist politics and served as Finance Minister for the previous seven years. Perhaps unsurprisingly, his priority was economic modernisation, responding to the long-term decline of Northern Ireland's staple industries in shipbuilding and textiles. The place needed to put its best foot forward to attract international investment. With a keen eye for presentation and big gestures, O'Neill saw himself as the right man in the right place at the right time to do just that.

There was also some politics to contend with as well. Given their hyper-sensitivity about losing control of the place (entirely unjustifiably), the electoral performance of the Northern Ireland Labour Party (NILP) was becoming a concern for the Unionists. The NILP's vote almost doubled between the 1958 and 1962 Stormont elections. If it became a vehicle for liberal Protestants and co-operated with the Nationalist Party and the assortment of independent Labour candidates (five other variations of 'Labour' were returned in 1962), it might pose the first proper electoral challenge to Unionist control in four decades. As it was, the Ulster Unionists won 66 per cent of the seats on just 49 per cent of the actual vote. (The system they had so assiduously geared in their favour was still a formidable advantage.) Nevertheless, Unionists were reading the runes across at Westminster, where the long period of Conservative rule through the 1950s and early 1960s was coming undone amid economic stagnation and a welter of espionage and sex scandals that had rocked confidence in the government, which looked and seemed out of kilter with the emerging society at the start of the 'Swinging Sixties'. The main beneficiary of these powerful new trends was the recently installed Labour leader, Harold Wilson, the youngest Cabinet Minister of the twentieth century in Clement Attlee's reforming post-war government and a whip-smart economist with a photographic memory. He became Leader of the Opposition just six weeks before O'Neill took over at Stormont and was widely expected to win the forthcoming British general election. Wilson represented Huyton, in Merseyside, and before that the Lancashire town of Ormskirk. Both seats had large Irish–Catholic communities, and unlike so many in Westminster he was all too familiar with the failings of Unionist rule in Northern Ireland.

It would do no harm, then, for Unionists to appeal to moderate Protestants both to avoid being on the wrong side of Wilson, but also to counter the local Labour threat in their Stormont backyard. The need for a fresh start for Northern Ireland, together with O'Neill's own temperament, were an optimistic portent. For once (and perhaps once only), Northern Ireland was part of the zeitgeist. Yet, writing his memoirs in 1971, just eight years after first coming to office and with the Troubles in full flight, O'Neill expressed his 'personal sorrow' that his attempts to bring about reconciliation in Northern Ireland had been 'wrecked by wicked men'.

O'Neill struggled to catalyse his rhetoric and good intentions into effective action through a combination of political ineptness and wretched luck. He was met by general indifference on behalf of Nationalist Northern Ireland, who saw him as another high-born, condescending Unionist. But that was a predictable response. He was hardly going to be thanked for reforming a system his party had deliberately created to do them down. His bigger dilemma, however, was how to handle his own party and, beyond that, the wider Unionist–Loyalist clan. He was unliked by many; seen as aloof and uninterested in their provincial minutiae and petty anti-Catholicism.

Perhaps O'Neill's signature success was to invite the Irish Taoiseach, Seán Lemass, to Belfast for talks in 1965. Looking back, it seems such an insignificant gesture, but in the mutually antagonistic world of intra-Irish politics, even as late as the mid-1960s, it was the equivalent of Nixon visiting China. Only his closest advisers knew of his plan, given the potential grief from his hard-line backbenchers, but also the very real prospect of violence from Loyalists towards the visiting Prime Minister of a sovereign state. On the day Lemass arrived, O'Neill pondered over his words of welcome. 'Welcome to Ulster' might 'rub salt into the wound', while 'Welcome to Northern Ireland' might seem like 'troublemaking'.[1] So, with great tact and sensitivity, O'Neill greeted Lemass with 'Welcome to the North'. Once inside, the Taoiseach remarked: 'I shall get into terrible trouble for this.' O'Neill responded: 'No, Mr Lemass, it is I who will get into trouble for this.'[2]

The last time the premiers of both jurisdictions had met face to face was in 1925, in Stanley Baldwin's parliamentary office, along with the Chancellor of the Exchequer, Winston Churchill, to agree the outcome of the Boundary Commission for Northern Ireland, which set the seal on the precise geography of the six-county statelet. No meeting between the Prime Minister of Northern Ireland and the Taoiseach of the Irish Republic had been held since that time. And, staggeringly, no Taoiseach had set foot in Northern Ireland. O'Neill hoped to 'break the chains of fear' that had kept Northern Ireland isolated and introverted for forty-three years. (So comprehensive was the lack of dialogue that it is said that civil servants from either side would hold impromptu meetings when they visited Belfast or Dublin for Irish rugby matches.) O'Neill records in his memoirs that in twenty years as Prime Minister, his predecessor, Sir Basil Brooke, had 'never crossed the border, never visited a Catholic school and never received or sought a civic reception from a Catholic town'. Both O'Neill and Lemass had similar goals when it came to their economies. Lemass wanted Ireland to look outwards for foreign investment, while O'Neill was determined to blow the cobwebs off Northern Ireland's archaic system. As he noted of Brooke, his 'pet aversions' were that he was 'determined never to recognise the trade unions, and second, [that] he condemned planning, which he regarded as a socialist menace'.[3]

O'Neill's memoirs record, in great detail, his international jet-setting in his first couple of years as Prime Minister and Northern Ireland's salesman-in-chief (and that it was Wilson's predecessor, Sir Alec Douglas-Home, who first suggested he meet with Lemass). There was clearly an air of optimism, normality even, in those early years. The Lemass visit prompted the Nationalist Party leader, Eddie McAteer, to form an official opposition at Stormont for the first time in Northern Ireland's history. The breakthrough meeting saw a return leg with O'Neill twice visiting Lemass in Dublin, and other ministers crossing the border for other meetings. On one such occasion, the car carrying Irish Finance Minister Jack Lynch was ambushed by Ian Paisley and his acolytes, who pelted it with snowballs, shouting 'No mass, no Lemass!' At this stage, Paisley was little more than a street preacher. The brickbats he would go on to hurl at, inter alia, Dublin, Westminster, the European Union, Catholics and homosexuals – and any Unionist politicians that he felt were insufficiently rabid in their effusions of loyalty to the Crown and denunciations of Catholicism – would do far more damage than a few snowballs. Even then, in the mid-1960s, Paisley was rehearsing his routine that O'Neill and his supporters were sell-outs. They were like bridges, he maintained. They both cross over to the other side.

Riding high in the moment, O'Neill called a general election in November 1965. The result, as ever, was a foregone conclusion. He had managed to slay the phantom menace of the Northern Ireland Labour Party by keeping liberal Protestants onside. The Ulster Unionist share of the vote was up ten points – taking 59 per cent of the votes cast. Both the NILP and the Nationalist Party fell back significantly. The voters seemed to warm to O'Neill's brand of modernising, non-sectarian Unionism. This, then, was the high watermark of his political project to move Northern Ireland on from the bitterness and division that had characterised it since partition.

Earnest though O'Neill's attempts were, the lot of Northern Ireland's Catholics was still a miserable one. His modernising rhetoric had not translated through into action. In the town of

Enniskillen, Protestants were allocated public housing at a rate of eleven to one over Catholics. Half the Catholics in West Belfast were unemployed. The Orange State was still the Orange State, albeit with a more progressive captain at the wheel. However, Catholics increasingly wanted to see reform in deed as well as word. Politics was now escaping the clammy grasp of Stormont's grey men. Change had waited long enough. A new generation, especially those that had benefited from going to grammar school and university, were not going to eke out an existence and put up with being second-class citizens like their parents and grandparents.

If Catholics were pulling one way, a new breed of assertive Loyalist was pulling in the opposite direction. O'Neill's liberalism – at least his gestures – were playing into the hands of people like Ian Paisley as the centre of Unionist politics started to disintegrate. An inveterate opportunist and talented self-publicist, Paisley converted every chance to divide and outrage with his poisonous rhetoric and built a following among grass-roots Loyalists as he did so. He responded to the visit of Princess Margaret and the Queen Mother to Pope John XXIII in April 1959 by denouncing the pair for 'committing spiritual fornication with the Antichrist'. When the 'Good Pope' died in 1963, Paisley declared that 'this Romish man of sin is now in Hell!' and opposed moves to lower the flags on public buildings as a mark of respect. An incident in the 1964 general election campaign epitomised Paisley's manic and destructive energy. The Republican candidate in the October election had placed an Irish tricolour in the window of his Divis Street office in West

Belfast. It was there for three weeks before it came to Paisley's attention. He called for Protestants to gather in their thousands outside Belfast City Hall before marching on the office to remove the flag. The similarity to the pogroms of the early 1920s was plain enough. In a bid to avert Paisley's plan, dozens of RUC officers smashed their way into the Republican election office and seized the flag before retreating.

Playing to the gallery, and by now wary of Paisley's growing strength, O'Neill ludicrously claimed that the seizure of the flag was the work of Republicans who were 'nothing more than modern anarchists who refuse even now to abjure the discredited policy of violence'.[4] Of course, the RUC had intervened to head off Paisley's followers from running rampant, using excessive force themselves to placate the mob's own bloodlust. Temporarily denied the confrontation he sought, Paisley held another rally at the City Hall and called upon Stormont to prosecute those responsible for displaying the flag. A notice was served on Billy McMillen, the Republican candidate, under the Flags and Emblems Act, which outlawed the 'display of the Tricolour flag or flags of the Irish Republic, or any other flag or anything purporting to represent the Irish Republic'. So total was Unionist control – and so palpable their paranoia – that even to fly the Irish flag was a criminal offence. Undeterred, the Republicans erected a fresh flag a few days later. Soon enough, the RUC was back in numbers and smashed the office window to remove it. This was the trigger for several days of rioting during which hundreds of people were injured.

This incident helped to set a pattern for the next few years.

Every time Catholics asserted their identity, or made demands for reform, Loyalists, usually whipped up by Paisley, would respond with unsubtle demonstrations of strength. Paisley's flair for the dramatic and undoubted oratorical prowess had been evident since he founded the Free Presbyterian Church of Ulster in 1951, after helping lead a breakaway from the Presbyterian Church in Ireland following a row about not being allowed to speak at a church gathering. He would be re-elected as moderator of his sect for the next fifty-seven years. But Paisley's attentions soon strayed into matters temporal. In 1956 he was instrumental in a bizarre and disturbing episode. A fifteen-year-old Catholic girl, working in a mainly Protestant garment factory, had been encouraged to convert to Protestantism by her workmates and visiting missionaries. Maura Lyons began visiting Paisley's church, much to the consternation of her family. One night she absconded through her bedroom window and was allegedly squirrelled onto the ferry to Liverpool and away from Northern Ireland. She was then moved around England before being settled in Scotland. The story became a sensation, not least because Maura was classed as a minor and those responsible for aiding her escape had committed a criminal offence. Her parents believed she had been kidnapped and made a public appeal for her return, fearing the worst. Paisley issued a statement denying knowledge of her whereabouts but, displaying his characteristic showmanship, promised an update at a Protestant rally at the Ulster Hall, leading to speculation that Maura might miraculously reappear.

On 21 December 1956, the 3,000-capacity hall heard a tape recording of Maura in which she renounced her Catholic faith

and reassured her parents not to worry about her welfare. Paisley maintained he knew nothing of her whereabouts. In May
1957, seven months after her disappearance, and on the day of
her sixteenth birthday, Maura reappeared in public at Paisley's
home. A court case was heard two weeks later following an application from Maura's father to have her made a ward of court,
as he feared that his daughter had been brainwashed. Northern
Ireland's Lord Chief Justice, Lord MacDermott, appointed Mr
Lyons guardian of his daughter and granted him custody on the
understanding that Maura be free to observe her new religion
(although she later returned to Catholicism). Paisley and his
supporters were not allowed near her.

It is the sort of story that seems utterly bewildering to an
English audience. Nevertheless, Paisley's dramatic entrance
onto the public stage would be followed by many other controversial episodes over the long decades of the Troubles. Later, his
main vehicle was Ulster Protestant Action, a grass-roots organisation created to offer street-level opposition to any perceived
weakness from mainstream Unionists, with Paisley providing
the outrage. Indeed, he earned his first criminal convictions for
public order offences. In 1959, he addressed a UPA rally in the
strongly Loyalist Shankill area of Belfast, after which the ad-
dresses of Catholic homeowners and businesses were attacked
and looted by the crowd, who daubed 'Taigs out' ('Taig' being a
derogatory term for a Catholic) on their doors.

In February 1966, Paisley established his own newspaper,
the *Protestant Telegraph*, to help spread his brand of muscular,
uncompromising Unionism. It was just in time to help raise

tensions as Nationalists and Republicans across Ireland commemorated the fiftieth anniversary of the 1916 Easter Rising. The spectre of a resurgent IRA and Republican subversion – real or imagined (usually the latter) – provided Paisley with a useful foil. But instead of the IRA returning from the past, it was another ghost – that of the Ulster Volunteer Force – that re-emerged, carrying out a series of random killings; the first of the Troubles. Led by Augustus 'Gusty' Spence, a former British soldier and shipyard worker, the disinterred organisation threatened that 'known IRA men will be executed mercilessly and without hesitation' as they sought to ensure 'continued rule by the Protestant majority in Northern Ireland'.[5] On 7 May 1966, the UVF showed its threats were not idle when it petrol-bombed a Catholic-owned bar in the Shankill Road area of Belfast. The attackers missed their intended target and instead set fire to the home of Matilda Gould, a 77-year-old Protestant who lived next door. Gould was severely injured in the attack and died of her injuries a few weeks later. The first victim of the Troubles, though, was a 28-year-old Catholic, John Scullion, who was shot by Loyalists in the Clonard area of Belfast and succumbed to his injuries on 11 June. His was the first death, but 3,500 other people would join him in losing their lives over the next three decades. Later that month, the UVF shot three Catholic men in Malvern Street in the Shankill area of Belfast. One of them, eighteen-year-old Peter Ward, died at the scene and the two other men were seriously injured. The events of summer 1966 – while England was basking in World Cup success – were a prelude to thirty-two years of death and destruction.

A few months earlier, in March, Harold Wilson called a fresh British election to try to improve his parliamentary position and won with a 96-seat majority. One of the new MPs elected to the House of Commons was Gerry Fitt, a Republican Labour representative who was returned for Belfast West. At this time, the affairs of Northern Ireland were effectively off limits and poorly understood by most people in Westminster. The convivial Fitt helped to redress the balance and found a sympathetic ear on the Labour benches. Labour MP Paul Rose had just established the Campaign for Democracy in Ulster, and around eighty Labour MPs were now taking an interest in the situation in Northern Ireland, demanding a reform of its rigged electoral system and the extension of anti-discrimination measures. In July, the *Sunday Times* Insight team carried out an investigation into Northern Ireland following a visit by the Queen. Entitled 'John Bull's Political Slum', it was an all-too-rare exposé of life in Northern Ireland, and highlighted the political gerrymandering and widespread discrimination against the Catholic minority.[6] Harold Wilson would need to decide whether to use the reserve powers of the British government to insist on measures to redress the balance, 'or simply allow Britain's most isolated province to work out its own bizarre destiny', the newspaper argued. 'During the forty-five years since partition the latter has often been negligently adopted with what looks like disastrous results.'

O'Neill's position was fast eroding, assailed now on all sides. Ministers were clamouring for reform, with added pressure coming from the Labour back benches; but he was not the one who needed convincing. He struggled to persuade his party to take the initiative and make reforms of their own volition – never mind the added headache of managing the wider Unionist clan – with Paisley breathing down his neck and even the UVF back in business. Indeed, the RUC had warned O'Neill about his own personal safety. Not from attack by the IRA, but from Loyalists.

In 1967, the Northern Ireland Civil Rights Association (NICRA) was formed. Catholics had drilled their frustrations down into a coherent set of demands, including the introduction of 'one man, one vote' – the universal franchise – for local government elections. At the time, only ratepayers and company directors could vote. The association also called for an end to the abuse of electoral boundaries. Just as important was an end to the rigging of the public housing system and public sector employment, both of which were skewed against Catholics. NICRA also demanded the repeal of the Special Powers Act and the disbandment of the hated B-Specials, which by now was unmistakably a Loyalist militia. What was significant, a year before 1968 and the birth of more radical protest movements across the Western world, was that NICRA was essentially working within the system. Activists wanted Stormont's reform, not its destruction – not that Unionists realised this. Unfortunately, the activists' polite letters and reasoned entreaties fell on deaf ears. Emboldened by the experience of the US civil rights movement, they took their efforts to the streets, and the embracing of direct action would become a watershed moment. In June 1968, civil rights activists highlighted the inequity of the allocation of housing by occupying a house in Caledon in County Tyrone. The building was part of a new development in Dungannon and had been allocated to a nineteen-year-old unmarried Protestant woman ahead of local Catholic families with children who were in greater need. The fact she was also the secretary of the local Ulster Unionist MP brought home just how nepotistic the process was. The protestors – including Stormont MP Austin Currie – were dragged out of the house by officers from the RUC (one of which was the woman's brother), but the incident chalked up another public relations victory for NICRA in the process.

Throughout 1968, civil rights protests were routinely banned ostensibly because of a threat from Loyalists to mount counter-demonstrations, but this was usually a convenient excuse to stifle dissent. In October, NICRA organised a march in Derry, only for the Apprentice Boys (another of the Loyal Orders) to announce they would also hold one. The RUC banned all marches, but the civil rights movement, inspired by the example of student radicals and Vietnam anti-war activists, ignored the ban and marched anyway. The result was grimly predictable. The RUC surrounded the NICRA group and beat them indiscriminately and without provocation. More than 100 people were injured, including several MPs who were present. Gerry Fitt sustained a nasty head injury, courtesy of an RUC officer's baton, which, given his canny knack for self-publicity, played well to the television cameras. It was a political catastrophe for the Stormont government, and portrayed Northern Ireland in all its ignominy. Yet, rather than undermining the civil rights movement, the treatment of the marchers merely emboldened them further. Thousands flocked to their cause. Northern Ireland went into one of its familiar tailspins, with street protests and violence, but something was different this time. Now, the eyes of the world could see what Catholics had been complaining about for decades. Stormont's hard-line Home Affairs Minister, William Craig, was unmoved: 'I wouldn't have given two hoots for the Labour MPs who were present, or the TV pictures.' His view was all too typical. As far as many Unionists were concerned, the civil rights movement was a Republican Trojan Horse. They believed the IRA was pulling the strings. It was just another front in their perennial campaign to destroy Northern Ireland. Therefore, any attempt to placate Catholic demands would simply see further demands for concessions. Where would that end? Better to hold the line as Unionists had been doing since partition.

Harold Wilson summoned O'Neill to Downing Street for a dressing down, and bluntly informed the Prime Minister of Northern Ireland that he was lower down the pecking order than the Prime Minister of the UK. If he could not put his house in order, then Whitehall would take over and do it for him. If that threat did not stir Unionists into action, then perhaps the loss of funding might focus minds? Wilson's Home Secretary, James Callaghan, warned O'Neill against 'stringing the UK government along' with further delay. He hurriedly pulled together a five-point reform programme, bowing to some of the demands for change from civil rights protestors. Ludicrously, he omitted the demand for 'one man, one vote' in local elections. Amid continuing unrest on the streets, O'Neill went on television to address Northern Ireland. 'What kind of Ulster do you want?' he asked plaintively. 'A happy and respected province, in good standing with the rest of the UK, or a place continually torn apart by riots and demonstrations and regarded as a political outcast?'[7]

Sensing it might be making a breakthrough, NICRA postponed further marches, but a breakaway group, People's Democracy, unsatisfied with the limited concessions on offer, was not similarly assuaged. A group of around forty students set off from Queen's University in Belfast on a four-day march to Derry in January 1969. They sought to emulate Martin Luther King's landmark march from Selma to Montgomery just four years previously. When they arrived at Burntollet Bridge on the outskirts of Derry on the fourth day, they were set upon by a gang of around 300 Loyalists. Rocks came first, then the RUC stepped back and allowed the Loyalists to swarm forwards. Heavily outnumbered by assailants armed with iron bars and clubs with nails driven through the end, the marchers were pulverised, with some jumping in the icy river Faughan for protection. The RUC stood idly by. Later, it would turn out that some of the mob were in fact off-duty police officers.

O'Neill was losing control of the political situation and becoming increasingly unpopular with both his colleagues and the Unionist grass roots. His Minister for Commerce, Brian Faulkner, resigned, as did William Craig, the Home Affairs Minister. In fact, so marginalised had O'Neill become that one of his lieutenants, George Forrest, had been pulled off a 12 July stage that he was speaking on in Coagh, County Tyrone and kicked unconscious by members of the Orange Order. He died the next year, which triggered a by-election in his Mid Ulster parliamentary seat. His widow stood in his place, but lost to Bernadette Devlin, one of the leaders of People's Democracy. She achieved instant celebrity, causing a sensation with her maiden speech in the House of Commons. Delivered on hand-written notes, and disavowing the convention that the new Member says something pleasant about their predecessor, 21-year-old Devlin let rip. She articulated the frustrations of the Catholic–Nationalist minority with a heady mixture of cold fury, moral outrage, socialist ethics and on-the-ground reportage. But she did something else; she made the point that poor Protestants were also victims of a system that perpetuated economic winners and losers. Scornful, in the best traditions of parliamentary debate, other MPs looked on as a young woman, plausibly of their daughters' age, laid out the charge sheet against half a century of Unionist misrule:

> Captain O'Neill listed a number of reforms which came nowhere near satisfying the needs of the people. Had he even had the courage of his convictions – had he even convictions – to carry out the so-called reforms he promised, we might have got somewhere. But none of his so-called reforms was carried out … He suggested that a points system [for housing] should be introduced, but he did nothing to force the majority of Unionist-controlled councils to introduce it.[8]

She went on:

The situation with which we are faced in Northern Ireland is one in which I feel I can no longer say to the people 'Don't worry about it. Westminster is looking after you.' Westminster cannot condone the existence of this situation. It has on its benches Members of that party [the Ulster Unionists] who by deliberate policy keep down the ordinary people. The fact that I sit on the Labour benches and am likely to make myself unpopular with everyone on these benches ... Any socialist government worth its guts would have got rid of them long ago.

Presciently, Devlin warned against deploying British soldiers to Northern Ireland and instead suggested abolishing Stormont and introducing direct rule from Whitehall as a temporary expedient (a policy that was adopted two years later by the British government, albeit for the next thirty-eight years). Yet, finally, here on the floor of the House of Commons was a reckoning for Stormont's record. Liberal Party leader Jeremy Thorpe (whose great-grandfather had been a superintendent in the Dublin police) spoke immediately after Devlin, stating that for far too long 'the problems and grievances of this unhappy part of the United Kingdom have been neglected by the House'. He added:

We regard the refusal of the Ulster Unionist Party to afford the full rights of citizenship to the Catholic minority in the province as not only offensive and wrong but crass folly. It is notorious that the delay in according full democratic rights to all citizens is the result of Paisleyite and other bigoted pressures which have been brought to bear on the Government there.[9]

Even though Northern Ireland was now under the microscope, with more MPs than ever sympathetic to the plight of Catholic–Nationalists, large parts of Westminster were still unmoved. Roy Hattersley, then a junior defence minister in Wilson's Labour government and later deputy leader of his party, wrote that Devlin's speech was 'the authentic, bitter and resentful voice of Catholic Ulster'. James Prior, who would later become Secretary of State for Northern Ireland, leaned over the bench to whisper to Edward Heath, who was then the Leader of the Opposition, remarking what a 'virtuoso' performance it was. 'Yes, but it's the only speech she's got in her, she can't make another one,' was Heath's dismissive reply.

On 1 May 1969, Terence O'Neill resigned as Prime Minister of Northern Ireland. He was facing the prospect of a 'no confidence' motion by his colleagues and decided to call a general election in February in the hope of reaffirming his mandate. It was to prove his undoing. The election offered little reprieve and resulted in the Ulster Unionists splitting – around 60/40 – with some candidates backing O'Neill and others standing on a platform opposing their own leader. (As well as being O'Neill's last election, it would prove to be the final election to Stormont.) His last weeks in office were marred by a series of bombings to utility infrastructure which led to water shortages and blackouts. It added to the general sense of chaos and was blamed on the IRA, though it was, in fact, the work of the UVF in an attempt to destroy what was left of O'Neill's credibility and usher him from office.

Although progress towards making Northern Ireland a less

egregiously divided and sectarian society was glacial, the pace was still too fast for many of O'Neill's colleagues. In a cruel irony, he finally managed to get agreement from his Cabinet colleagues for the introduction of 'one man, one vote' reforms to the electoral system. To add insult to injury, O'Neill had faced a stiff challenge in his own Bannside constituency from his nemesis, Ian Paisley. A few days after his resignation, O'Neill gave an interview to the *Belfast Telegraph* in which he summed up, in his unfortunate manner, the political dilemma he faced:

> It is frightfully hard to explain to Protestants that if you give Roman Catholics a good job and a good house they will live like Protestants because they will see neighbours with cars and television sets; they will refuse to have eighteen children. But if a Roman Catholic is jobless and lives in the most ghastly hovel he will rear eighteen children on National Assistance. If you treat Roman Catholics with due consideration and kindness they will live like Protestants in spite of the authoritative nature of their Church.[10]

If these were the comments of liberal Unionism's 'Great White Hope', one can only imagine the views of O'Neill's more austere critics. O'Neill's successor was James Chichester-Clark, a former major in the Irish Guards turned Stormont career politician (and, in the nepotistic world of Northern Irish politics, O'Neill's cousin). He had recently resigned from the Cabinet in protest at the granting of 'one man, one vote'.

The political and security situation in Northern Ireland

continued to deteriorate during the summer of 1969. In Derry, the numerically superior Catholic community (accounting for around 60 per cent of the city's population) had already established a no-go area – 'Free Derry' – in the Bogside part of the city, blocking off roads which it then patrolled to deny the RUC entry. Problems reached their peak in the middle of August following a Loyalist march. Coin-throwing turned into fighting, which progressed into rioting, which then escalated into a three-day battle with Loyalists and the RUC pitched against Nationalist residents, with both sides hurling rocks and petrol bombs, while the RUC fired 1,000 cannisters of CS gas at protestors – this was the first time the gas was used in Northern Ireland, although it would not be the last, despite never having been deployed anywhere else in the UK. Officers from across Ireland were drafted in to try to restore order. However, the 'Battle of the Bogside' quickly spread to other parts of Northern Ireland, particularly as there was a view that by widening the protests RUC resources would be pulled back from Derry.

Over in Belfast, events were even more tumultuous. Amid the general confusion, Catholics feared that a pogrom was in the offing, with Loyalist attacks coming from all sides in the various flashpoint areas across West Belfast. The fighting was intense, with regular clashes and running gun battles between the IRA and marauding Loyalist gangs, who were burning and looting houses. The RUC deployed Shorland armoured cars, fearsome military vehicles – replete with machine-gun turrets – designed for the RUC before the Troubles broke out. They were now roaming the streets of Belfast with devastating consequences.

One incident gained immediate notoriety. Three Shorlands opened fire on Divis Tower, a newly built high-rise block at the bottom of the mainly Nationalist Falls Road, mistakenly assuming that IRA gunmen were using it as a vantage point. The vehicles' machine guns raked the building with bullets, which tore through the walls of the building, in one journalist's description, 'as if they were cardboard'. Inside, a nine-year-old boy, Patrick Rooney, was killed as he lay in his bed. He was the first child to be a victim of the Troubles. The Shorlands opened fire again later. This time twenty-year-old Hugh McCabe, a Catholic but also a serving British soldier at home on leave, was killed. Given the RUC's high-velocity gunfire hit a total of thirteen flats in Divis Tower, it was amazing not more people were killed.

Northern Ireland's grisly sectarian secrets, so long concealed, were pouring forth and being transmitted around the world by television news crews. As they had done the preceding year, the RUC generally did not think twice about knocking lumps out of any Catholic that stood in their way, whether cameras were present or not. As events continued to deteriorate, the Irish Taoiseach, Jack Lynch, made a televised address. He began by stating that the Irish government had acted with 'great restraint' over recent months while it applied diplomatic pressure behind the scenes, as the situation in Northern Ireland deteriorated, but this had proven futile. Indeed, it was 'evident' that Stormont was 'no longer in control of the situation' and that the present state of affairs was 'the inevitable outcome of the policies pursued for decades by successive Stormont governments'.[11] The Irish government could 'no longer stand by' while people were injured 'and perhaps worse'. Lynch's remarks – calibrated to cause a diplomatic frisson – were a marker of how bad Anglo-Irish relations were in those days. Scolded into action by Westminster's inertia, Lynch then played his main card:

> The Irish Government have, therefore, requested the British government to apply immediately to the United Nations for the urgent despatch of a peace-keeping force to the six counties of Northern Ireland and have instructed the Irish permanent representative to the United Nations to inform the secretary-general of this request. We have also asked the British government to see to it that police attacks on the people of Derry should cease immediately.

Not content with causing diplomatic embarrassment by invoking the UN, Lynch went further still:

> Very many people have been injured and some of them seriously. We know that many of these do not wish to be treated in six county hospitals. We have, therefore, directed the Irish Army authorities to have field hospitals established in County Donegal adjacent to Derry and at other points along the border where they may be necessary.

UN peacekeepers and field hospitals to protect Northern Ireland's citizens from the brutality of their own police force? Lynch was treating Britain like some despotic regime. Tellingly, his list of demands – the internationalisation of the management of Northern Ireland's Troubles; a role for the Irish Republic in its affairs; the replacement of the RUC; and the granting of universal civil rights for all and the eventual unification of the island of Ireland – were all met in the Good Friday Agreement settlement thirty years later. Yet again, the analysis of what needed to happen was clear at the start of the Troubles.

Northern Ireland's new Prime Minister, James Chichester-Clark, said that Lynch's remarks were 'deplorable' and that they would inflame tensions. He told Stormont that the trouble was 'not the agitation of a minority seeking by lawful means the assertion of political rights'.[12] Rather, it was a 'conspiracy of forces seeking to overthrow a Government democratically elected by a large majority'. Even at this stage there was a complete unwillingness to countenance the role played in proceedings by half a century of Unionist control. 'What the teenage hooligans seek beyond cheap kicks I do not know,' he added. 'But of this I am quite certain – they are being manipulated and encouraged by those who seek to discredit and overthrow this Government.' On 14 August 1969, British soldiers were despatched to Northern Ireland to help restore order after days of intense rioting. A request for military support to 'come to the aid of the civil power' had already been received from Stormont, but Whitehall had initially refused in an attempt to avoid such an escalation, if at all possible. Roy Hattersley, then a defence minister, recalled the sequence of events:

A group of civil servants came to my house. They all advised delay. That, to my relief, was Callaghan's instinct. Next day, I went to Downing Street to 'debrief' the Prime Minister. Did the Ministry of Defence, Harold Wilson asked, share the Home Secretary's view? Rather nervously, I told him that it did. 'Quite right,' he said. 'Once they're on the streets, the soldiers may be there for weeks.' They were there for thirty years.[13]

However, events continued to worsen. 'On the following Sunday, we had no choice,' Hattersley recalled, as the request from Stormont was repeated.

> Again, we agonised. Then a message came in the name of Bernadette Devlin. If troops did not close the bridges across the river Foyle there would be mayhem that would end with Catholics being slaughtered. If both the police and the Republican irregulars thought that the time had come for military intervention, we had no choice. Callaghan agreed. I solemnly signed the required document and awaited the wrath of my Irish constituents for the sin of 'sending in the troops'.[14]

'Operation Banner', as the deployment was known, would last for the better part of the next four decades, with up to 20,000 soldiers deployed in Northern Ireland at its peak. Over the course of four days in August, eight people were killed, including five Catholics slain by the RUC. More than 750 Catholic homes and nearly 300 businesses had been destroyed. During the summer of 1969, a total of 1,800 families had been forced to flee their homes – four-fifths of them were Catholics. Many initially welcomed the army's presence – anything to stop the

Loyalists' attacks. This was not, however, a sentiment that survived contact with reality for long. Under Stormont's direction, soldiers became an adjunct of the Orange State. Liberators soon enough were regarded by Catholics as persecutors, as Northern Ireland slid ever deeper into the mire. The Troubles had begun.

*   *   *

The first thing to say about the period between 1963 to 1969 is that the echoes of the earlier Edwardian period are strikingly apparent. It began with Catholic–Nationalists calling for reform not revolution – seeking concessions from the Unionist-controlled state. This was met with aggression, both by the sectarian police and by Loyalist mobs. It involved crushing peaceful, progressive dissent and unleashing mindless attacks on Catholic communities, driving thousands from their homes – the pogroms of the early 1920s revisited. It ended with an alienated Catholic community pushed towards radicalism. In summing up those critical few years, it is hard not to offer Marx's famous quote as summation: 'History repeats itself, the first time as tragedy, the second time as farce.' What happened in the mid- to late 1960s in Northern Ireland, and the British government policy that helped shaped it, might be considered farcical. After all, the historical parallels were there as a warning. But farce is hardly the appropriate term to describe the blood, fury and division that was unleashed. It was a time of rapid change, where the Stormont regime reaped the whirlwind of its half-century of mismanaging Northern Ireland, and an absentee British government came to learn the price of assuming the stale political settlement there could endure. O'Neill's mood music around reform helped to both validate Nationalist criticisms and encourage the civil rights movement, as well as inspiring a Loyalist backlash. If Stormont was prepared to bend a little, then perhaps the whole edifice would crumble? Nationalists and Loyalists alike shared that belief. O'Neill was simply not equal to the demands of the times. He could not catalyse his good intentions and deliver results quickly enough. In mitigation, no one else within Unionism was going further than O'Neill, so his efforts represented the farthest point it was possible to go to placate Catholic–Nationalist demands. After leaving office, O'Neill had lunch with an SDLP MP who told him that 'the Protestants were mad not to support you, if they had done so, partition would have become permanent'.

That O'Neill tried to be an agent of change was apparent, even amid the gales of sectarianism that befell his earnest attempt to create a better Northern Ireland. He tried to bring about change through talk of modernisation and hoped, by bringing new investment and industry into Northern Ireland, that all would benefit from it. That a rising tide would raise all boats, as Kennedy put it. At no time did he really try to address the structural inequalities at the heart of Northern Ireland. If he had done so, if he had had more success or fortitude, another future might have been possible. One where Northern Ireland's ruling elite would accept that a new generation would not put up with the discrimination and privations that previous generations had been subjected to. In this scenario, Unionism would have reacted to, amended and accommodated the eminently reasonable demands of the civil rights movement. If so, many of the subsequent events would have been avoided. Northern Ireland's centenary might have been a more benign affair.

Alas, events did not take this turn and we have an altogether different legacy to contend with. In retrospect, O'Neill's analysis of what needed to change in Northern Ireland was accurate. He talked a good game but simply did not bring about real change. Northern Ireland's second university went to Protestant Coleraine rather than Catholic Derry, Northern Ireland's second-largest city. Indeed, when a new city was created it was called Craigavon, after James Craig, with perhaps only Paisley being a more divisive figure for Catholics. Although the pace of events sprinted past him, O'Neill's memoirs, written in 1971, remain prescient.

As I look back, my overwhelming sentiment is one of regret. What could have been solved in peace had to be settled in bloodshed. Continuous one-party rule in any country breeds all sorts of attendant evils. The knowledge that any splits or rows which develop will still leave the party in control of the government, tends to encourage political boat-rocking, in the hope that a new crew can clamber on to the bridge. This is particularly true if a prime minister is trying to carry out long-overdue reforms, in a country where any reform can be described as treachery.[15]

CHAPTER 3

THE POINT OF NO RETURN

As a new decade began, British soldiers were patrolling the streets of British cities. A problem that had lain dormant for two generations had exploded – metaphorically and literally – back into the centre of political life in Westminster. Was it still possible to pull Northern Ireland back from the brink? Could its system of government be reformed? Was there sufficient goodwill to make that happen? 1970 was the year that moderate Nationalists and civil rights activists would come together to form the Social Democratic and Labour Party, and pursue reform and eventual Irish unification through constitutional means. The same year saw the launch of the cross-community Alliance Party. A year later, in 1971, the Ulster Unionists, so wary of the Paisleyites for the past decade, had further reason to feel a chill run down their collective spines when Ian Paisley launched the Democratic Unionist Party.

This was also the moment the Republican movement split between Marxists who, broadly, wanted to explore greater class consciousness with working-class Loyalists – and those radicalised by the Troubles who got involved defending Catholic enclaves from Loyalist gangs and now wanted to take the fight to the British and drive them from Ireland once and for all. The division within the Republican movement between the 'Official' and 'Provisional' IRA would be reconciled by the 'Provos' becoming pre-eminent. After all, the outlook for progressing the Republican movement's aims through political means or cross-community dialogue looked decidedly bleak. Engaging with Stormont and Westminster was viewed as a waste of time. (This point was brought home when Bernadette Devlin was arrested and jailed after losing an appeal against a six-month prison sentence imposed for taking part in riots in Derry.) In March 1970, there were further riots in the Springfield Road area of Belfast following an Orange Order parade. The British Army used 'snatch squads' to arrest Catholic youths. The ugly confrontations saw the army use CS gas in Belfast for the first time, with thirty-eight soldiers injured as well as an unknown number of civilians. The army's honeymoon period with the Catholic–Nationalist community was already a distant memory, even ahead of more dramatic events that would soon unfold.

At the end of April, the B-Specials were officially disbanded. Seen as an oppressive Orange militia by Catholics, they had become an embarrassment to both the British government and Stormont itself. Indeed, the General Officer Commanding of British troops in Northern Ireland, Lieutenant-General Ian Freeland, had strongly recommended abolishing the unit. The force was replaced by the creation of the Ulster Defence Regiment (UDR), a largely part-time division of the British Army

that was recruited locally. Initially, Catholics comprised nearly
a fifth of recruits, although this would rapidly wane. It would
go on to become the largest regiment in the army and play a
prominent role for the rest of the Troubles, either working to
stabilise the security situation, or as a rebranded version of the
B-Specials, depending on taste. Announcing the creation of
the UDR in November 1969, defence minister Roy Hattersley
told the House of Commons that although overall defence matters were for the British government, 'the tasks for which this
new force will be raised are of the greatest importance to the
Government of Northern Ireland'. Crucially, the deployment of
the UDR, under control of the General Officer Commanding,
would be expected to engage in 'the fullest possible consulta-
tion with the Government of Northern Ireland about the use
of this force'. For all intents and purposes, the UDR became
an extension of Stormont. Freeland signalled a new 'get tough'
policy and announced that those throwing petrol bombs could
now be shot dead or face ten years in prison. That same month,
Ian Paisley was elected in a Stormont by-election caused by the
resignation of Terence O'Neill, who had accepted a peerage in
January 1970. There could be no starker example of where the
power and energy now lay in Unionist politics. The pre-eminent
moderate from the Unionist elite first ousted and then replaced
by the one-time fringe radical.

Harold Wilson went to the country in June 1970. The assumption was that victory was his for the taking; however, Labour
lost to the Conservatives, and the new Prime Minister, Edward
Heath, inherited a rapidly deteriorating situation in Northern

Ireland. In July, the British Army sealed off part of the Falls Road area of West Belfast and introduced a curfew following an escalation in rioting caused by a previous army incursion into the area. For thirty-six hours soldiers raided hundreds of houses and arrested 300 people in a search for the IRA and their arms. Homes were smashed to pieces and people beaten in the process, which cast the army as an occupying force in the eyes of the Catholic–Nationalists. Indeed, four people were killed and sixty others injured during the raids. Fifteen soldiers were shot by the IRA (both wings), who, in the confusion, suspected another Loyalist pogrom was in the offing. A Catholic man was killed when he was run over by a Saxon armoured vehicle, deliberately so as many onlookers insisted. The curfew was broken by a 'march of mothers' who pulled the barbed-wire blockades to one side and brushed past the soldiers to bring in food and medical supplies.

The switch at Westminster resulted in a hardening of policy, with Heath's Home Secretary, Reginald Maudling, stating quite openly in the House of Commons that the government was now 'at war with the IRA'.[1] From this point, rubber bullets were commonly used, as were counter-insurgency methods previously seen in former British colonies. This would eventually see interrogation programmes against Republican suspects and British security agencies work with Loyalists to target suspected IRA members for assassination. But before that, the Military Reaction Force – plain-clothed soldiers – were sanctioned to drive around Nationalist parts of Belfast shooting at suspected IRA figures, or, more usually, innocent bystanders. The British government was intent on flogging a broken system, while Irish Republicans, more cognisant of their history, saw it as another episode in a long-running saga and were digging in for a long fight. Amid the gunfire and explosions, neither side could hear the alarm bells. Yet amid these rising tensions, incremental reforms to Northern Ireland's system of government were taking place. A housing executive was created to take over control of the building and allocation of public sector housing to help address the systematic bias against Catholics. Local councils, many of which were Unionist-controlled thanks to blatant gerrymandering, were stripped of powers. A boundary commission was established in 1971 to help address electoral chicanery. Yet none of this was equal to the scale and pace of events. If reforms had been pushed through even five years earlier, much of what followed might have been avoided. If Stormont had shown it was capable of reform, then Catholic–Nationalists might have remained engaged in trying to work within the system.

Instead, the parameters were now clear. On the one hand there was the Provisional IRA, committed to defending Catholic areas from attack and, more broadly, ending British rule by military force. Then there was the SDLP, representing moderate Catholic opinion and trying to establish a political way forward. On the other side of the equation was Stormont, now with the British Army on hand to help them re-establish control. Loyalists too. The divisions within the Ulster Unionist Party were less acute now given that no one was talking about reform anymore. Behind them, the British government, looking on with increasing concern, but now pulled into the conflict and obliged to back the soldiers come what may. Maudling had warned that direct rule would be considered if the situation was not recovered. In turn, Stormont ministers put pressure on army chiefs to assert control. It was a vicious circle. Westminster wanted to put Northern Ireland back in a box. Stormont wanted to tighten its grip. And the army, under local control, did as it was told, relying on senior officers entirely unsuited to dealing with this kind of civilian uprising taking place within the confines of the British state itself. They defaulted to the handbook from previous colonial conflicts, albeit ones where the television cameras were not privy to their dubious methods.

Throughout 1971, the same pattern continued unabated. In February, the first British soldier was killed since troops had first been deployed. Robert Curtis, a twenty-year-old gunner, was shot by the IRA. He had just learned that his wife was expecting a child. In March, Brian Faulkner succeeded James Chichester-Clark as Northern Ireland's Prime Minister after defeating the hard-line William Craig. Faulkner suggested a system of Stormont committees to oversee control of key government departments as a means of bringing the SDLP on board. The idea foundered after the SDLP, which was still, in essence, a civil rights protest group, withdrew from Stormont in protest after ministers refused an inquiry into the shooting of two Catholic men in Derry by soldiers.

That year's main event was the imposition of internment without trial. A misplaced belief that rounding up the 'ringleaders' would deprive the IRA of its momentum saw a co-ordinated swoop across Northern Ireland, with 342 people arrested and taken to makeshift camps. The overwhelming majority of them were ordinary Catholic men and a few known Republicans. In the furore that followed, seventeen people were killed by soldiers over the next forty-eight hours. These included a Catholic priest, who was giving the last rites to a dying man, and a mother of eight. Interment lasted until December 1975 and would eventually see 1,981 people imprisoned over that time. In total, 1,874 of them were Catholics and just 107 were Protestant–Loyalists.[2] The reverberations were quickly apparent. Over the coming days, an estimated 7,000 Catholic families were forced from their homes by marauding Loyalist mobs. The SDLP and many other non-Unionist councillors withdrew from their public roles. Thousands of Nationalist council house tenants withheld rent and rates as part of a rolling campaign of civil disobedience. David Bleakley from the Northern Ireland Labour Party, whom Faulkner had appointed as Minister for Community Relations, resigned his position. In Westminster, a group of five Northern Ireland MPs, including Bernadette Devlin and John Hume, held a 48-hour hunger strike in protest at the internment rules. All of which had little effect. The British government was sleepwalking into a prolonged confrontation and subsidising the incompetence of a Stormont regime that simply learned nothing from its mistakes. Yet, it would take even more dramatic events to dislodge British complacency.

At the end of January 1972, on a cold, bright winter's afternoon in Derry, a civil rights march against internment began to wend its way into the city centre. Two hours later, twenty-seven people had been shot by British soldiers. Thirteen of them were killed outright and a fourteenth would die later. No soldiers were injured. It was the largest loss of life committed on British soil by state forces since fifteen people were killed by Yeomanry at the Peterloo Massacre in Manchester in 1819. 'Bloody Sunday' – as it invariably became known – made a difficult situation incalculably worse. Northern Ireland's bleak history would see lots of turning points, but perhaps none would become so totemic.

The context is important. Two weeks prior to Bloody Sunday, Faulkner had banned all marches. Undeterred at this age-old tactic to rob the Irish of their right to protest, an anti-internment march was held on a strip of coastline at Magilligan Strand in County Derry, near to where an internment camp had been established. Several thousand people took part and as they neared the site they were confronted by British soldiers. When they refused to disperse, CS gas and rubber bullets were fired at them. Some of the soldiers were from the Parachute Regiment and had been brought across from Belfast, where they had recently been deployed in the Falls Road curfew. The soldiers were set loose on the marchers and many were severely beaten. John Hume, one of the march organisers, accused the soldiers of 'beating, brutalising and terrorising the demonstrators'.

Despite the experience at Magilligan, a subsequent march was scheduled in the centre of Derry for Sunday 30 March. The organisers informed the RUC, who in turn discussed their approach with the army. The Chief Superintendent of the RUC, Frank Lagan, recommended that the army hold back and allow the march to take place. The local army chief recommended this course of action to General Robert Ford, Commander of Land Forces, and the top soldier in Northern Ireland, who had taken over the previous July at the height of the Falls Road curfew. A security hardliner, he ignored the advice and placed Derek Wilford, who was then a lieutenant colonel and commander of the 1st Battalion of the Parachute Regiment on the day, in charge of a snatch operation.

To avoid a repeat of the violence they had been subjected to at Magilligan, the protest leaders pleaded for a peaceful and dignified march. Ivan Cooper, a Stormont MP and leading civil rights campaigner, had even liaised with the local IRA and had an assurance that their members would withdraw from the area on the day. The march began at 2.50 p.m., setting off from the Creggan estate to the Bogside area, just outside the city walls, near to the centre of Derry. As it approached its destination some estimates had the crowd of marchers as high as 20,000. By 3.45 p.m. most of the group departed for a rally. Some of them broke away and headed to nearby barricades, where British soldiers were waiting, for one of their regular stand-offs. Away from both the rally and the barricade lines, soldiers opened fire, shooting a fifteen-year-old boy, Damien Donaghy, and 59-year-old John Johnston. The boy survived his injuries, but Johnston succumbed to his five months later (making him the first to be shot but the last victim of Bloody Sunday to die).

At precisely 4.07 p.m. that afternoon, an order was given for the 1st Battalion Parachute Regiment to begin an arrest operation against 'rioters', with a clearly expressed instruction that soldiers were not to begin a 'running battle'. Exactly three minutes later, the shooting started. By 4.40 p.m., twenty-seven people had been shot. Thirteen lay dead. Much of the carnage was covered by television cameras and watching journalists. On a day of stark imagery, the sight of Fr Edward Daly waving a blood-stained handkerchief as he led a group of men carrying a mortally injured teenager, Jackie Duddy, became a harrowing vignette.

Bloody Sunday was a human rights disgrace. A reckless and unjustified slaughter. But, militarily, it was a disaster; revealing the limits of the British Army's ability to police a civilian theatre. And it was also a political catastrophe with deep, abiding ramifications. It was caused by a poisonous cocktail of ill-disciplined soldiers, inept commanders and hand-wringing politicians. This was not a 'fog of war' incident. It was a sustained attack from soldiers that had already earned notoriety for casual brutality that lasted for half an hour. It was the result of a culture where 'getting stuck into them' had become an unwritten rule of engagement to deal with 'hooligans'. But it is difficult not to read Bloody Sunday as a warning. A hard lesson meted out for Derry's insubordination. It was a tactical mistake, but it served a strategic purpose. The message was clear: we will stop at nothing, so get into line.

The cover-up was instantaneous: it was all the fault of the deceased; they were IRA men; they shot first; they had pipe bombs. Of course, these were all lies; proven to be so by Lord Saville's landmark inquiry thirty years later. Bloody Sunday failed the elementary test of handling a political crisis by not future-proofing the position. 'Is what I'm saying today going to

make sense next week/month/year?' The army's excuses, amplified by the disingenuousness of their political masters, were as
nonsensical in 1972 as they have proven to be decades later. The
essential facts are indisputable. Twenty-seven people shot and
thirteen dead on the day. The fundamental injustice of Bloody
Sunday should have been reconciled immediately. Democratic
governments do not shoot protestors down in the street – especially their own citizens. Moreover, not people with a justifiable
cause that Westminster had failed for decades. The smart move
would have been to admit it was a horrible sequence of mistakes
and take responsibility. But that did not happen. The British
state leaned into its failures. It protected the incompetence of
senior officers and the stupidity of a small group of bloodthirsty
soldiers.

The result was that Bloody Sunday turbo-charged the Provisional IRA, bringing in volunteers and donations and val-
idating their argument that the Orange State and the British
Army could never be engaged with and had to be confronted
and defeated. They must be the enemy because, in turn, they
perceived ordinary Catholics as the enemy. Ultimately, hundreds
of other British soldiers would lose their lives because of the actions of British commanders and a handful of trigger-happy soldiers on Sunday 31 January 1972. Speaking years later, one of the
paratroopers on the day, whose whistle-blowing helped secure
Lord Saville's fresh judicial inquiry, described the 'rottweiler'
mentality in the 1st Battalion Parachute Regiment. 'I had the
distinct impression', he said, 'that this was a case of some soldiers realising this was an opportunity to fire their weapon and

they did not want to miss the chance.' He added: 'There was no justification for a single shot I saw fired ... the only threat was a large assembly of people and we were all experienced soldiers who had been through riot situations before.'[3]

There then followed a dizzying sequence of events. The next day, British Home Secretary Reginald Maudling made a statement in the House of Commons. 'The Army returned the fire directed at them with aimed shots and inflicted a number of casualties on those who were attacking them with firearms and with bombs,' he told MPs.[4] His biographer, Lewis Baston, recounted:

> He sat down without a word of regret ('deep anxiety' was as far as he went), or sympathy for the relatives of those who had been killed, having smeared all those who died as having been armed with guns or bombs. It was a deplorable statement, inadequate to the occasion as well as inaccurate.[5]

Unable to catch the Speaker's eye so she could rebut his falsehoods, Bernadette Devlin launched herself across the chamber of the House of Commons, grabbed Maudling by the hair and slapped him repeatedly, calling him a 'murdering hypocrite'. Maudling tried to make light of it by saying that he was used to his grandchildren pulling his hair. Devlin later remarked that she wished she had grabbed him by the throat. (Tellingly, Bloody Sunday does not merit a single mention throughout the 268 pages of Maudling's own memoirs.)

The following day, Edward Heath announced that an inquiry

would be conducted by the Lord Chief Justice, Lord Widgery. Meanwhile, the Ministry of Defence set out the army's version of events claiming that throughout the incident soldiers only fired at 'identified targets', which it described as 'attacking gunmen and bombers'.[6] 'At all times,' it went on, 'the soldiers obeyed their standing instructions to fire only in self-defence or in defence of others threatened.' Harold Wilson, by now Leader of the Opposition, openly stated that Irish unity was the only way out of the quagmire, while William Craig, the Unionist hardliner, suggested that the western part of Derry should now be ceded to the Irish Republic. The Irish custom of quick burials saw eleven funerals on the Wednesday. Tens of thousands attended, including leading politicians from Northern and southern Ireland. In Dublin, there was a widespread shutdown as workers stopped work to pay their respects to the dead, while a huge march on the British embassy saw the building stoned before it was eventually burnt to the ground. Two weeks later, Brian Faulkner was summoned to London to be given the news that direct rule was going to be imposed. It was a minor courtesy.

At the end of February 1972, the Official IRA attacked Aldershot Barracks – home of the Parachute Regiment – killing six people. The nature of 'asymmetric warfare' is that the 'wrong' people are repeatedly killed. For every targeted assassination there is a random atrocity. A faulty timer. Botched warning calls. A lack of precision caused, invariably, by a lack of regard for human life. The next few years would see many such examples, carried out by the IRA, the British Army and Loyalists, in this three-pronged conflict. In this instance, the targets were presumably paratroopers. In reality, six civilians, including five women and a Catholic army chaplain, were slain. Seven more people were killed in March, including two RUC officers and a soldier from the Ulster Defence Regiment, as the Provisional IRA launched its first car bomb attack in Belfast City Centre.

On 24 March, just seven weeks after Bloody Sunday, Stormont was shut down. Edward Heath made a statement in the Commons confirming that Whitehall would now be taking charge. Northern Ireland was not deemed fit to run its own affairs any longer and Unionists had tested the patience of Westminster to breaking point. An abiding irony was that the legislation used to prorogue Stormont was entitled the Northern Ireland (Temporary Provisions) Act. It would be needed for a further twenty-six years until it was superseded by the Good Friday Agreement. A new Northern Ireland Office would be created, overseen by a Secretary of State. Willie Whitelaw got the job. A wily operator from the 'One Nation' tradition in his party, Whitelaw had an instinct for cutting a deal, and one of his first acts was to intervene to avert the hunger strike of the Provisional IRA's jailed Belfast commander, Billy McKee, by meeting his demand that Republicans should be treated as political prisoners and conceding him special category status.

And this was still only March. That year, 1972, was the bloodiest of the Troubles, with 10,000 shooting incidents – up from fewer than 2,000 a year earlier. Nearly 500 people would be killed and 5,000 injured. There was no pause for reflection after Bloody Sunday. No point at which everyone – British ministers, the army, Loyalists or Republicans – looked over the precipice and recoiled. Each of them pressed on. This was the point of no return. The remainder of the year saw atrocity after atrocity. Shootings, bombings and killings committed by all sides and against all sides. April saw eleven-year-old Francis Rowntree become the first person to be killed by a rubber bullet fired by a British soldier. This ammunition would eventually give way to plastic bullets and then 'attenuating energy projectiles'. Their purpose, however, was the same. Whatever the iteration, these weapons killed seventeen people during the Troubles and they have never been used anywhere else in the UK at any time.

Amid the carnage, the Official IRA announced a ceasefire at the end of May 1972, marking the end of its military campaign, except for what it regarded as defensive measures (which included spats with the larger and now dominant Provisional IRA). Worried about the growing sectarianism of the conflict, its members would eventually spin off to become the Workers' Party, achieving some success in the Irish Republic and eventually merging into the Irish Labour Party. The Provisional IRA had grown powerful as the defenders of Catholic areas and, while sharing some of the Marxist theoretics of the Official IRA, the group was solely focused on a military response and driving the British from the 'Occupied Six Counties'. On 21 July, twenty-two Provisional IRA bombs exploded across Belfast in the space of seventy-five minutes. Nine people were killed and 130 injured. The sheer scale of it, let alone its randomness, reduced Belfast, one of the most important cities in the United Kingdom, to a battleground. If Republicans were willing to up the ante in pursuit of their objectives, so were the British. The propaganda damage of not being able to maintain control saw the biggest peacetime deployment of British troops since the Suez incident in 1956 as 12,000 soldiers and armoured vehicles swept into Republican redoubts in Belfast and Derry to retake 'no-go' areas under the control of the IRA, which, having got wind of the plan, simply vacated its positions. Still, Operation Motorman – as the deployment was codenamed – saw two people killed, including a fifteen-year-old schoolboy who was out with his cousins doing nothing more than watching what was going on.

As the security situation deteriorated, the political climate was also curdling. In February, William Craig, the former Home Affairs Minister sacked by O'Neill, launched Ulster Vanguard. A crypto-fascist organisation, replete with uniforms and salutes, Vanguard was a reaction against direct rule and a warning against any drift from Unionist grandees towards power-sharing with Catholics. In March 1972, in what became a notorious speech, Craig urged his supporters to 'build up the dossiers on the men and women who are a menace to this country, because one day, ladies and gentlemen, if the politicians fail, it may be our job to liquidate the enemy'.[7] Addressing the far-right 'Monday Club' of Conservative MPs and activists, Craig boasted that he could mobilise 80,000 men and that he was ready for conflict: 'I am prepared to come out and shoot and kill, let's put the bluff aside.'

On the other side of the political equation, Harold Wilson made a speech calling for a constitutional commission that would lead to a united Ireland with a 'fifteen-year period of transition'. Following Bloody Sunday, he called for a ceasefire and the release of all internees that had not been brought to trial. After this, his office was approached by representatives of the IRA. Wilson agreed to meet their 'friends' in person during a trip to Dublin (a euphemism, given the IRA was an illegal organisation in Dublin as much as it was in Belfast). In March, Wilson, together with his shadow spokesman, Merlyn Rees, met mainstream political leaders in Dublin and restated his view in a television interview that internment should end, adding that the IRA's terms should at least be discussed. Wilson and his team were then taken to the home of an Irish Labour politician to meet three senior members of the Provisional IRA. That the meeting even took place was remarkable, given the context of the time, and would prove impossible in future years and even decades. The talks lasted for four hours, stretching into the early morning. Wilson was keen to know if Gerry Fitt and the new SDLP would be acceptable as a political vehicle for Republicans. Fitt was keen to talk to the IRA, Wilson reported, but was fearful he might get a bullet in the back for his efforts. 'Hardly in the back,' quipped veteran Republican Dáithí Ó Conaill, one of Wilson's interlocutors.[8] 'What politicians have you confidence in in Northern Ireland?' Wilson enquired. 'None of them,' Ó Conaill responded. Joe Haines, Wilson's press secretary, who was in the meeting, summed up the disconnect: 'We were planets apart; words had different meanings.' Despite this, Wilson, an inveterate pragmatist, wanted to try to find a way through, to the chagrin of some. As his biographer, Ben Pimlott, observed:

Wilson – who had first sent the troops in two and a half years earlier – did not ... alter his fundamental belief that progress

required their withdrawal. His speeches continued to urge conciliation, to the public fury of Ulster Protestants, and the secret
fury of some members of the British security forces, who marked
him down as a dangerous political enemy.[9]

He was not the only Westminster figure interested to see if there
was still a way of ending the Troubles by talking directly with the
IRA. Willie Whitelaw, the first Secretary of State for Northern
Ireland with responsibility for the enlarged brief hived off from
the Home Office, also wanted to see where talking might lead.
At the end of June 1972, Whitelaw convened an unprecedented
face-to-face meeting between the British government and the
Provisional IRA, following earlier discussion with officials. A
bilateral ceasefire had first been called as a symbol of good faith,
while a delegation flew across to London to conduct talks with
Whitelaw, his minister of state, Paul Channon, and officials from
the security services and the new Northern Ireland Office. The
IRA delegation was led by its chief of staff, Seán MacStiofáin, a
British-born former RAF veteran, along with Dáithí Ó Conaill
and long-standing Belfast IRA figures Séamus Twomey and
Ivor Bell. Their delegation also included two up-and-coming
figures who were still in their twenties: Gerry Adams and
Martin McGuinness. The venue was the Cheyne Walk home of
Paul Channon in Chelsea, which was deemed far enough away
from Westminster to allow an open discussion without any
prying eyes and ears. The row of fashionable three-storey town
houses by the river Thames had seen their fair share of celebrity
and notoriety. Bertrand Russell had lived there, as had Ralph

Vaughan Williams, Ian Fleming and half the Rolling Stones. Irish residents had included Bram Stoker, Erskine Childers and George Best. Channon was a multi-millionaire and scion of the Guinness family, the Anglo-Irish brewing and banking dynasty, and together with the equally aristocratic Whitelaw offered a contrasting perspective to the other attendees. For their part, the IRA delegation was there on business. The offer of a drink was declined, and Ó Conaill refused to sit alongside Whitelaw. 'MacStiofáin set out the familiar demands,' Whitelaw's biographers recounted. 'British troops were to be removed from "sensitive areas" immediately, and must leave the province before 1 January 1975; there would be an amnesty for all "political prisoners", and an end to internment; the key demand, however, was for an all-Ireland referendum on the border.'[10]

Whitelaw promised that the Cabinet would examine the last point 'very carefully', but he pointed out that the basis of the Ireland Act 1949 was that it was a matter for the people of Northern Ireland to decide their fate. 'The mood deteriorated further', his biographers noted, 'when Willie asserted that British soldiers would never fire on unarmed civilians; he was forcefully reminded of Bloody Sunday by the twenty-two-year-old Martin McGuinness from Derry.' Frank Steele, an MI6 agent who was in attendance, later said he was 'appalled' at the IRA delegation's 'naivety and lack of understanding of political reality'. Yet, as Whitelaw's biographers noted, the same allegation could have been made of the British. 'They had assumed the Provos would never negotiate unless they felt they were losing their fight; they failed to realise that the Provos were likely to interpret Willie's willingness to talk as a symptom off the same defeatism.'

After the three-hour meeting concluded without resolution, Whitelaw headed straight to his golf club to indulge his favourite pastime, depressed about the lack of progress. As Harold Wilson had previously found, there was not enough common ground to hope to achieve much. Too much blood had been spilled by either side – and both had lost too much to give anything way. What might have happened if such a meeting had taken place sooner? Without the cumulative weight of internment and Bloody Sunday, progress might still have been possible. Indeed, Whitelaw confessed in his memoirs that he wished he had arrived in Northern Ireland two years earlier. He was at least politically astute enough to entertain dialogue and limit confrontation. He had already announced that proportional representation would be introduced to counter the gerrymandering of electoral boundaries. 'The minority in the North have been deprived of their rights,' he later wrote in his memoirs. 'I set myself the task of conquering this.'[11] Whitelaw's successors were often a mixed bag and certainly lacked his lightness of touch. Especially as he was dealing with military officers who were simply ill-equipped to act as ersatz police officers. 'I have been engaged in campaigns against blacks, yellows and slant-eyes. Why should we have one rule for the white and one for the coloureds?' was how one senior military officer indelicately summed up their role in Northern Ireland.

The next year brought little relief. The IRA exported its campaign to Britain for the first time since the 1940s. On

8 March 1973, an eleven-strong IRA team planted a series of bombs in central London. Two eventually exploded, one at the Old Bailey – the Central Criminal Court – and one outside the Ministry of Agriculture. Two others were defused. This signalled a major escalation in the IRA's campaign – bringing the Troubles to the very heart of London – and was a symbol that they could strike outside Northern Ireland. It was hoped that this switch in tactics might also raise morale after a wave of arrests of leading IRA figures in Belfast and Derry. The Old Bailey bomb caused extensive damage and injured as many as 280 people. One man died after having a heart attack. The entire IRA unit was arrested at Heathrow airport trying to fly back to Belfast before the bombs went off. What is striking is the ages and backgrounds of those involved. As the *New York Times* report of the trial put it:

Among the eight, members of the militant Provisional wing of the Irish Republican Army, were two women, Dolours Price, twenty-two years old, described by the prosecution as the leader of the group, and her sister Marian, nineteen. Both are student teachers. The others were Hugh Feeny, also a student teacher; Robert Armstrong, a window cleaner; Robert Walsh, and Paul Holmes, roof tilers; Martin Brady, a driver, and Gerard Kelly, unemployed. All are in their twenties and come from Belfast.[12]

None of the group were older than thirty and four of them were still teenagers, while three were student teachers who, in any other society, would be starting out in promising careers. All of them were given lengthy sentences (apart from the youngest in the group, who was acquitted after providing information and was given a new identity). If the symbolism of the attack was to strike at British authority, the date made it doubly significant. On the day of the bombings there was a referendum held in which Northern Ireland voters were asked: 'Do you want Northern Ireland to remain part of the United Kingdom?' or 'Do you want Northern Ireland to be joined with the Republic of Ireland outside the United Kingdom?' It resulted in a 99 per cent vote for the status quo on a 59 per cent turnout. The SDLP led a boycott of the poll, regarding it as a foregone conclusion and merely a stunt designed to paper over Northern Ireland's widening cracks. Some estimates suggest that as little as 1 per cent of the Catholic–Nationalist population bothered voting.

In June, Northern Ireland held elections to a new assembly, following talks and an agreement between the main parties and the Irish government. The Sunningdale Agreement (named after the British government's Civil Service College where the talks took place) held out the promise of restoring devolved government, but a new, improved version. A 78-member assembly with power-sharing was at the heart of the new deal. Crucially, most parties were on board.

Elections to the new assembly saw the Ulster Unionists retain their top spot with thirty-one seats, but the new parties – the SDLP and the Democratic Unionists – began to make ground, with the former gaining nineteen seats and the DUP gaining eight. The cross-community Alliance Party also took eight, with Craig's Vanguard managing seven. A new pattern was asserting itself. Catholic–Nationalist support congregated around the

SDLP, while the Unionist vote was beginning to splinter. Meanwhile, liberals who did not want to be defined by the constitutional question had a new home in Alliance. A new executive was formed, with Brian Faulkner becoming 'chief executive', alongside five other Unionists in the executive, and Gerry Fitt taking a role as his deputy, leading three of his colleagues. At the very least, the look of the new executive was a marked departure from what had gone before. Even the language – chief executive and deputy chief executive – sounded businesslike and forward-thinking. The problem was that Unionism had not undergone a wholesale conversion. Faulkner's party – never mind the broader Protestant–Unionist–Loyalist community – was split over the very principle of sharing power with Catholics, and trouble was brewing. For Republicans, such an 'internal settlement' to Northern Ireland's affairs was now anathema to them. Sinn Féin boycotted Sunningdale and it would still be a decade before the party routinely contested elections. The IRA's focus remained fixed on armed struggle. In October, it mounted an audacious break-out of three leading IRA figures (including Séamus Twomey, who had been part of the Cheyne Walk delegation) from Mountjoy Prison in Dublin. A helicopter was hijacked and landed in the prison yard, scooping up the three prisoners before making good its escape. Despite the men being recaptured over the next few years, it was a propaganda coup and another measure of the gulf between politics and realpolitik during the Troubles.

Events the following year would extinguish whatever optimism Sunningdale had created. First, the IRA stepped up its campaign in England with a devastating series of bombings. In

February, eight soldiers, the wife of one of them and two children were killed when a bomb ripped their coach apart on the M62 motorway in West Yorkshire. In June, the IRA bombed the Houses of Parliament, causing serious damage. In October, four British soldiers were killed when two bombs went off in pubs in Guildford, Surrey. The next month, two people (one of which was a soldier) were killed when a shrapnel bomb was thrown inside a pub in Woolwich, south London. A fortnight later, twenty-one people were slain when bombs went off in two pubs in Birmingham city centre – the biggest single loss of life in England during the Troubles. The Ulster Volunteer Force was conducting a parallel bombing campaign and killed six Catholics at the Rose and Crown bar in Belfast in May. Much worse was to follow when they exploded a series of bombs in Dublin and Monaghan three weeks later, killing thirty-three people and injuring 300. It was the largest loss of life from a single incident during the Troubles.

Two days earlier, the Ulster Workers' Council – a front for Loyalist paramilitaries – started a general strike with the aim of bringing down the new executive. Northern Ireland was once again plunged into pre-meditated turmoil. As the economy ground to a halt, the political pressure grew. By the end of the month, the power-sharing executive collapsed. Harold Wilson, who had returned to power in the February 1974 general election, was governing without an overall majority and had a bulging in-tray of political and economic woes. His frustration was obvious, and he denounced the Loyalists' tactics in a stinging television address:

The people on this side of the water – British parents – have seen their sons vilified and spat upon and murdered. British taxpayers have seen the taxes they have poured out, almost without regard to cost – over £300 million a year this year with the cost of the army operations on top of that – going into Northern Ireland. They see property destroyed by evil violence and are asked to pick up the bill for rebuilding it. Yet people who benefit from all this now viciously defy Westminster, purporting to act as though they were an elected government; people who spend their lives sponging on Westminster and British democracy and then systematically assault democratic methods. Who do these people think they are?[13]

There was no plan B. Sunningdale was supposed to be the answer. Not only was it the best chance of bringing things back to balance, but its demise now set a bar for any subsequent arrangement. If power-sharing was not guaranteed, along with an all-Ireland dimension, then, clearly, no other model for cross-community devolved government would now work (and this is how it turned out to be until the Good Friday Agreement in 1998). Perhaps trying to normalise the political situation while Northern Ireland was in utter chaos was a strategy doomed to fail. While forcing power-sharing on Unionists, with so many of them unprepared for such a concession, was always going to result in a backlash. 'No solution could be imposed from across the water,' Wilson ruefully wrote in his memoirs.

But why not? Sunningdale was the barest minimum that Catholics had a right to expect. To bring it crashing down, simply to destroy the principle of power-sharing in what was (and is) such a deeply divided society, merely underscored the depth of the problem. Unionist leaders and the British government needed to show greater resolve. Getting the executive into the water was one thing; stopping it capsizing was clearly something else. But Sunningdale should have been made to float. It should not have been allowed to sink. The job of reviving any cross-community working arrangements would only get harder, and it was surely better to see they did not fail to begin with. Without strong leadership from the Ulster Unionists, and with Ian Paisley gaining on them in the polls, their resolve was always going to buckle; that much was predictable, which makes the British government's failures all the worse. The whole episode represents another 'what if?' moment. If Sunningdale had succeeded, guaranteeing power-sharing, and book-ending the abuses of the Stormont era, might it have been enough to curtail the Troubles at that point?

With the political situation in Belfast in tatters, and with Westminster unable or unwilling to press down hard to secure a political way forward, Republican and Loyalist paramilitaries had free rein. But first there was an interlude. The Provisional IRA announced a ceasefire just before Christmas 1974 – immediately after it had tried to blow up Edward Heath's home in London.

Merlyn Rees, Wilson's Northern Ireland Secretary, believed the backlash from the Birmingham bombing, which had resulted in emergency legislation being rushed through Parliament in the form of the Prevention of Terrorism Act, had provided pause for thought in the Republican leadership. It would be a short-lived hope and 1975 would become yet another bloody year of bloody carnage, especially as the failure to save Sunningdale meant there was no realistic political opportunity to focus on.

In April 1975, five Catholics were killed in a gun and bomb attack on a bar in the Short Strand area of Belfast. In June, the UVF attempted to derail a train in County Kildare in the Irish Republic. A man was stabbed to death when he tried to stop the saboteurs, which ensured the plot was delayed long enough for the train to pass safely. The next month, four soldiers were killed by a remote-controlled bomb in County Armagh. Later that month, members of a popular Irish showband were stopped at an army checkpoint in County Down after playing a gig in Belfast. Two off-duty UDR soldiers planted a bomb in their minibus, which was intended to explode after the band crossed the border into the Irish Republic; however, it detonated prematurely and killed the soldiers. The other gunmen then opened fire on the musicians, killing three of them. One survived to identify the assailants.

In August, the Provisional IRA carried out a gun and bomb attack on a bar in Belfast frequented by UVF leaders, killing four Protestant civilians. Two weeks later they bombed a pub near an army barracks in Caterham in Surrey. Thirty-three people, including ten soldiers, were injured, some seriously, with one soldier losing both legs and an arm. On 1 September, five Protestant men were killed, and seven others were injured in a gun attack on an Orange hall near Newtonhamilton in County Armagh. The attack was claimed by the South Armagh Republican

Action Force. The next month, the UVF killed seven civilians in a series of attacks across Northern Ireland. Four UVF members were killed in Coleraine when the bomb they were transporting prematurely exploded.

Throughout the autumn, the IRA launched a series of attacks in England. In September, it exploded a bomb in the lobby of the London Hilton hotel, killing two people and injuring sixty-three. In October, one person was killed and twenty injured in a bomb attack on Green Park tube station in central London. Later in the month, three people were killed and forty injured in two separate attacks on central London restaurants. In December, the gang responsible for the London campaign was cornered in Balcombe Street in Marylebone after police had observed a pattern in their attacks. Members of the gang were identified and pursued by the police and after a running shoot-out the gang took a couple hostage. A six-day siege then followed before the four men eventually surrendered.

The obvious question, sincerely meant but mordantly expressed, is if this was a year in which one of the main perpetrators of the violence had called a ceasefire, how much worse would it have been if it had not? The chasm between what Irish Republicans wanted and what the British government was able to concede was politically unbridgeable. This was the price for failing to make Sunningdale hold. If the moderate SDLP could not be accommodated in a cross-party executive, then the government would need to deal directly with the IRA. The choreography of being seen to accede to the IRA's demands meant there was no realistic prospect of anything coming of the dialogue.

Loyalists took full advantage of the truce and stepped up their campaign of sectarian killings, murdering 120 Catholics during 1975, mostly in random attacks. Many in the Provisional IRA opposed the ceasefire and used front organisations to retaliate in the hope that it gave them plausible deniability. Both Loyalist and Republican attacks showed little rhyme or reason, the targets were just identified as being from the other side, with the so-called Shankill Butchers showing anything but homicidal hatred of Catholics. The name of this gang was apposite; they would torture and slash the throats of their Catholic victims, who were picked at random on the street (although they also had several Protestant victims, who were either mistaken for Catholics or killed in personal vendettas). Sentencing members of the gang in 1979 for the twenty-three people they had murdered, the trial judge, Lord Justice O'Donnell, described their rampage as 'a lasting monument to blind sectarian bigotry'.

In all, 247 people were killed and 2,663 injured during 1975. There were 1,805 shootings, 635 bombs planted, 825 weapons and 20,000lb of explosives found, and 1,197 people charged with terrorist offences.[14]

During the 1970s, Northern Ireland's bloodshed saw one year simply melt into another. However, January 1976 was one of the bleakest months in the entire Troubles. It started with an horrendous series of murders and ended with the collapse of the Provisional IRA's ceasefire. On 4 January, the UVF killed six Catholics in County Armagh. Although the number of deaths was not unusual in terms of what had already been seen in the early 1970s, what was particularly appalling was that all the victims came from just two families. In fact, three of the dead were brothers, while the remaining victims were an uncle and two nephews. By the standards of the Troubles, where so many families on all sides suffered so much bereavement, it was an incalculable loss for them. The killings of the Reavey and O'Dowd families in County Armagh was followed by a reprisal attack the following day. The South Armagh Republican Action Force, a front for members of the Provisional IRA, stopped a minibus carrying workmen at Kingsmill, County Armagh. The men were forced out of the bus, lined up and then shot. Ten were killed and one man survived, despite being shot eighteen times. It was a brutal and sectarian attack on men simply going to work. As far as the IRA was concerned, the men were repairing an RUC station and were therefore 'legitimate targets'.

March saw the ending of special category status for paramilitary prisoners, which was a measure that would have severe consequences over the next few years. It also saw Harold Wilson's resignation as Prime Minister, with James Callaghan replacing him a month later. On St Patrick's Day, the UVF killed four Catholics, including two children, in a bomb attack on a bar in Dungannon. The attack was the work of the Glennane Gang, a ruthless Loyalist murder squad that operated in the Mid Ulster area and would go on to earn notoriety for the scale of their murderous rampage, killing as many as 120 people. But that was only half of it. They included in their number members of the RUC and the UDR.

May saw a brace of attacks on the same day. The UVF killed four Catholics in a gun and bomb attack on two pubs in

Charlemont, County Armagh, while the IRA killed three RUC officers in County Fermanagh and a fourth in County Down. June and July saw twenty-four people murdered in a series of shootings and bombings across Northern Ireland. This included the British ambassador to Ireland, Christopher Ewart-Biggs, who was killed by a large landmine planted near his official residence.

In August, an IRA volunteer was shot dead as he drove along a Belfast road. The car he was driving ploughed into three children, killing them all. It was one of the few moments throughout the Troubles that created an inflection point. A series of rallies were organised and a campaign group called 'Peace People' was established, bringing the community together across the sectarian divide in a renewed effort for an end to violence. Meanwhile, a different sort of direct action was stirring inside HM Prison Maze in County Down. Republican prisoners began refusing to wear prison uniforms following the removal of special category status, adorning themselves in nothing more than their blankets.

Despite the main organisers of the Peace People, Mairead Corrigan and Betty Williams, jointly receiving the Nobel Peace Prize, there was little reprieve in the violence. There was further bloodletting in 1977 between the Provisional and Official IRA, which saw four people killed and eighteen wounded. A body calling itself the United Unionist Action Council, an iteration of the Unionist co-ordinating body that had helped to bring down Sunningdale, called for a tougher security response from the British government and a return to Unionist-majority rule. That response came, after a fashion, in the form of the Labour government's latest Secretary of State for Northern Ireland, Roy Mason, who had been appointed by James Callaghan. A former Barnsley coal miner, Mason was clear that he was not sent to Northern Ireland to get a political deal. As he recorded in his memoirs: 'I had to reassure the people of Ulster [the preferred term of Unionists] that Her Majesty's Government was not going to be pushed around ... I wanted criminals caught by the RUC and punished as criminals, not as "political".'[15] To Mason, Republicans and Loyalists were simply 'gangster groups' and had 'violence in their souls'. They just needed to be taken on and taught a lesson.[16]

In February 1978, twelve people were killed and thirty more injured by an IRA bomb at the La Mon restaurant in Belfast city centre. In November, the group carried out dozens of bombings at locations across Northern Ireland, declaring that it was digging in for a 'long war'. In 1979, eleven members of the Shankill Butchers were sentenced to life for at least twenty-three murders. In March, the IRA killed the British ambassador to the Netherlands, Richard Sykes, and his assistant. A week and a half later, the Irish National Liberation Army assassinated an even more high-profile target. Airey Neave was the shadow Northern Ireland Secretary and one of Margaret Thatcher's closest confidants. A bomb had been attached to his car and it exploded as he was leaving Parliament's underground car park in Westminster. In May, Thatcher became Prime Minister after defeating James Callaghan. His government had soldiered on for three years and had become reliant on stitching together majorities by appealing to the smaller parties to get its business through, including the Ulster Unionists (who tried to make their numbers count in much the same way the Irish Parliamentary Party had done in the Edwardian period). By the summer, Thatcher would face a violent reminder of how much time and political energy Northern Ireland could consume. On 27 August, the Provisional IRA launched what was probably its most audacious series of attacks. It detonated a bomb on the fishing boat of Lord Mountbatten, who was lobster fishing off County Sligo in the Irish Republic. The Queen's cousin, the last Governor-General of India and former Commander of British Forces in Singapore faced an ignominious death along with three other people, including his young grandson, a local boy helping for the day and the 83-year-old Lady Brabourne. But this was only half the day's events. Two roadside bombs exploded in Narrow Water, near Warrenpoint in County Down, killing eighteen British soldiers, sixteen of whom were from the Parachute Regiment.

CHAPTER 4

AND ON IT GOES

January 1980 started miserably. Two Catholic teenagers were killed – one as she was joy-riding in a stolen car and one young man was beaten to death near the Loyalist Shankill Road. Two undercover soldiers were killed by other undercover soldiers in County Armagh while they were on an operation. In addition, three members of the UDR were killed by an IRA landmine in County Down. Three people, including the bomber himself, were killed and two more injured when a bomb planted by the IRA exploded prematurely on a train at Dunmurry, near Belfast. Amid the death and destruction, another tragedy happened that was quiet and personal, but no less devastating. Anne Maguire was found dead after apparently committing suicide. She was the mother of the three children who were killed when a car driven by a wounded IRA volunteer careered into them in August 1976, which spurred the Peace People into existence. The death toll for those killed in the Troubles in Northern Ireland had now reached 2,000.

This grim milestone coincided with the start of the latest

political initiative. Humphrey Atkins, Margaret Thatcher's new Northern Ireland Secretary, called a constitutional convention with the parties to try to revive a political way forward. The SDLP, Alliance and even the DUP were on board, but the Ulster Unionists refused to participate. To address the SDLP's concerns that any settlement needed an all-Ireland dimension, Atkins conceded a parallel set of talks. These, however, were anathema to the DUP and, unsurprisingly, the convention fizzled out. In February, Charles Haughey, the Irish Taoiseach, called for the two governments to launch a new joint initiative to drive progress forwards at the Fianna Fáil *ard fheis* (party conference). In May, Thatcher made plain her opposition. 'The future of the constitutional affairs of Northern Ireland is a matter for the people of Northern Ireland, this government and this parliament and no one else,' she stated.[1] The timing was deliberate and provocative. Haughey was flying into London the next day for talks with her. A communiqué released following their meeting referred to the 'unique relationship' between Britain and Ireland and promised greater political co-operation between the two governments over Northern Ireland. Undeterred, Haughey appeared on the BBC's *Panorama* programme three weeks later to argue that it was in both Britain's and Ireland's best interest if Britain would withdraw from Northern Ireland.

In July, Atkins tried again to kickstart talks, but his proposals were met with indifference. Unionists were not interested in power-sharing, while the SDLP and Alliance were not interested in a return to anything that smacked of Unionist majority rule. As the political situation outside atrophied, inside the

Maze there was growing unrest. Back in March, Atkins had announced the complete abolition of special category status for paramilitary prisoners. This had long been a bone of contention for Unionists and Conservative backbenchers. The idea that IRA volunteers should be treated as political prisoners rather than ordinary criminals rankled. As Northern Ireland Secretary, Willie Whitelaw had been smart enough not to entertain the issue, but his Labour successor, Roy Mason, had done just that, and ended the status for new prisoners from 1976 onwards. Now, Atkins threatened to abolish the caveat altogether.

At the end of October, Republican prisoners began a hunger strike in protest at the removal of the special category status, which, among other concessions, meant they did not have to do prison work and could wear their own clothes, rather than prison uniforms, and remain housed within their paramilitary groups. Thatcher vowed that she would not back down, telling the House of Commons: 'The government will never concede political status to the hunger strikers, or to any others convicted of criminal offences in the province.'[2] Meanwhile, Atkins reported that there was little prospect of meaningful talks or any restoration of devolved government in Northern Ireland. At the start of December, three women Republican prisoners joined the strike and two weeks later twenty-three more Republicans joined the initial seven hunger strikers. The situation was becoming serious for those at the head of the strike, who showed no signs of backing down. At the same time, there had been a sudden upsurge in political activity between the two governments. Despite Thatcher and Haughey having a frosty relationship, the British Prime Minister, accompanied by Atkins, Lord Carrington, the Foreign Secretary, and Geoffrey Howe, the Chancellor of the Exchequer, travelled to Dublin for talks with Haughey and his senior ministers. This was the first trip by a British Prime Minister to Dublin since partition. Although the talks did not officially include discussions about Northern Ireland's constitutional future, there was dialogue about how the two governments could work more closely together in future and embrace the 'totality of relationships' (a phrase that would go on to become synonymous with the Good Friday Agreement process). A week later, and with the health of the hunger strikers continuing to deteriorate, the Catholic Primate of All Ireland, Cardinal Tomás Ó Fiaich, pleaded with the prisoners to call off their protest and asked Thatcher to intervene personally. There was talk of the government acceding to their demands, which might have carried greater weight than Ó Fiaich's intervention, but, nevertheless, his intervention paid off and the next day the Republican strikers at the Maze prison, as well as those in other prisons in Northern Ireland, ceased their hunger strike after fifty-three days – and before anyone died.

As with the previous year, January 1981 started violently. Bernadette Devlin and her husband were shot and seriously injured in a gun attack in their home near Coalisland, County Tyrone. It was believed that members of the Ulster Defence Association (UDA) were responsible. She was shot multiple times in front of her children, but both she and her husband went on to recover from their injuries. RUC officers were positioned nearby but did not come to their aid. Meanwhile, a few days later the

IRA murdered Stormont's former Speaker, 86-year-old Norman Stronge, and his 48-year-old son, James, in their home, Tynan Abbey.

At the start of February, the IRA warned there would be further hunger strikes if Republican prisoners were not granted special category status. The next evening, Ian Paisley led a group of 500 men up a hillside in County Antrim for a photo opportunity. The crowd waved their firearms certificates above their head to force home the point that as well as the army's weapons, and the illegal weaponry of paramilitaries, Northern Ireland was also awash with legally held guns – more than 100,000 of them, in fact. Three days later, Paisley spoke at a major rally at Belfast City Hall where those present signed a declaration to defend Ulster, which was modelled on the 1912 version, but this time in opposition to any bilateral deals between the Margaret Thatcher and Charles Haughey governments. It was a big week for Paisley and, to round it off, he got thrown out of the chamber of the House of Commons for repeatedly calling Humphrey Atkins a liar.

On Sunday 1 March 1981, another hunger strike began. Bobby Sands, the IRA's officer commanding in the Maze, began refusing food. The day marked the fifth anniversary of the ending of special category status and the strike aimed to reverse that decision. The next day, other Republican prisoners called off their blanket strike so as not to detract attention from Sands. A day later, Humphrey Atkins made a statement in the House of Commons reiterating the by now familiar formulation that the British government would not cave in to the strikers' demands.

On Thursday 5 March, Frank Maguire, the independent Republican MP for Fermanagh and South Tyrone, died suddenly of a heart attack at fifty-one. There was some horse-trading to be done among Nationalist politicians about who would stand in the by-election, and given that Maguire had a majority of less than 5,000, a good campaign would be needed to retain the seat. Various SDLP figures expressed an interest; however, Bernadette Devlin suggested she would prefer it if the prisoners in the Maze made the choice. Raymond McCreesh became the third hunger striker, joining Sands and Patsy O'Hara. The strategy was to bring on other hunger strikers in phases to prolong the campaign if – and when – the first of them started to die. On 26 March, Sands was formally nominated as a candidate in the by-election in Fermanagh and South Tyrone. Three days later, the SDLP decided to withdraw its candidate to increase Sands's chances, making it a two-horse race between the hunger strike candidate and the Ulster Unionists' Harry West.

In the week or so before the by-election, Ian Paisley organised a series of rallies as part of his ongoing campaign to stymie any joint working between the British and Irish governments. On 28 March he addressed around 30,000 supporters at Stormont. A few days later, he organised a series of late-night rallies on hillsides near Armagh, Gortin, in County Tyrone and in Newry. At one of them, two RUC vehicles were overturned by the crowd. Once again, those present waved firearms certificates. Outside the Maze, Sinn Féin called on its supporters to boycott that year's census as a demonstration of civil disobedience and as a supportive gesture to the hunger strikers. In one appalling

incident that followed, a 29-year-old Protestant census enumer-
ator, Joanne Mathers, was shot dead by the IRA while she was
out collecting forms.

On Thursday 9 April 1981, voters in Fermanagh and South
Tyrone went to the polls. Bobby Sands was returned as their
new Member of Parliament after two days of counting. He had
accrued 30,492 votes, beating his Unionist opponent by just
1,446. The turnout was huge, with 87 per cent of the electorate
coming out, either to spur him on – or to stop him. The by-
election was a propaganda victory for the hunger strike and
a media sensation that was widely covered around the world.
However, the position of the British government was unmoved.

A couple of weeks later on Monday 20 April, three members
of the Irish Dáil, along with Bobby Sands's election agent, Owen
Carron, came to visit him at the Maze and later called for urgent
talks with Margaret Thatcher. The next day, on a foreign trip to
Saudi Arabia, the Prime Minister flatly denied their request,
adding: 'We are not prepared to consider special category status
for certain groups of people serving sentences for crime. Crime
is crime is crime, it is not political.'[3] More than six weeks into a
hunger strike that had already seen him elected to the House of
Commons, Bobby Sands remained defiant. A flurry of international visitors now came to see if there was a way of convincing
him to avert his course of action. His sister, Marcella, made an
application to the European Commission on Human Rights
over the treatment of Republican prisoners. On 25 April, representatives from the commission tried to visit Sands, but he refused to see them unless he was accompanied by representatives

of Sinn Féin. A few days later, Sands was visited by the private secretary of Pope John Paul II. But even a Pontifical emissary was unable to convince him to change his mind. The Pope's representative, Fr John Magee, held talks with Humphrey Atkins the next day, but to no avail. He was unflinching. 'If Mr Sands persisted in his wish to commit suicide, that was his choice. The government would not force medical treatment upon him,' was Atkins's condescending response. On Monday 4 May, the European Commission on Human Rights announced that it had no power to proceed with the case brought against the British government by Marcella Sands.

The following day, Tuesday 5 May 1981, 27-year-old Bobby Sands, Member of Parliament for Fermanagh and South Tyrone, died after sixty-six days on hunger strike. His death, the result of the journey he embarked upon just over three months previously, was preordained, but still shocking. The news sparked widespread rioting and the British government sent 600 extra soldiers to Northern Ireland. On Thursday 7 May, an estimated 100,000 people attended Sands's funeral in Belfast. For Republican prisoners in the Maze, the loss of their figurehead did not sway their resolve. The next day, 29-year-old Joe McDonnell replaced him as leader. The determination of the strikers to follow through was no longer theoretical. Their resolve had been tested and it had been proven. The strike would go on. As each hunger striker died for the cause, another man stepped up to take his place who was prepared, if it came to it, to do exactly the same.

Saturday 9 May 1981 saw an IRA bomb explode at an oil terminal in the Shetland Isles, a quarter of a mile from where the Queen was attending the plant's official opening. The following Tuesday – a week after Sands's death – a second hunger striker, Francis Hughes, died. He was twenty-five. Once again, rioting and protests were widespread. A group of up to 2,000 people tried to storm the British embassy in Dublin. On 13 May, fourteen-year-old Julie Livingstone was shot dead in Belfast, killed by a plastic bullet that was fired by a soldier (a fifteen-year-old, Paul Whitters, had been killed by one two weeks previously).[4] The SDLP's John Hume pleaded with Margaret Thatcher to make concessions to allow prisoners to have free association on their wings and to permit them to wear their own clothes. But as so many others found, the Iron Lady was not for turning. The local elections saw Paisley's DUP edge the Ulster Unionists by 26.6 per cent to 26.5 per cent, while the SDLP dropped back to 17.5 per cent. Media coverage of the hunger strike was pervasive, but without a Republican option to vote for as a result of Sinn Féin's policy of abstentionism – given the party did not recognise the legitimacy of Northern Ireland – many Catholics simply sat on their hands. On the following day of Thursday 21 May, two further hunger strikers died. Raymond McCreesh, who was twenty-four, and Patsy O'Hara, who was twenty-five. Both had spent sixty-one days on hunger strike. As the third and fourth men died on hunger strike, outside the Maze on the streets of Northern Ireland the third and fourth people were killed by plastic bullets fired by British soldiers. A 45-year-old man, Henry Duffy, was killed in Derry and twelve-year-old Carol Ann Kelly in Belfast.

The Catholic Church's attempts to either dissuade the hunger strikers from continuing their protests, or in pleading for clemency from the British government, were repeatedly unsuccessful. The Irish Commission for Justice and Peace, set up by the Irish Bishops' Conference, tried to persuade the British government to accept some of the strikers' demands without necessarily conceding political status. Their efforts ended with accusations of bad faith against the Northern Ireland Office. On 11 June, two Republican prisoners were elected to the Dáil (the lower house of the Irish Parliament) in the general election in what became another successful attempt to raise awareness of the hunger strike by standing candidates in elections. The following day, British ministers published proposals to amend the Representation of the People Act 1918 to stop any other serving prisoners from standing in parliamentary elections. Undeterred, Sinn Féin stated that a Republican prisoner would join the hunger strike every week.

The political situation was now in stasis. The British government was unflinching, having been prepared to stand by while four prisoners died. There was a new Fine Gael–Labour Party coalition in Dublin that had yet to make a public intervention. While Sinn Féin and the wider Republican movement (the hunger strikers were a mixture of IRA and INLA prisoners) were attracting huge attention and sympathy for their cause. Humphrey Atkins floated fresh proposals that would see a fifty-member advisory council established to help run Northern Ireland – another of his untimely and unrealistic proposals that was subsequently shelved.

On 8 July, Joe McDonnell – the first prisoner to join the

hunger strike after Bobby Sands's death – died himself after sixty-one days without food. Once again, by grim coincidence, the fifth hunger striker to die was matched by the fifth Catholic to be killed by a plastic bullet. Thirty-year-old Nora McCabe was shot by an RUC officer. Joe McDonnell's funeral on the Friday saw an attempt by the British Army to arrest the honour guard who were firing a salute over his coffin. The following Monday, Martin Hurson became the sixth man to die after forty-six days on hunger strike.

The Irish government then approached US President Ronald Reagan to see if he could use his leverage with Thatcher, after he had previously stated that he was 'greatly concerned' about the situation in Northern Ireland. Atkins invited the International Committee of the Red Cross to inspect HM Prison Maze and speak to the hunger strikers – he was particularly eager to demonstrate to the committee that conditions inside the prison were as they should be. However, the hunger strikers rejected the suggestion that the committee become involved, as they did the suggestion from the political leaderships of the IRA and INLA that the hunger strike be suspended for three months to assess prison reforms.

Out on the streets, another Catholic was killed by a plastic bullet. The 36-year-old Peter Doherty was the latest victim, shot dead by a British soldier in Belfast on 31 July 1981. On the same day, Paddy Quinn, who was then on the forty-seventh day of his hunger strike, was reprieved when his family intervened and asked for medical treatment to save his life. On 1 and 2 August, the seventh and eighth hunger strikers died. Kevin Lynch, who was an INLA prisoner aged twenty-five, had survived for seventy-one days. The next day, Kieran Doherty, who was also twenty-five, died after seventy-three days on hunger strike. He was one of the two prisoners who had been elected to the Dáil in the general election back in June. A week later, on 8 August, Thomas McElwee became the ninth hunger striker to die after sixty-two days. He was just twenty-three years old. This date also marked the tenth anniversary of the introduction of internment without trial. A day later, another Catholic, 41-year-old Peter McGuinness, was shot dead by a plastic bullet fired by the RUC outside his home in Belfast.

The by-election caused by Bobby Sands's death took place the following week. The SDLP refused to stand a candidate to maximise the chances of a candidate from the Catholic–Nationalist–Republican tribe holding the seat. Owen Carron, who had been Bobby Sands's election agent, was chosen as the candidate and held the seat as an 'Anti H-Block' candidate – taking its name from the H-shaped blocks in the Maze, this label was used by pro-hunger strike candidates standing for election. Carron beat veteran Unionist politician Ken Maginnis, a recently retired major in the UDR, by just over 2,000 votes. On the same day, the tenth and final hunger striker, 27-year-old Michael Devine, died after sixty days on hunger strike. Although there was no shortage of Republican prisoners willing to join the hunger strike, there were also those who were forced to come off of it. The Catholic Church and the SDLP stepped up efforts to get family members to intervene to save their loved ones. Laurence McKeown's family asked for medical intervention to save his life. He had endured seventy days on hunger strike. As did the family of Matt Devlin, who had managed fifty-two days. And Liam McCloskey, who had lasted fifty-five days.

Midway through September, the ineffectual Humphrey Atkins was replaced by James Prior as Secretary of State for Northern Ireland. Prior went straight to the Maze and met with the hunger strikers and Republican prisoners for three hours. Three weeks later, on 3 October, the hunger strike was called off. At that point, six prisoners were still fasting, with the longest strike having lasted fifty-five days. The next day, Republican prisoners issued a statement citing pressure from families and the Church for the end of the strike. Two days later, Prior announced a new prison regime. Prisoners would be allowed to wear their own clothes at all times, which had been one of the strikers' key demands. They would also be allowed extra visitors, half their lost remission would be restored and free association in the Maze's H-blocks would be allowed. To outside observers, the whole episode was bewildering. Both sides saw the strike as an issue of principle. The hunger strikers were common criminals according to Unionists and Margaret Thatcher. The strikers, in turn, saw themselves as political prisoners and demanded to be treated accordingly. Had they not been caught up in the maelstrom of the Troubles, it is unlikely any would have ever seen the inside of a prison cell. After he left school in 1969, Bobby Sands took up an apprenticeship at a firm as a coach builder. He worked there diligently for nearly a year, even though he had to endure constant sectarian harassment from his workmates in the mainly Protestant company. After his shift one day he was accosted by some of them, Loyalist wannabes, and held at gunpoint. He was told that he was 'Fenian scum' and warned not to come back. With such formative experiences, it was little wonder the Republican paramilitaries had an endless supply of recruits who were deeply disillusioned in the hostile society into which they were born. James Prior, for his part, intervened swiftly to clear up the mess made by his predecessor and provide Thatcher with cover for a political retreat. During the seven months that the hunger strike lasted, ten Republican prisoners had died the most excruciating, protracted deaths. Sixty-two civilians also perished over this period, six of whom were killed by plastic bullets.

There was also political fallout from the hunger strike. Ian Paisley called for the establishment of a 'Third Force' – a Loyalist militia intended to take the war to the IRA.[5] He held a series of rallies throughout the autumn of 1981, threatening to make Northern Ireland ungovernable and claiming he had up to 20,000 volunteers signed up, with tens of thousands regularly turning out to hear him speak. At the end of November, he organised a 'day of action' with both the Democratic Unionists and Ulster Unionists taking part. Several Unionist-controlled district councils voted to adjourn council business in protest at what they claimed was the deteriorating security situation in Northern Ireland. Prior made it clear he would not tolerate private armies being established. However, Paisley's extremism meant that he did not get everything his own way. In late 1981, more than 100 US Congressmen lobbied the State Department to revoke his visa for a planned trip to the US, citing his divisiveness.

At the end of October, Sinn Féin held its *ard fheis* in Dublin. Danny Morrison, the then editor of the Republican movement's weekly newspaper, *An Phoblacht*, gave a speech urging the abstentionist party to fight elections and open up a new front in its campaign. 'Who here really believes we can win the war through the ballot box?' he said. 'But will anyone here object if, with a ballot paper in one hand and an Armalite in the other, we take power in Ireland?'[6] So would begin the Republicans' two-pronged approach, with Sinn Féin contesting elections and the IRA waging its guerrilla war. The hunger strike had been a propaganda triumph and, as a result, people around the world were paying attention to the situation in Northern Ireland. Streets in far-flung corners of the globe were even being renamed after Bobby Sands. In Iran, the name of the road where the British embassy was based was changed in his honour, forcing embarrassed diplomats to change the address to the street that ran along the other side of the building. The tumultuous events of 1981 drew to a close with the murder of a Unionist MP, Robert Bradford, who was gunned down by the IRA in a Belfast community centre, along with its 29-year-old caretaker.

As Secretary of State for Northern Ireland, James Prior had a familiar list of issues to contend with. Improving the security situation, which had destabilised following the hunger strike, remained paramount and, as a part of this, maintaining the appearance of normality wherever possible. His other ongoing issue was the task of moving the political situation forwards through yet more rounds of talks with the main parties in the hope of re-establishing devolved working. But as 1982 began, he was faced with a more mundane problem. The effects of the Thatcherite economic revolution, which, as a leading opponent of her policies, he abhorred, had reached Northern Ireland. ·

The DeLorean Motor Company was facing collapse, with the prospect of 2,500 jobs being lost in Belfast. Famous, now, as the car used in the *Back to the Future* films, American John DeLorean, the founder of the company, had initially sought incentives from the government to locate its manufacturing hub in an area of high unemployment. With joblessness running at 22 per cent, Northern Ireland fitted the bill and the British government underwrote the building of the plant near Belfast with a grant of £80 million (tellingly, the Irish government declined to have anything to do with DeLorean). However, by February 1982 the company had laid off nearly half its workforce and Prior told them there would be no more bailouts. A week later, it went into receivership and the remaining 1,500 workers were made redundant. The House of Commons Public Accounts Committee would later declare that the loss of £77 million of public money was one 'of the gravest cases of misuse of public resources in recent years'. In the same week, Belfast's Harland & Wolff shipyard announced 1,000 job cuts. And then in March, British Enkalon, the Anglo-Dutch nylon manufacturer, closed its base in County Antrim with the loss of 850 jobs.

If the economy was creating a headache for the Secretary of State, the other familiar problem pains would not go away. Prior's big idea for restoring the local management of Northern Ireland came to be known as 'rolling devolution'. A white paper published in April 1982 set out proposals for a new 78-member assembly, which would be tasked with finding agreement over which powers could be devolved to it on a piecemeal basis. There would need to be agreement among 70 per cent of the members for this to happen. There was also evident frustration in the Northern Ireland Office at the repeated failure to make any arrangements stick since the collapse of Sunningdale. One of Prior's junior ministers, Lord Gowrie, described direct rule as 'very un-British' and that a form of dual citizenship, for those that considered themselves British or Irish, might be considered. In a debate on the proposed assembly, Prior himself said that continuing with direct rule did not offer a long-term answer. 'We either move to a position of total integration', he said, 'or we seek a gradual devolution of power.'[7] In July, Prior announced that there would be fresh elections to the new assembly on 20 October. A week later, the IRA planted two bombs, one near Hyde Park and the other under the bandstand in Regent's Park in central London. Eleven soldiers were killed, and dozens of civilians were injured. The soldiers targeted in the first attack were from the Blues and Royals (Royal Horse Guards and 1st Dragoons) and were on horseback at the time of the attack, and the scenes of devastation in Hyde Park also included dead and injured horses. The second attack killed seven bandsmen from the Royal Green Jackets who were performing an open-air concert. The grinding, relentless nature of the conflict made finding a political accommodation even more urgent; however, Prior's plans looked as doomed to fail as all of those of his predecessors. The election to the new assembly in October was the first that Sinn Féin contested during the Troubles. The party gained

10 per cent of the vote and won five seats, roughly half the SDLP, with the Ulster Unionists and DUP taking 30 and 23 per cent respectively. The result raised the prospect of Sinn Féin eventually competing with – and even supplanting – the SDLP as the electoral vehicle of choice for Catholic–Nationalists. And over the next two decades this is exactly what happened.

As Christmas approached, there was a flurry of developments. First, the INLA planted a bomb in the Droppin' Well Bar and Disco in County Derry that killed eleven soldiers and six civilians. The bomb caused a central pillar in the bar to collapse, with many of the victims killed by falling masonry. A day later, the Irish Supreme Court ruled that paramilitaries could be extradited to the UK, rejecting the claim they were politically motivated. Then, in a bid to thwart Gerry Adams and Danny Morrison from visiting London to speak at the Greater London Council, Home Secretary Willie Whitelaw placed a banning order on the two men, under the terms of the Prevention of Terrorism Act, which stopped them crossing the Irish Sea – a form of internal exile. Then, a week before Christmas, the ailing economy once again demanded Prior's full attention as Michelin announced 2,000 jobs were to go at its factory in County Antrim.

The New Year brought the Secretary of State little respite. The IRA killed two RUC officers in County Down, and then shot a county court judge, the Catholic William Doyle, as he left Sunday Mass. Ken Livingstone, the leader of the Greater London Council, came over to Belfast at the invitation of the internally exiled Gerry Adams. The Irish Foreign Minister, Peter

Barry, also paid a fact-finding visit to Belfast, drawing the ire of Unionists who resented his presence. To make matters worse, he told Prior that the new assembly was doomed to failure. The Irish government also had an alternative plan up its sleeve. In March, it announced it was setting up the 'New Ireland Forum'. The aim was to bring together various parties and discuss the 'manner in which lasting peace and stability can be achieved in a new Ireland through the democratic process'. It was the brainchild of SDLP leader John Hume and Fine Gael Taoiseach Garret FitzGerald. Fianna Fáil and the Irish Labour Party were also involved. Sinn Féin was not invited to participate, due to the forum's insistence on non-violence (and in a naked bid to bolster the SDLP's standing). Although invited, the DUP and Ulster Unionists, along with Alliance, boycotted the forum when it met at the end of May.

The forum did engage a range of academics, and even Protestant clergy, and produced several reports from a 'constitutional Nationalist' perspective. Their main proposals concerned laying out a range of constitutional models for the future governance of Northern Ireland. The first was a single, unitary, 32-county Ireland. The second was a federal Irish state with maximum autonomy for Northern Ireland. The third was joint authority, with the British and Irish governments sharing sovereignty and responsibility over Northern Ireland. The response from Westminster was decidedly lukewarm and Thatcher would go on to denounce the proposals of the New Ireland Forum. 'I have made it quite clear', she said, 'that a unified Ireland was one solution. That is out. A second solution was confederation of two states.

That is out. A third solution was joint authority. That is out ...
The majority [of people in Northern Ireland] wish to stay part
of the United Kingdom.'[8]

Thatcher had just won the Falklands War and she was in no
mood to countenance 'losing' Northern Ireland. A week after
the report came out in June 1983, Britain went to the polls. The
result was a landslide victory for Thatcher and her Conservatives, crushing the Labour opposition that had committed to
Irish unity by consent and the outlawing of plastic bullets and
had objected to provisions in the Prevention of Terrorism Act.
Unionist candidates took fifteen of Northern Ireland's seventeen
Westminster seats, with the SDLP taking one and Sinn Féin
the other. Gerry Adams, whom Willie Whitelaw had banned
from crossing the Irish Sea, was now the Member of Parliament
for Belfast West and the ruling had to be rescinded. He had
beaten Gerry Fitt and continued the long, steady process of
Sinn Féin usurping the SDLP as the main political representatives of Northern Ireland's Catholic–Nationalists. James Prior,
hardly a favourite of Thatcher and a known critic of her economic policies, was kept at the Northern Ireland Office – a punishment from the perspective of Westminster. Once again, the
challenges he was facing were grimly predictable. In attempts at
improving the security situation, there were a series of so-called
supergrass trials, in which large numbers of suspected paramilitaries were convicted on the evidence of a single informer. It
was a tactic used against both Loyalists and Republicans. In
August, one such trial involving thirty-eight alleged members
of the IRA resulted in twenty-two of them receiving custodial

sentences – equivalent to 4,000 years in prison. This exemplified the dilemma that was faced by those trying to govern Northern Ireland: how do you keep up the appearance of being part of a Western democratic state, while using methods that would not be out of place under a dictatorship? As it happened, eighteen of the convictions were overturned on appeal – in what was to become a common flaw in supergrass trials.

The autumn brought a significant tilt in the inner workings of Sinn Féin. At the party's *ard fheis*, Gerry Adams, the vice-president and recently elected (abstentionist) MP for Belfast West, became president of the party, replacing veteran Republican Ruairí Ó Brádaigh. This signalled a generational shift towards those who were now in their thirties and had come of age at the start of the Troubles, with figures like Adams, who had been interned in the Maze, now stepping up to lead the Republican movement. The party would need people who were willing to appear in the media and provide an account of what was going on, and Adams proved himself adept at this. This development also represented a decisive shift away from the movement being run by southerners, many of whom lacked first-hand experience of life on the streets of Belfast and Derry.

As ever, there was no shortage of appalling killings to contend with. Two that took place over the space of a few weeks in the autumn of 1983 were particularly haunting. On 20 November, three elders of a Pentecostal Church in the small village of Darkley in County Armagh near the Irish border were murdered by members of the INLA, who used the nom de plume 'Catholic Reaction Force'. One of the three wounded men managed to stagger into the main hall, where a service was taking place, before dying. Outside, the gunmen opened fire, spraying the little wooden church with bullets, injuring a further seven people. It was said to be a retaliatory attack following a series of killings by the UVF on ordinary Catholics under the aegis of the 'Protestant Action Force'. Even by the standards of the Troubles, the Darkley attack was a disgrace. A sectarian bloodbath. It even forced the INLA's leader, Dominic 'Mad Dog' McGlinchey, to issue an apology in which he claimed it was the work of rogue elements. Three weeks later, on 7 December, a promising young barrister and academic was shot dead at Queen's University in Belfast by the IRA. Edgar Graham was also a Northern Ireland Assembly member and a rising star for the Ulster Unionists. Like Robert Bradford's killing in 1981, this was a particularly heinous murder. Even for those who viewed Northern Ireland as a deeply flawed system, murdering the public's elected representatives was hardly a strategy that would bring about reconciliation or political progress.

The following year started with a rebuke for Margaret Thatcher from an unexpected quarter. The Catholic Primate of All Ireland, Tomás Ó Fiaich, criticised the Prime Minister for a visit she made to soldiers of the UDR just before Christmas. There was growing attention to the issue of collusion between members of the UDR, the RUC and security services and Loyalist paramilitaries. The cardinal did not hold back and said that he viewed Thatcher's visit as nothing short of 'disgusting'.[9] While condemning violence unequivocally, Ó Fiaich, who was a native of the Republican stronghold of Crossmaglen in South Armagh, considered that he had a pastoral duty towards all Catholics in Northern Ireland, which saw him intervene both to deter the hunger strikers from their course of action and to lobby Thatcher to relent to their demands. After the deaths of Bobby Sands and Francis Hughes he wrote to the British leader and pleaded: 'In God's name, don't allow another death.' Catholic Church leaders before and after him tended to adopt a more circumspect approach, but Ó Fiaich had fallen out with Thatcher at a meeting he had with her as early as 1981, when he recounted to a diplomat that she mused whether the motivation of the hunger strikers 'wasn't to demonstrate their virility'.[10]

Throughout 1984 there was a continuation of extreme violence, perpetrated by all sides, punctuated by attempts to resuscitate a political process that might lead to a deal that most parties could accept. Therein, of course, lay the difficulty. In the south, the Taoiseach, Garret FitzGerald, was lobbying the Americans to support the recommendations coming out of the New Ireland Forum discussions. However, British ministers were having none of it. On a visit to Ireland, President Reagan made supportive noises about the forum, piling more pressure on the British government, which had no viable political project to counter the Irish initiative. Meanwhile, the security situation remained precarious and any improvement looked unlikely. Loyalists were enraged by the decision of Londonderry District Council to change its name to Derry District Council and to stop the routine flying of the Union Flag. In March, the deputy governor of the Maze was killed outside his home by the IRA. A week later, Gerry Adams, the Sinn Féin president, was himself shot and wounded by Loyalists as he was travelling in a car. Three other Sinn Féin figures were also injured.

Over in Westminster, the Labour opposition had adopted a position of 'unity by consent' under its new leader, Neil Kinnock, with one of his frontbenchers advocating the harmonisation of Northern Ireland with the Republic of Ireland as a prelude to eventual unification. At the party's conference in October, Labour backed proposals to scrap Diplock courts (non-jury trials for serious offences), supergrass trials and the use of plastic bullets.

Politically significant though this was, it paled into insignificance in light of events that occurred just a week later. At 2.54 a.m. on 12 October, a bomb exploded at the Conservative Party conference hotel in Brighton, tearing through the Grand Hotel where the Prime Minister and most of the Cabinet were staying. Five people were killed, including Sir Anthony Berry MP, while thirty-one were injured, some seriously so. It was an audacious attempt to decapitate the British government itself, with one journalist likening it to the Gunpowder Plot in its ambition.[11] It brought home that the 'acceptable level of violence', that Reginald Maudling had once claimed the British government was willing to countenance in relation to the Troubles, only applied to attacks in Northern Ireland. Once the Troubles became an everyday fact of life for the British people, it was a different matter, not least because of the international embarrassment that accompanied this very visible loss of control. Indeed, it was the

IRA's plan to invert the British government's attempt to contain the Troubles on the streets of Belfast and Derry and bring it to the doorsteps of the British establishment. The IRA's statement claiming responsibility for the attack was phlegmatic: 'Today we were unlucky, but remember we only have to be lucky once. You will have to be lucky always.'[12] Undeterred, Thatcher summoned her Churchillian defiance as she pressed on with the conference, claiming that 'all attempts to destroy democracy by terrorism will fail'. The next day, her latest Northern Ireland Secretary, Douglas Hurd, poured more cold water on the New Ireland Forum proposals, echoing Thatcher's own disdain. Garret FitzGerald was dismayed, not only at the British government's response but the manner of it, privately describing Thatcher's reaction as 'gratuitously offensive'.[13] In the same month, two major supergrass trials collapsed with charges dropped and sentences overturned against thirty-five Republicans and fourteen Loyalists. The year 1984 ended much as it had begun, with the Catholic Primate of All Ireland, Tomás Ó Fiaich, claiming that Northern Ireland's Catholics felt an 'unprecedented level' of alienation with their lot. *Plus ça change.*

The next twelve months would prove to be significant. By the end of 1985, two of the key building blocks of what would later become the Good Friday Agreement would be put in place, and it would be Margaret Thatcher that laid one of them. It would involve the very thing – a bigger role in Northern Ireland's affairs for the Republic of Ireland – that she had previously set her face against. Before then, however, the familiar pattern of killing and destruction continued, interspersed with regular and invariably fruitless attempts to divine a political way forward. In February, SDLP leader John Hume took the first, faltering step to try to engage the Irish Republican movement in politics. There was no love lost between his party of moderate constitutional Nationalists and the radicals of Sinn Féin. Nevertheless, Hume consistently tried to create an initiative that would persuade them to embrace politics. He was attacked on all sides for his troubles, with Unionists, Dublin and London all critical of his efforts. A meeting with IRA leaders lasted only a few minutes after he refused to have the meeting tape-recorded. Nevertheless, it was the first foray in a strategy to engage Republicans that would later bear fruit and become a cornerstone of the peace process. From the Republicans' perspective, there was a need to develop their approach to politics, especially as this long war was now entrenched and looked set to continue for the foreseeable future. Sinn Féin achieved another electoral breakthrough in the 1985 local elections, winning 12 per cent of the vote and the election of fifty-nine local councillors.[14] But other opportunities were being lost along the way. Gerry Adams had been refused a visa to enter the US to address members of Congress, while the Irish government was introducing measures to seize the assets of those suspected of being involved with terrorism. But the scale of the challenge in ending the IRA's campaign was brought home at the end of February, when a mortar attack on an RUC station in Newry, County Down killed nine officers and injured thirty. It was the RUC's largest loss of life in a single attack throughout the Troubles. In addition, a UDR soldier was killed in a separate attack in County Tyrone. Until the Armalite was put down, the strategy of the ballot box alone would not prevail.

The British government was also operating on different fronts, increasingly keen to counter Republican propaganda. There followed a row over a proposed BBC programme, *Real Lives: At the Edge of the Union*, which, among other interviews, included a section with Martin McGuinness, the former IRA commander in Derry who was now assuming a leadership role in Sinn Féin. The government and its appointed governors exerted pressure to get the programme stopped, which resulted in a revolt by programme makers and a strike by BBC and ITN journalists that shut down the BBC's World Service for the first time ever – a revised version of the programme was later broadcast on 5 June. Eager though it was to maximise media opportunities to get its message across, the IRA's campaign continued. In August it killed a Catholic businessman in Dublin who sold portable buildings to the RUC. Aiding the enemy, as Republicans saw his business, made him a 'legitimate target'. The following month, a married couple, Gerard and Catherine Mahon, were shot in West Belfast after being accused of being informers.

In September, there was another change at the Northern Ireland Office as Douglas Hurd was succeeded by Tom King. He inherited growing Unionist suspicions that something was afoot between the British and Irish governments. The leader of the Ulster Unionists, James Molyneaux, in a rare demonstration of unity with Ian Paisley's Democratic Unionist Party, met with Thatcher in Downing Street to protest about any involvement by the Republic's government in the affairs of Northern Ireland.

They did not have long to wait to have their suspicions confirmed. On 15 November, the two governments signed the Anglo-Irish Agreement, a concordat signed in an attempt to help manage political developments and security issues and seek out areas of cross-border co-operation. The treaty would see Irish civil servants work alongside Northern Ireland Office staff at a joint secretariat in Belfast.

The agreement ignited Unionist fury more significantly than at any other time during the Troubles. In essence, it validated their long-held belief that Westminster was willing to sell them out. Doubly galling was that the 'treachery' came courtesy of Margaret Thatcher – who had consistently set her face against deeper ties with Dublin. What it showed was the disconnect between what went on in Northern Ireland and how the rest of the UK reacted. Westminster was plainly unmoved. There might have been a frisson of disapproval on the right of the Conservative Party, but the fact the agreement was so comprehensively voted through tells its own tale about how concerned British MPs were about assuaging Unionist sensibilities. There were no votes to be lost in taking a decisive move that might improve the security situation in Britain. Unionist-controlled local councils threatened to refuse to set a rate and the Northern Ireland Assembly voted 3:1 in favour of a referendum on the agreement, but this appeal went unheeded. So, all fifteen Ulster Unionist and Democratic Unionist MPs resigned their Westminster seats to trigger by-elections. With Thatcher commanding a three-figure majority in the House of Commons, the move was all gesture and no effect. At the end of November, there was a massive rally of up to 100,000 protestors outside Belfast City Hall. 'Ulster Says No' was the voluble, unmistakable message from Unionists and Loyalists, as a parallel effort to challenge the agreement in the court failed. In the House of Commons a few days later, MPs voted 473:47 to approve it. Opposition to the Anglo-Irish Agreement barely scraped together a tenth of the votes. This was the British government taking its own initiative after the repeated failure to establish effective devolved working, to the general disinterest of Parliament. Over in Belfast the mood was febrile. The initial meeting of the British–Irish Intergovernmental Conference – the key body established by the agreement that would see Irish and British civil servants working together – was picketed by angry Loyalists, resulting in violent clashes that saw thirty-eight RUC officers injured.

So, 1985 ended with two of the building blocks in place of what would gradually become the peace process. John Hume's brief but symbolic meeting with the IRA would form the basis of an ongoing dialogue with the Republican movement that would eventually lead to the end of their armed struggle and shift towards a focus on politics. Meanwhile, the Anglo-Irish Agreement, codifying the role of the Irish government in the affairs of Northern Ireland, would provide a framework for the two governments to work in partnership in managing Northern Ireland from now on. As ever, the pace of events was often glacial and there would be much more pain and blood before these developments would pay off in a decade's time.

Reverberations from the Anglo-Irish Agreement continued to cause problems throughout 1986 with a warning from Northern

Ireland Secretary Tom King that the British government would not be swayed by the results from the fifteen parliamentary by-elections caused by the mass resignation of Unionist MPs. Unionists wanted to use the occasion as a proxy referendum on the agreement and although they increased their overall share of the vote, the effect was undermined when one of the seats was lost to the SDLP's Seamus Mallon. 'Ulster Says No' remained the campaign slogan. 'Westminster isn't bothered' was the position of the government. At the same time, the High Court in Belfast ordered Belfast City Council to end its adjournment of business and to remove a large 'Ulster Says No' poster from the front of City Hall after the cross-community Alliance Party complained.

At the beginning of March 1986, Unionists called a 'day of action' – a wildcat strike in opposition to the agreement – orchestrated by the Ulster Unionists and Democratic Unionists who were, for now, putting up a united front. Molyneaux and Paisley had been across the Irish Sea for talks with Thatcher, pressing the case for the restoration of devolution and calling for the agreement to be scrapped. As ever, Unionism's political leaders distanced themselves from the ensuing violence that broke out across Northern Ireland, which resulted in forty-seven police officers being injured and led to dozens of arrests. In the House of Commons, Tom King criticised Unionist politicians for colluding with masked thugs. Extra soldiers would be despatched from Britain to assist with the upsurge in Loyalist violence. A week later, three DUP representatives were arrested by police after cutting through a perimeter fence at Stormont while a session of the Intergovernmental Conference was underway.

Meanwhile, the refusal of eighteen Unionist-controlled councils to set a rate saw the Northern Ireland Office intervene and set one for them.

Thatcher wrote to Unionist leaders reiterating that there would be no concessions made about the agreement. Having staked her credibility on it, it was now the turn of the Unionists to experience what it meant when the lady said she was not for turning. In a mark of the animosity towards Thatcher, the Ulster Unionist Party's executive committee voted to end the special relationship with the Conservatives that had begun during the Home Rule era. Through March and April there were waves of Loyalist rioting, petrol bomb attacks on Catholic communities and intimidation of RUC officers. Echoing Tom King, who had already made the same point, the Chief Constable of the RUC, John Hermon, alleged that Unionist politicians were 'consorting with paramilitary elements' after fifty RUC families and seventy-nine Catholic families had their homes firebombed in a single month.[15] Six months on from the signing of the Anglo-Irish Agreement, and opposition to it was becoming more desperate. A group of DUP activists stormed the switchboard room at Stormont. Comical though this episode was, there was a sinister undercurrent to these actions and the RUC was taking the brunt of it. Not usually the target of Loyalist fury, hundreds of officers had been subjected to intimidation, with 500 homes attacked and 150 families forced to move. Perhaps the greatest irony about the agreement was that it wrongfooted both Sinn Féin's Gerry Adams and Fianna Fáil's Charles Haughey. Both spoke out against it, believing it to be a means of copper-fastening partition, while Unionists were furious because they thought the exact opposite.

In June, Tom King officially dissolved the Northern Ireland Assembly. Once again, political developments had stalled and it was not apparent where things should go next. A large group of Loyalist protestors gathered outside Stormont, forcing the RUC to baton charge them. Two dozen Unionist politicians refused to leave, with Ian Paisley muttering darkly about Northern Ireland descending into civil war. Unionist politicians established their own version of the assembly in Belfast City Hall, but the initiative petered out a few months later. This was all a new experience for Unionists and Loyalists. However, Westminster was unmoved by their plight. Even someone as hard-line as Thatcher in her opposition to the IRA could not be relied on to instinctively side with them. The RUC, too, now stood in opposition to them.

The summer months brought further trouble. Ian Paisley and his DUP deputy, Peter Robinson, led 4,000 Loyalists in an early morning protest where they tried to occupy the village of Hillsborough in County Down as part of their ongoing action against the Anglo-Irish Agreement. There followed a week of mass disturbances around the traditional 12 July celebrations, which led to the RUC firing 300 plastic bullets at Loyalists, and hundreds of civilians and police officers were injured over the course of the week. In addition, around fifty Loyalists attacked Catholic homes in the village of Rasharkin, County Antrim. To bookend the trouble, the IRA shot dead three RUC officers in Newry, County Down as they sat in an armoured patrol car.

At the start of August 1986, Peter Robinson led a mob of 500 Loyalists across the Irish border into the village of Clontibret, County Monaghan, where they attacked two members of *An Garda Síochána* (the Irish police).[16] Robinson was later convicted over the raid and received a hefty fine. With Loyalists preoccupied with their campaign against the agreement, the IRA was broadening the remit of its offensive. Contractors working for the British state were now also deemed to be 'legitimate targets', and were liable to be assassinated. This was no idle threat. In July and August, the IRA killed two Protestant men, a forty-year-old and a 22-year-old, who had been working as contractors for the RUC.

The Ulster Unionist Party and the DUP continued to work together in opposition to the agreement, commanding vast numbers of Loyalists in the process, sometimes overlapping with paramilitaries as they did so. One such occasion was the funeral of Loyalist John Bingham, a leading figure in the Ulster Volunteer Force and a sectarian gunman who had allegedly murdered several Catholics and had been killed by the IRA.[17] Several MPs from the UUP and the DUP attended, blurring the lines between the constitutional and paramilitary and adding to the impression that Unionism and Loyalism were not separate categories, but simply a continuum. Less dubious co-operation came in the opposition to the agreement in the town halls of Northern Ireland. By September, both the UUP and the DUP had decided to call off a rate strike and now urged people to pay their council bills. They had also decided against mass resignations from council chambers following the lack of impact the resignation of their MPs had made on opinion over at Westminster. In November, Molyneaux and Paisley attended an Orange Order rally in Glasgow to try to launch a campaign in Britain against the agreement, but there was a palpable lack of progress for their efforts. Unionist gestures were having little effect, even if they were proving to irritate British ministers, as happened when Belfast's Lord Mayor, the DUP's Sammy Wilson, banned Northern Ireland Office ministers from attending the annual Remembrance Day service at Belfast City Hall.

The Republican movement, sensing the potential to further develop its political front, decided to end its policy of abstentionism, in effect recognising the southern Irish state for the first time and, with it, partition. This was a big moment for Sinn Féin and its president, Gerry Adams. To avoid splits, the move had been carefully teed up with a General Army Convention of the IRA (the supreme authority of the organisation) first agreeing to the move, which was followed by a subsequent motion at Sinn Féin's *ard fheis* echoing the call and agreeing that candidates would in future take their seats in the Dáil. To outsiders it probably seemed like a minor development, but it was enough to trigger a sizeable walkout led by veteran Republicans, Ruairí Ó Brádaigh, the former president of Sinn Féin, and Dáithí Ó Conaill, the former vice-president. Both men had sat side by side with Adams at the Cheyne Walk talks with Willie Whitehall fourteen years earlier.

As Republicans started to cleave towards politics, the DUP moved towards militarism. In a private meeting at Ulster Hall, attended by 3,000 people, Ian Paisley, together with

Peter Robinson and others, escalated their opposition to the Anglo-Irish Agreement with the launch of Ulster Resistance – a paramilitary movement established to procure arms. Donning a red beret, Paisley referred to the need to take 'direct action as and when required', in opposition to the agreement.[18] On the first anniversary of its signing, there was a large rally held outside Belfast City Hall, while Robinson led a cohort in full paramilitary garb at a protest march in Portadown. The forming of Ulster Resistance had distinctly sinister undertones, and the group would go on to import a major cache of arms into Northern Ireland to be shared out among the various other Loyalist paramilitaries. Paisley and the DUP claimed to have severed contact with it as early as 1987, but the connection through this group makes a mockery of attempts to divide 'Unionist' and 'Loyalist'. In their opposition to the Anglo-Irish Agreement, Paisley was quite happy to consort with anyone to pursue his agenda. As 1986 drew to a close, he was found in familiar form, haranguing Margaret Thatcher as she addressed the European Parliament in Brussels, holding up an 'Ulster Says No' poster and bellowing: 'I would like to indict you, Mrs Thatcher, as a traitor to the loyalist people of Northern Ireland in denying them the right to vote on the Anglo-Irish Agreement!'[19]

In early 1987, a discussion paper entitled 'Common Sense' was published by the Ulster Political Research Group on behalf of the UDA.[20] It proposed fresh talks leading to the establishment of a new assembly and power-sharing executive and a bill of rights. It was a useful and thought-provoking intervention, even more so because it came from Loyalists and bypassed Unionist politicians. It was mainly the work of John McMichael, a senior commander in the UDA, with input from David Trimble, who was then a law lecturer at Queen's University. 'Whilst we have no doubt that compromise and accommodation can be reached between Catholics and Protestants in Northern Ireland,' it said, 'it is impossible to compromise on the existence of Northern Ireland itself – it either exists or it doesn't.' The statement recognised that the current constitutional status 'may not be the whole-hearted wish of everyone in the province', but it did, currently, represent majority opinion. And while 'the vast majority' in both communities longed for peace, 'there must be a mechanism created to harness the love, generosity, courage and integrity of Ulster people in both religious communities and direct its great power towards the light of a new beginning'. Creditably, the statement recognised there 'is no section of this divided Ulster community, which is totally innocent or indeed totally guilty, totally right or totally wrong'. Both sides must share the blame and the responsibility 'of maintaining good government'.

The pamphlet's flaw was that it offered an 'internal' British solution, eschewing any all-Ireland dimension which by then was a red line for Irish Nationalists and Republicans. They would not settle for being cut off from the rest of the country any longer. Nevertheless, the language was emollient and the energy in the approach would later be reflected in the positive contribution that Loyalists would make during the talks that led to the Good Friday Agreement. Meanwhile, the two main Unionist parties, the Ulster Unionists and the Democratic Unionist Party, were still in the business of mass mobilisation against the Anglo-Irish

Agreement. In February, they delivered a petition of 400,000 signatures to Buckingham Palace, bypassing Margaret Thatcher and Westminster, where they were still getting a cold reception. British public opinion remained decidedly lukewarm, with a poll in the *Daily Express* finding that 61 per cent of the British public wanted to withdraw from Northern Ireland entirely.[21]

In May 1987, Sinn Féin published its own proposals for moving the stalled political process forward. 'A Scenario for Peace' suggested an all-Ireland 'constitutional conference' to draw up a new system of government, repealing the Government of Ireland Act and 'publicly declaring that the "Northern Ireland" statelet is no longer part of the United Kingdom'.[22] Furthermore, a date for British withdrawal should be agreed and all political prisoners 'unconditionally released'. It also called for the army and 'system of political administration' to be removed in the 'shortest practical period'.

While not minimising the 'great trauma' that Unionists would experience, the statement stated that 'we believe that Loyalism derives an artificial psychological strength from the British presence, from the Union'. In any event, most opinion polls showed 'the majority of people in Britain want to wash their hands of Ireland'. Like 'Common Sense', 'A Scenario for Peace' was impossible for the other side to accept, but was at least cordial in its tone. 'We do not intend to turn back the pages of history, or to dispossess the Loyalists and foolishly attempt to reverse the Plantation,' it said. 'We offer them a settlement based on their throwing in their lot with the rest of the Irish people and ending sectarianism. We offer them peace. We offer them equality.'

Later that month, an eight-man IRA unit was killed at Loughgall in County Armagh after they were ambushed by forty SAS soldiers. It was the organisation's single biggest loss of life during the Troubles. A civilian was also killed in the exchange. This exemplified the dual policy that the British government was pursuing: trying to normalise the situation in Northern Ireland with a hope of restoring cross-community devolved working, while, at the same time, waging an unrelenting war against the IRA. In the minds of British ministers, the limitations of either approach necessitated the other policy. If you could not guarantee security then there would never be political progress, but because there was no viable political development to invest in, the security situation was out of control. All of which meant the real policy was one of treading water and hoping for the best. June saw a British general election and Margaret Thatcher safely returned for a third term. Earlier in the year, Garret FitzGerald had been ousted in the Irish election to be replaced, once again, by Charles Haughey presiding over a Fianna Fáil-led coalition. Thatcher's victory would be her last, and by the end of 1990 she would be forced out. The election result in Northern Ireland was predictable, with the caveat that Enoch Powell, who by now sat as an Ulster Unionist, lost his seat to the SDLP, fulfilling his own famous prediction that 'all political careers end in failure'. In a sign of their continued co-operation, the Ulster Unionists and Democratic Unionists stood on a joint manifesto. Tom King was reappointed as Northern Ireland Secretary and the political inertia and sporadic violence continued.

The carnage reached a new low in November 1987 with an

explosion at an annual Remembrance Day ceremony in Enniskillen in County Fermanagh. The IRA detonated a bomb that killed eleven people – including three married couples – and injured dozens more. It was one of the gravest atrocities of the Troubles, with the IRA claiming the bombing was a mistake and the intended targets were parading soldiers. Nevertheless, the Enniskillen explosion had deep political ramifications for Republicans, ranging from the Irish government acquiescing to British proposals to make it easier to extradite IRA suspects from the Irish Republic, through to Colonel Gaddafi stopping weapons shipments to the IRA. More prosaically, it undermined Sinn Féin's electoral standing, setting back the 'ballot box and Armalite' strategy. One of those injured in the explosion, Gordon Wilson, had to endure watching his daughter, Marie, succumb to her injuries as they both lay in the rubble from the blast. He immediately forgave the bombers and urged that there be no reprisals. His extraordinary moral courage would see him go on to become a prominent peace campaigner in future years and to sit in the Irish Senate.

Just before Christmas, the deputy leader of the UDA was killed on his drive by a bomb that was attached to his car. The killing was part of a Loyalist feud and the Troubles saw many similar 'Orange on Orange' assassinations. A new generation that wanted to step up the violence was to blame. If Republicans had set back their political progress with the Enniskillen bombing, Loyalists could be just as myopic. The victim, John McMichael, had been the architect of the forward-thinking 'Common Sense' proposals.

Sinn Féin's need to reinforce its political front following the debacle at Enniskillen saw a restoration of the dialogue between Gerry Adams and the SDLP's John Hume. Throughout 1988, the two men met privately to discuss a way of ending the Troubles and what was needed to bring Republicans in from the cold. Their initiative would eventually become a cornerstone of the peace and political process; however, for now, that was some way off. Indeed, it was difficult for Adams to convince his side that an exclusively political track was possible when the war against the British government and Loyalist paramilitaries was still in full flight. In March, three IRA members were ambushed and killed by the SAS in Gibraltar. They were unarmed and said to have been reconnoitring potential targets. Eyewitnesses maintained they were given no warning to surrender. It would provoke a firestorm of reaction, with sixty Labour MPs criticising the killings amid mounting accusations that Britain was operating an extra-judicial 'shoot to kill' policy.

Worse was to come over the next few weeks. The funerals of the 'Gibraltar Three' at Milltown Cemetery in Belfast were attacked by a lone Loyalist, Michael Stone, throwing hand grenades at mourners. Three people were killed, with a further fifty injured. The whole affair was captured by television cameras. Stone fled and was pursued by other mourners before being captured, the police arriving to arrest him before he was killed by the crowd.

Three days later, at one of the subsequent funerals of a victim at Milltown, a car approached the procession at speed. Inside were two plain-clothed soldiers. Assuming this was another attack on mourners, the crowd surrounded the car and one of the soldiers inside discharged a pistol as a warning. This seemed to confirm the crowd's fears and the two men were dragged out of the car and beaten before being taken to a nearby waste ground, stripped and shot dead by members of the IRA. Again, much of this was captured on camera (and it has never been satisfactorily explained what the soldiers were doing at the procession). A few weeks later, Thames Television screened a documentary, *Death on the Rock*, about the Gibraltar shootings. Journalists had interviewed several eyewitnesses who claimed soldiers fired on the three IRA members while they were trying to surrender. The Thatcher government unsuccessfully tried to get the programme banned, creating a major row with the broadcaster and merely adding to the programme's lustre. In seeking to avoid what they perceived to be a propaganda coup for the IRA, ministers simply guaranteed that it would become one. The perception that the government did not play by the rules in its dirty war with the IRA undermined the British claim that it was a neutral referee. An editorial in the staunchly Conservative *Daily Telegraph* summed up the dilemma:

Unless it wishes Britain's enemies to enjoy a propaganda bonanza it [the government] should explain why it was necessary to shoot dead all three terrorists on the street rather than apprehend them with the considerable force of police and SAS which appears to have been deployed in the locality ... It is an essential aspect of any successful anti-terrorist policy to maintain the principles of civilised restraint which obtain in a democratic society. A failure to do so argues that terrorism is succeeding in one of its critical aims: the brutalisation of the society under attack.[23]

Having lost its battle to have *Death on the Rock* withdrawn, the British government introduced a broadcasting ban in the autumn of 1988, aimed at muting Sinn Féin or, using Margaret Thatcher's eponymous turn of phrase, denying them the 'oxygen of publicity'. The tactic backfired when broadcasters circumvented the ban by dubbing the various Sinn Féin spokespeople with the voices of actors.

Despite Gerry Adams continuing to engage in talks with John Hume, the IRA remained committed to armed conflict every bit as much as the British government. In June, an IRA bomb killed six off-duty soldiers in Lisburn, County Antrim. In the same month, the group planted a bomb on a school bus in an attempt to kill the driver who was a part-time member of the UDR. He was injured in the explosion along with some of the children on the bus. One of the passengers was seventeen-year-old Arlene Foster, who would go on to become leader of the Democratic Unionists twenty-seven years later. In August, the IRA killed one soldier and injured nine others in a bombing at a London army barracks. Days later, it killed two Protestant workers in Belleek, County Fermanagh, who were carrying out repairs to a police station. The rest of the month was just as bloody. Two Catholic men were killed by the so-called Protestant Action Force before eight British soldiers died in a bomb attack at Ballygawley in County Tyrone. Twenty-eight other soldiers were injured in the blast. Shortly after this, three members of the IRA were killed by the SAS near Drumnakilly in County Tyrone.

September saw the inquest into the Gibraltar killings, which found that the authorities had acted lawfully. Views about the verdict predictably split along political lines. For the British, the act was a necessary measure in showing the IRA that they meant business. For Republicans, it validated their argument that there was no British justice to be had. Earlier in the year, Patrick Mayhew, the Attorney General (and later Secretary of State for Northern Ireland), confirmed that there would be no prosecutions emanating from an outside review into allegations of a British 'shoot to kill' policy on the grounds of 'national security'. The review had caused controversy when the senior police officer initially heading it, John Stalker, the Deputy Chief Constable of Greater Manchester, was removed over his alleged connections to underworld figures. He maintained that the real reason was that his findings would have caused major political embarrassment for ministers. Neither was there any movement in the gathering controversy around the 'Birmingham Six' – the men who had been convicted of the IRA bombings of two city-centre pubs in Birmingham in 1974, which killed twenty-one people and injured 182 others. Fresh evidence supporting their claim that they were the victims of a miscarriage of justice were rejected by appeal judges (although they would be freed three years later). To compound matters, Ian Thain, the first British soldier to be convicted of murder while on duty in Northern Ireland in 1984, was freed after just twenty-six months and allowed to rejoin his regiment.

The year rounded off with a series of legal wrangles. In October, Tom King announced legislation that would allow courts to infer guilt from the silence of witnesses when questioned by police. He also proposed that the remission of sentences for prisoners would be reduced from a half to one-third. The European Court of Human Rights was also causing problems for the government after ruling that Britain was in breach of the European Convention on Human Rights by detaining suspects for more than four days. There was also a problem with the Irish government, which was refusing to extradite a renegade priest who had been arrested in Belgium and was wanted in connection with his support for the IRA.

The New Year began with movement on the case of the 'Guildford Four' (those convicted of the bombing of two pubs in Guildford in October 1974, which killed four soldiers and a civilian) being referred to the Court of Appeal. As with the case of the Birmingham Six, there was mounting concern over the soundness of the convictions for those found guilty of the IRA bombings in Britain in the early 1970s. Amid the clamour at the time for arrests and convictions, innocent Irish people had been fitted up by corrupt police officers, so the accusation went. After many years in prison, and with their legal challenges gaining ground – thanks to new evidence emerging and a concerted effort to raise the profile of their cases from a range of campaigners, not least Cardinal Basil Hume, the most senior Catholic in Britain – there was growing unease in government. By October, their convictions had been overturned after the court accepted that the confessions used to convict the men were fabricated. No police officer was ever charged with conspiracy or miscon- duct, adding to the suspicion that the legal process had been weaponised in the propaganda war against the IRA.

The growing effectiveness of legal challenges against gov- ernment policy in Northern Ireland was beginning to grate with ministers. In the House of Commons, a junior Home Office minister, Douglas Hogg, made a cryptic remark about 'a number of solicitors' in Northern Ireland who were 'unduly sympathetic to the cause of the IRA'.[24] Less than a month later, on a Sunday evening as he was sitting down to eat dinner with his family, 38-year-old Pat Finucane, a prominent Belfast solic- itor, was gunned down by Loyalist gunmen who had smashed in his front door and started opening fire. In what was a hor- rendous attack, he was shot fourteen times at point-blank range in front of his wife, who was also injured by a stray bullet, and their young children. The attack immediately gained notoriety considering Hogg's inferences the previous month, with allega- tions of security force collusion in his killing. A series of inves- tigations followed over many years, each concluding that there was indeed collusion between the two gunmen and the British Army's Force Research Unit, a covert unit running agents and informants in Loyalist paramilitary groups.[25] That was the con- clusion of an inquiry led by Sir John Stevens, the former Com- missioner of the Metropolitan Police. Two subsequent judge-led reviews of the case found the same.

The late 1980s were grim times. There was weariness on all

sides. The Troubles were becoming unsustainable – for everyone. By now, the Republican movement, particularly under the leadership of Gerry Adams, was looking for a political pathway. It was clear the British would not be bombed out of Northern Ireland and, as such, there was little incentive for Unionists to give any ground. It was equally clear that the IRA would never be militarily defeated. Irish Republicans had been resisting British rule since the 1790s and there was little prospect of them laying down their arms and acquiescing to a return to a failed status quo that had ignited the Troubles in the first place. Each side, in their own way, had exhausted their options and was left without a viable new way forward. Collusion between British state agencies and Loyalist paramilitaries was, however, a particularly dark chapter. In August, a Catholic man, Loughlin Maginn, was killed by the Ulster Freedom Fighters (UFF) – a front name for the UDA to avoid it becoming proscribed as a terrorist organisation. The UFF claimed they had received intelligence on IRA suspects from the security services. The following month, further documents containing details of suspected IRA members went missing and the RUC eventually arrested twenty-eight members of the UDR who were suspected of passing them to Loyalists. August saw the twentieth anniversary of the deployment of the British Army in Northern Ireland. It was a milestone that came and went. A few weeks later, the IRA killed eleven soldiers from the staff band of the Royal Marines at Deal Barracks in Kent. In November, the new Northern Ireland Secretary, Peter Brooke, conceded that the IRA could not be defeated militarily, holding out the prospect of talks with Sinn Féin if the IRA would end its campaign. As the 1980s drew to a close, an opinion poll in the *Observer* newspaper found that 51 per cent of the British public wanted the army withdrawn from Northern Ireland.[26] It would be another decade before the circumstances would allow that to happen.

CHAPTER 5

THE END IS IN SIGHT

The 1990s would bring a cessation of the IRA's campaign and equivalent ceasefires from Loyalists. It would see the beginning of a peace process that would eventually lead to the signing of a comprehensive agreement ending the Troubles and put Northern Ireland on an exclusively political track. It would result in paramilitary prisoners being released from prison, with many of them, on both sides, going to work in the community and local politics, putting their weight behind an agreement that managed to restore devolved working with genuine power-sharing at its heart, along with an all-Ireland dimension and the promise, down the road, of a referendum on Irish unity.

But all this was some way off at the start of 1990. The decade that would take us to the signing of the Good Friday Agreement was long and arduous, typified by the killings and bombings to which Northern Ireland was grimly familiar and the long, slow, stop–start attempts at political engagement that would lead to talks that, eventually, led to agreement. On the political front, a senior Ulster Unionist MP, John Taylor, suggested that his party recommence talks with British ministers. Their unilateral boycott – a hangover from their opposition to the Anglo-Irish Agreement – was clearly now counter-productive with smarter Unionists realising they were cutting off their noses to spite their face, especially as Peter Brooke was urging them to restart political dialogue and to try to find a way through the impasse. April 1990 saw the first visit to Northern Ireland by the Taoiseach since Terence O'Neill invited Seán Lemass in 1965. Charles Haughey headed north to speak at a business conference, flying in by military helicopter. Hundreds of Loyalists, including Ian Paisley and figures from the Ulster Unionists, came to protest outside the venue and scuffled with the RUC. The lack of progress in normalising relations between north and south was underscored by the death of O'Neill in June 1990, who had spent his final days living in Hampshire.

Throughout the early 1990s, Peter Brooke led an ongoing effort to construct a process of multi-party talks that might lead to a political accommodation. This slow, time-consuming and often frustrating process was set against the backdrop of a volatile security situation. By now, the combatants each accepted that they would not succeed in their aims militarily. It was an assumption for the British as much as for the Republicans. But without a viable political settlement to invest in, the killing continued. In July, the IRA planted a bomb at the London Stock Exchange. It was a small device and did not cause extensive damage or interrupt trading, but in a bid to bring the conflict to British shores, London became a frequent target, especially its high-profile financial centre. In 1992, the IRA planted a bomb at the Baltic Exchange, which killed three people and in-jured ninety-one. In contrast to the Stock Exchange bomb, this 2000lb device was the largest bomb exploded in Britain since the Second World War. The historic building was so severely damaged that it was later demolished and eventually replaced by the 'Gherkin'. But the attacks were not just large and random. Sometimes they were intimate and specific. In July 1990, the IRA murdered the Conservative MP Ian Gow with a car bomb outside his home. An outspoken critic of the IRA, Gow was a long-time confidant of Thatcher and had once served as her parliamentary private secretary – her 'eyes and ears' in the House of Commons. He had parted ways with her over the signing of the Anglo-Irish Agreement and had resigned his role as a junior Treasury minister. Even as an early political process was starting to take shape, the killing continued unabated. Later in the year, the IRA continued with a tactic it had first developed in the late 1980s, namely the use of the 'proxy bomb'. To minimise the risk of operatives being caught, taxi drivers were forced to drive to checkpoints with explosives in their vehicles, whereupon the explosives would be detonated. This inhumane method was used on numerous occasions in the late 1980s and early 1990s.

By the middle of 1990, Brooke was no further forward in establishing a viable programme of talks. The SDLP's insist-ence on an all-Ireland dimension to any deal was anathema to Unionists, who were insisting that the Irish government should not be involved unless it first dropped Articles 2 and 3 of the Irish Constitution, which claimed 'the national terri-tory' of the country consisted 'of the whole island of Ireland'.

On a visit to Dublin, Nelson Mandela (a long-time supporter of Irish Republicanism) remarked that the British government should begin direct talks with the IRA. Brooke's quiet diplomatic efforts would increase in tempo during November as he made his most significant intervention to date. In a scheduled speech, he said that Britain had no 'selfish strategic or economic interest' in Northern Ireland.[1] Ireland could be unified, but only by the consent of a majority of the people living there. At one remove, it was an unremarkable formulation. 'Nothing will ever change unless a majority wants it to' would have been another way of saying the same thing. And yet it was full of carefully coded symbolism. It provided Unionists with a constitutional guarantee, while enticing Republicans with the prospect of securing their political objectives via exclusively political means. The implicit message was: 'We won't stay here longer than we are wanted.' Brooke would later explain that it was part of an attempt to get the various participants, the British government included, to re-evaluate their aims 'in the context of the 1990s'.

Conservative MPs were also thinking about their aims, and began re-evaluating their support for Margaret Thatcher. After eleven years in Downing Street, they forced her out. The cumulative impact of the botched implementation of the poll tax, her increasingly hostile approach to Europe, as well as general political fatigue meant it was time for a change. Her replacement, the little-known John Major, had been her Chancellor of the Exchequer. A quiet, unassuming man who wanted to build a 'classless society' and a country 'at ease with itself', he was to bring pragmatism where Thatcher had brought stridency. On his watch, political reform would rapidly accelerate. Eventually. For now, though, he was merely another British Prime Minister and therefore a 'legitimate target' for the IRA. In February 1991, Republicans made that clear by launching an audacious attempt to wipe out the British Cabinet with a home-made mortar fired at Downing Street from a nearby van. The shot landed close enough to shatter windows, prompting ministers to dive under the Cabinet table. More positive developments were in the offing, however.

The following month, Peter Brooke, who had retained his role as Northern Ireland Secretary under Major, succeeded in establishing the choreography for a series of multi-party talks between the UUP, the DUP, the SDLP and Alliance, which would, crucially, also include participation from the Irish government. Over time the Brooke–Mayhew talks (the joint billing referred to Brooke and successor Patrick Mayhew) were based on finding agreement between the parties in Northern Ireland ('strand one'), the relationship between Northern Ireland and the Irish Republic ('strand two'), and between Ireland and Britain ('strand three'). This model would create the rapport and build the momentum that eventually carried things towards the Good Friday Agreement, but that was a long way off, especially as Sinn Féin was not yet represented in the talks process. In a bid to avoid any of the parties cherry-picking the parts they liked, the underpinning rule was that any agreed package of measures had to be accepted in totality under the principle that 'nothing is agreed until everything is agreed'. British public opinion was jaded by the long shadow cast by Northern Ireland. A poll in

The Guardian found that 43 per cent of the British public favoured Irish unification, with only 30 per cent backing Northern Ireland to remain part of the UK.[2]

Away from the talks, March 1991 saw a long-running injustice resolved as the Birmingham Six were finally released from prison following a lengthy campaign by supporters and some deft case management by their legal team. They had originally been convicted on forensic evidence that was now deemed unreliable and from confessions that had been beaten out of them by corrupt police officers, who had also forged notes and given false evidence at the original trial. As one injustice was resolved, another was committed, as the officers involved faced no charges. Later in the year, the convictions of the 'Maguire Seven' – an Irish family from the Kilburn area of north-west London falsely convicted of supplying the bombs used in the Guildford and Woolwich bombings in 1976 – would also be quashed by the Court of Appeal.

Northern Ireland's census for 1991 revealed one of the quiet ironies of the conflict. Catholics were the largest confessional group and now accounted for over 40 per cent of the population, but after decades of incremental steps to halt discrimination they still only accounted for 35 per cent of the total workforce in companies with more than twenty-five employees – according to a report from the Fair Employment Commission – a gap equivalent to tens of thousands of jobs.[3] Meanwhile, the Northern Ireland civil service produced a report on the religious composition of the civil service that showed that 57 per cent of civil service roles were held by Protestants and 36 per cent by

Catholics, mirroring the discrepancy in the private sector.[4] Moreover, just one-fifth (21 per cent) of senior roles were held by Catholics.

As the multi-party talks began, the IRA campaign of violence showed no signs of slowing, with a series of huge bomb attacks. In February, members loaded a 500lb bomb into a van and forced a man working as a contractor for the security forces to drive into a UDR base in County Derry. Amazingly, he managed to get out of the vehicle before the explosion, but it caused massive damage to the base and nearby houses. In April, a 1,000lb bomb caused major damage in Banbridge in County Down. In May, the group planted another large bomb in a mainly Protestant housing estate in Cookstown in County Tyrone. No one was killed, but more than 100 homes were damaged. Days later, a 2,000lb truck bomb killed three members of the UDR at a base in Glennane, County Armagh. In June, a 600lb bomb exploded in a mainly Protestant housing estate in Donaghcloney, County Down but fortunately there were no fatalities. In August, a 500lb bomb was planted near an RUC station in Kilrea, County Derry, which again caused widespread damage to property but resulted in no loss of life. (In the same month, the IRA was also responsible for forty bomb hoaxes in Belfast.) December saw three major bombings: a 1200lb bomb in the centre of Belfast, which injured sixteen people; a 2,000lb bomb planted outside a police station in Craigavon, County Armagh, injuring sixty; and a 500lb bomb at the Belfast law courts, which caused serious damage to the court building and neighbouring properties and vehicles. All of this was in addition to bombing campaigns in

London and other British towns and cities. Loyalists, too, were oblivious to the political moves being made as their sectarian campaign continued. In October, the Ulster Freedom Fighters, the UDA's front organisation – announced that members of the Gaelic Athletics Association would in future become 'legitimate targets' given the association's long connection with peaceful Irish Nationalism. A few weeks later, a UFF member threw a hand grenade at Cliftonville football supporters – a team supported mainly by Catholics – during a game against rivals Linfield at Northern Ireland's Windsor Park stadium. The subsequent blast mercifully missed the fans, which included young children.

The talks process continued tentatively until the summer of 1991. Maintaining buy-in from all sides was clearly paramount, which dictated the pace. Diplomacy and compromise were hardly in abundance to begin with. As an illustration, Ian Paisley's daughter, Rhonda, who was a councillor for the DUP, remarked that a UFF bomb attack had been 'perfectly understandable' given the 'betrayal' of Northern Ireland by British ministers, while Ulster Unionist MP John Taylor told a gathering of the party's youth wing that one in three Catholics were either a 'supporter of murder or worse still a murderer'.[5] Peter Brooke was reported to believe that the Irish Republic's continued claim to sovereignty over the whole island contained in Articles 2 and 3 of the Irish Constitution was 'not helpful' and should be changed. Tellingly, Garret FitzGerald, the former Taoiseach, told an Irish newspaper at the start of the year that he had considered holding a referendum on scrapping the articles.

(Eventually, this would happen as part of the Good Friday Agreement package.) In November 1991, John Major travelled to Dublin to meet with the Taoiseach, Charles Haughey. This was the first such visit to Britain's nearest neighbour since 1980. The two premiers agreed to hold more regular meetings in future, while Peter Brooke worked in the background to restart the talks process, which had been stalled since July.

Major was perhaps being overly optimistic about holding further meetings. Although he had been in power for barely a year, his thoughts necessarily turned to the forthcoming British general election. January 1992 saw what was, by now, a familiar pattern. Two large IRA bombs were exploded in quick succession and a sectarian attack was carried out by the UVF on two Catholics in their butcher's shop in County Tyrone. The IRA then planted a bomb at a rural crossroads at Teebane, between Cookstown and Omagh, which killed eight Protestant civilians who were travelling in a minibus. The IRA claimed they were 'collaborators' who had been working on a British Army base in Omagh. A week later, the UFF killed five innocent Catholics in a betting shop in Belfast. One of the dead was a fifteen-year-old boy. The statement admitting responsibility ended with the words 'Remember Teebane'. On the night of the first attack, Peter Brooke was booked to go on RTÉ's *The Late Show* in Dublin. The convivial format of the programme saw Brooke accept the invitation to provide a rendition of 'Oh My Darling, Clementine', much to the disgust of opinion back in Northern Ireland, with Unionists citing his insensitivity over the day's events.

The run-up to May's British election offered little respite. In February, an off-duty RUC officer walked into Sinn Féin's offices on the Falls Road in Belfast and shot three people, two of whom died. The assailant left the scene only to shoot himself dead later. In March, two UDR soldiers were convicted of 'aiding and abetting' the UFF in murdering Loughlin Maginn in 1989. Also, the double agent Brian Nelson pleaded guilty to multiple charges, including conspiracy to murder and possessing information useful to terrorists. He had been an intelligence officer for the UDA and an agent of the security services. He admitted the charges and was sentenced to ten years in prison. His guilty plea meant he was not cross-examined about his activities working for the security services, which included planning the assassination of the human rights lawyer Pat Finucane.

March 1992 saw a plenary session of the political parties as Peter Brooke tried to maintain momentum in a talks process that was, by now, akin to encouraging pandas to procreate. The parties met only to agree to reconvene meaningful conversations after the election. This was perhaps understandable, as opinion polls indicated that it was set to be a close result, with Neil Kinnock's Labour Party in real contention for the first time since James Callaghan's government had fallen thirteen years previously. In addition, Charles Haughey had made way for a new Taoiseach in the south in the shape of Albert Reynolds.

A MORI poll for *The Times* on the attitudes of people living in Britain towards Northern Ireland found that just 29 per cent wanted it to remain part of the UK. Nearly a quarter (23 per cent) were in favour of Irish unity and the remaining 31 per cent were in favour of Northern Ireland becoming an independent state.[6] The election itself did indeed turn out to be a closely fought affair. However, John Major's Conservatives were returned, albeit with a significantly reduced 21-seat majority, which would have ramifications later in the parliament as his majority dwindled through a series of by-election losses. As ever, little changed in the Northern Ireland landscape, although the big loser of the night was Gerry Adams, who was defeated in Belfast West by the SDLP's Joe Hendron. The two Unionist parties maintained the equilibrium by agreeing not to stand against each other in seats that they had a theoretical risk of losing. In April 1992, Patrick Mayhew, the former Attorney General, took over from Peter Brooke as Northern Ireland Secretary. A tall, imposing man of military bearing and with a somewhat condescending manner, Mayhew was from an Anglo-Irish family on his mother's side that traced its roots in County Cork back centuries.[7] He would now be charged with turning the nascent talks process that his predecessor had laboured over into something substantive. One of the other post-election changes saw the security service, MI5, take control of intelligence gathering from the Special Branch of the Metropolitan Police. This was said to be part of an effort to counter the IRA's efforts in Britain, particularly in London, which was now being measured not only in the loss of lives but in the significant disruption to the economy.

Multi-party talks resumed after the election, with Mayhew leading on the British side and the new Minister for Foreign Affairs, David Andrews, leading for the Irish. In the background, the work of the British–Irish Intergovernmental Conference

– the body made up of officials from both governments at the time of the Anglo-Irish Agreement – was suspended to avoid Unionist complaints that there was a dual-track process. Sinn Féin was frozen out of the talks process at this stage, so the IRA responded by exploding a 1,000lb bomb at a border post in County Armagh, killing a British soldier and injuring others. The middle of the year saw slow progress in the all-party talks, particularly in relation to strand one (arrangements for the running of Northern Ireland). The SDLP, keen to ensure there was no 'internal settlement' with Northern Ireland returning to being run as a Unionist backwater, suggested a six-person commission should govern, with three of the positions directly elected by proportional representation and three nominated – one each by the British and Irish governments and one by the European Commission. There was some movement, however, from Unionists who were now prepared to deal with the Irish government in relation to strand two (relations between the two jurisdictions). The run-up to the 'marching season', in July, in which Loyalists celebrate the 1690 victory at the Battle of the Boyne, was predictably difficult. A parade through the mainly Catholic Lower Ormeau Road area of Belfast saw Orange Order members shouting 'Up the UFF!' while holding up five fingers – a crude reminder of the five Catholic civilians killed earlier in the year in a nearby bookmaker's shop. Mayhew denounced the marchers, remarking that they 'would have disgraced a tribe of cannibals'.[8] A few weeks later he proscribed the UDA, the organisation behind the Ulster Freedom Fighters. The move was long overdue and, among other things, removed the scintilla of respectability that the organisation had. Later in the year, the UDA responded by threatening to increase its campaign 'to a ferocity never imagined'.[9]

Political talks between the parties resumed in September. The early promise of Unionists engaging with the all-Ireland dimension contained in strand two foundered when Ian Paisley and his deputy, Peter Robinson, marched straight out of the talks – in one of their pre-rehearsed routines – because the agenda did not immediately focus on the Irish state's territorial claim to Northern Ireland contained in Articles 2 and 3. Briefing and counter-briefing between the parties continued through the autumn, which at least indicated there was a level of engagement in the process. In a first, James Molyneaux, the leader of the Ulster Unionists, even went to Dublin for talks with the Irish government over strand two issues. No similar meeting had taken place between a Unionist leader and the Irish government since partition. After two years of careful positioning, with all sides wary of being blamed for the collapse of yet another political initiative, Mayhew drew the talks process to a close, for now at least. Informal dialogue between the government and the parties would continue.

In December, Mayhew made a speech at the University of Ulster floating the prospect that Sinn Féin could become involved in the talks if the IRA campaign ended. A week later, Gerry Adams made his own speech suggesting not only that Sinn Féin should be admitted to the talks, but that the United Nations and the European Commission be involved as well. As it turned out, efforts to establish a viable and sustainable political process in Northern Ireland would indeed become internationalised and another election would have a profound bearing on Northern Ireland. Bill Clinton had just won the US presidential race and had made a series of commitments to court the Irish–American lobby, a demand of which was to agree a visa for Gerry Adams to visit America and to appoint an envoy to Northern Ireland.

The year 1993 turned out to be pivotal. The tentative, on–off talks process started to bear fruit, but this was set against a series of horrible atrocities as Northern Ireland began a slow but hopeful journey from conflict and towards, if not normal politics, then something that was at least less abnormal. Hope and nihilism may have been mutually exclusive but were now on parallel tracks. The year began violently – with the threat of more bloodshed to come. In a particularly heinous attack, even by the standards of the Troubles, the UVF gunned down a Catholic father and his twenty-year-old son near Dungannon, County Tyrone. Their killing and the unimaginable loss for the family was amplified weeks later when the son's grief-stricken girlfriend committed suicide. The now-banned UDA announced that in future it would target any Catholic that was part of the so-called 'pan-Nationalist front'. According to the UDA, all Catholics were colluding against the interests of Loyalists, including the IRA or Sinn Féin politicians, but also the SDLP or even just members of the Gaelic Athletics Association. As ever, it was merely a fig-leaf justification for the murder of any Catholic, but this was no idle threat. Days later, the UDA shot dead a 28-year-old Catholic man at his home in County Derry, while two incendiary bombs were planted outside the homes of two SDLP councillors.

On the political front, the new Irish Minister for Foreign Affairs, Dick Spring, floated the suggestion that Articles 2 and 3 of the Irish Constitution might be up for negotiation, tentatively remarking that they were not 'cast in bronze' and that amending the Constitution could form part of an overall package of measures.[10] Patrick Mayhew described Spring as someone he could 'do business with', and in a speech in Bangor said that while there could be no change to Northern Ireland's constitutional status unless a majority wished it, the British government would remain 'neutral' about the prospect.[11] But some issues were still too controversial, and ahead of the twenty-first anniversary of Bloody Sunday, John Major wrote to SDLP leader John Hume ruling out any new inquest into the killings of the thirteen civilians by soldiers from the Parachute Regiment. The following month, in March 1993, he also banished any prospect of devolution in Scotland and Wales.

On 20 March, the IRA detonated two bombs in Warrington. They had targeted the Cheshire town the previous month with an explosion at a gas installation, but this time the bombs were left in litter bins on a main street in the town centre. They exploded moments apart at lunchtime on a Saturday and killed two small boys: three-year-old Jonathan Ball and twelve-year-old Tim Parry. Dozens of people were injured and one of them, 32-year-old Bronwen Vickers, had to have one of her legs amputated and then died of cancer the following year. The IRA claimed it had made a specific warning about the location of the bombs, which the police denied. Even with the political wheels starting to turn, the horror of armed conflict was ever-present, underlining the fact that political failure was measured in lost lives and unbearable trauma. And, as ever, the violence came in waves. A few days later it was the turn of the UFF. On 25 March, they shot and killed four Catholic men as they arrived for work at a building site in Castlerock, County Derry. Later in the day, they launched another attack, killing a seventeen-year-old Catholic boy and injuring another young Catholic. The Unionist-supporting newspaper, the *News Letter* published a poll of its readers showing that 42 per cent of them supported Loyalist paramilitary violence.[12]

Without a political solution it seemed as if the killing would never stop. In April, John Hume held another series of talks with Sinn Féin's president, Gerry Adams. Nowadays, such a meeting between the leaders of the Irish Nationalist and Republican parties would be innocuous enough, but back then it was controversial, with Hume once again coming in for criticism for engaging with the political wing of the IRA while it was still waging its violent campaign. The talks were long and detailed as Hume tried to encourage Adams to end the armed struggle and adopt an exclusively political way forward. Hume had recently floated the suggestion that a deal might be constructed by the two governments and put to the people of Northern Ireland in a referendum. Everyone wanted a breakthrough, and this was Sinn Féin's opportunity to move centre stage. For now, though, the Republicans wanted it both ways. The dialogue between the two men had an immediate price, as the Unionist parties said they would not re-enter talks with the SDLP while Hume was talking to Gerry Adams.

Just days after the talks, the IRA detonated a massive bomb at Bishopsgate in the heart of the City of London. The damage caused was extensive and ran into hundreds of millions of pounds. It led to a 'ring of steel' being introduced in central London as a large-scale stop-and-search operation went into effect, while the police desperately tried to keep up the appearance of business as usual, especially to foreign investors. Around this time it probably dawned on both the IRA and British government that these sorts of so-called spectaculars, which caused huge economic damage but many fewer casualties than smaller bombs detonated in Belfast and Derry, were considerably more effective in focusing minds.

The middle of the year saw a familiar pattern of IRA bombings and sectarian murders by the UVF and the UDA/UFF. In June, the Irish President, Mary Robinson, paid an unofficial visit to Belfast. Amid the usual retinue of community group meetings, she met with Gerry Adams and shook his hand, which caused a stir with Unionists. It was another small gesture of acceptance that helped to shift Republican thinking, convincing them that there was a political route to their age-old objective of Irish unity and that armed conflict was now actively inhibiting that. A few weeks later, it was revealed that the British Labour Party had previously produced a discussion document ahead of the 1992 election advocating joint authority of Northern Ireland if political talks were unsuccessful. In an interview with the Irish *Sunday Tribune* newspaper a few weeks later, Gerry Adams suggested that Republicans might accept joint authority as 'part of the process towards an end to partition'.[13] In September 1993, John Hume visited Downing Street for talks with the Prime Minister. Afterwards he dismissed criticism of his meeting with Gerry Adams, adding that he did not give 'two balls of roasted snow' what his critics thought. The following day, Ian Paisley went in to see Major. He left after criticising Hume for being the spokesman for 'pan-Nationalism' – the exact phrase the UDA had used at the start of the year to justify their attacks on just about any Catholic in Northern Ireland.

As ever, optimism remained a commodity in short supply. The Ulster Unionist MP David Trimble dismissed the Hume–Adams dialogue as 'misconceived and bound to fail'.[14] However, Martin McGuinness, the former IRA commander and Sinn Féin deputy, told *The Guardian* that there was a way forward if the British would respect the right to the 'self-determination of the Irish people'.[15] At the end of September, John Hume and Gerry Adams issued a joint statement: 'Our discussions, aimed at the creation of a peace process which would involve all parties, have made considerable progress,' they said. 'We are convinced … that a process can be designed to lead to agreement among the divided people of this island, which will provide a solid basis for peace.'[16] One that would 'respect[s] the diversity of our different traditions and earn[s] their allegiance and agreement'.

The Hume–Adams proposals were put to the British and Irish governments but remained private. As ever, Republican tactics flitted between the political and the military. Two days after the statement was issued, the IRA exploded two large bombs in Belfast. A few days later, Patrick Mayhew made a speech referring to the 'self-determination of the people living in Northern Ireland'.[17] This was a subtly different remark to that used by Martin McGuinness a few weeks earlier. McGuinness wanted self-determination to be an all-Ireland concept, whereas Mayhew was limiting it to Northern Ireland, but echoing the language and sentiment. Clearly, the British government could not be seen to roll over easily and Mayhew said Sinn Féin could only join political talks if it had given up violence 'for real'. But these were holding tactics. For the first time since the Troubles erupted there was a prospect – remote at this stage and one that would certainly need careful management – of Republicans ending their armed campaign. But the sense, even the hint of an emerging deal, even if that was just around a process, was enough to spook Loyalists. In October 1993, the UFF shot up a bar in Twinbrook in Belfast, killing one man and injuring two others. They explicitly blamed the Hume–Adams initiative for inciting the attack. For good measure, the UVF left a bomb outside a Sinn Féin office on the Falls Road in Belfast. However, the initiative also received an equally negative reception among mainstream Unionists. James Molyneaux told a fringe meeting of the Conservative Party conference that the Hume–Adams proposals had destroyed the multi-party talks. Typically, the DUP's Ian Paisley went further and wrote to John Major claiming that the initiative was 'aimed at Ulster's destruction'.[18]

At the same time, John Hume went to see Albert Reynolds and Dick Spring in Dublin to update them in person about his talks with Gerry Adams. This was the best chance of peace in twenty years, Hume told them. If they could agree on the choreography and package of measures, they could end the IRA's campaign and, by extension, the Troubles. That weekend the Irish *Sunday Independent* ran a poll which showed that 72 per cent of the population supported the Hume–Adams initiative. Nelson Mandela was once again visiting Dublin and he too endorsed the direction of travel. As for Adams, he was prevented from attending a speaking invitation from veteran Labour MP Tony Benn because he was subject to an 'exclusion order' by the Home Secretary, Michael Howard.

As ever in Northern Ireland's tortuous history, it was a case of two steps forward, one step back. Later that month a bomb that was being planted by an IRA unit in a fish shop on the Loyalist Shankill Road exploded prematurely. Ten people were killed, including the bomber. Another fifty-seven people were wounded. This represented the largest loss of life in a single attack since the Enniskillen bombing in 1987. The IRA maintained that they were targeting the UFF, who were thought to be meeting upstairs at the time. Nevertheless, the fallout from the attack was immediate, thousands of Protestant workers from the shipyards came to the site to pay their respects, while a dozen Catholics were murdered over the following week. The funeral of the IRA volunteer who was killed planting the bomb saw a British soldier fire at the mourners and injure a prominent Republican, Eddie Copeland. (The soldier was later sentenced to ten years for attempted murder.) It also caused outrage among Unionists when Gerry Adams was pictured carrying the bomber's coffin. Again, this decision represented the tightrope that Adams had to walk; he needed to keep his movement and community onside, while trying to lead them in a radically different direction without making it either look or feel like defeat. A week later, on 30 October, UFF gunmen walked into a crowded bar in Greysteel, County Derry. One of them shouted 'Trick or treat?' to the patrons inside, before they opened fire with automatic rifles, slaying seven people, six of whom were Catholic and one Protestant. The UFF claimed it was retaliation for the Shankill bombing, but it fitted with their broader modus operandi of indiscriminately targeting Catholics. Even with the prospect of a peace deal, October 1993 was the bloodiest month in seventeen years, with twenty-seven deaths.

Following a row about whether the British government had been engaged in a secret dialogue with the IRA – which turned out to be true – John Major and the Taoiseach, Albert Reynolds, issued a joint declaration from the two governments on the steps of Downing Street. It was the culmination of strenuous efforts on behalf of the two governments and the various parties, but the kernel of their announcement was inspired by the Hume–Adams dialogue. The Downing Street Declaration was 'the starting point of a peace process designed to culminate in a political settlement', they said.[19] The aim was to heal divisions and end a conflict that 'has been so manifestly to the detriment of all'. To foster agreement and reconciliation 'leading to a new political framework founded on consent and encompassing arrangements within Northern Ireland, for the whole island, and between these islands'. The declaration stated: 'It is for the people of the island of Ireland alone, by agreement between the two parts respectively,

WHAT A BLOODY AWFUL COUNTRY

to exercise their right of self-determination based on consent, freely and concurrently given, North and South, to bring about a united Ireland, if that is their wish.'

The Irish government held out the prospect of rewriting their constitutional claim to Northern Ireland, with the two Prime Ministers asking Unionists to 'look on the people of the Republic as friends, who share their grief and shame over all the suffering of the last quarter of a century, and who wants to develop the best possible relationship with them, a relationship in which trust and new understanding can flourish and grow'.

After scrambling up a mountain face for the previous few years amid the incessant death and carnage, the Downing Street Declaration marked a plateau. A chance to rest, reassess and prepare for the next arduous ascent. A moment of optimism. A breakthrough. But what was the reaction? Sinn Féin remained hesitant, keen, as ever, to assess the reaction before committing a view. They were not buying into anything without reading the small print, although Gerry Adams demanded 'direct and unconditional dialogue' with the British government. James Molyneaux for the Ulster Unionists said they could live with the declaration (with the government announcing a new House of Commons select committee on Northern Ireland, a long-standing Molyneaux hobbyhorse, as a sweetener). Ian Paisley was not so easily assuaged and threatened to organise mass protests against the declaration, presumably on the basis that 'if you don't understand it, kill it'. Surprisingly, the UVF demurred, saying it was not threatened by the declaration's intentions and would not support Paisley's 'publicity stunt'.

The New Year saw the various parties still trying to make sense of the declaration. It was a big moment and required a strategic response from all parties. Gerry Adams wrote to John Major seeking clarification on a series of points. An official wrote back refusing to do so (as it would amount, in their opinion, to directly negotiating with Sinn Féin). Albert Reynolds, a no-nonsense former businessman by background, said that the Irish government would happily provide it. He also moved to scrap the broadcasting ban, which had been in place since 1971 as a way to keep Sinn Féin off the Irish airwaves. Reynolds was to grow increasingly frustrated at the lack of pace that John Major was willing to bring to proceedings. Mayhew floated the prospect of troop withdrawals if it looked like the level of violence was dropping, but balanced his remarks with the caveat that the government would not 'join the ranks of the persuaders' for Irish unity.[20] As it circled around the declaration cautiously, Sinn Féin received a boost from the other side of the Atlantic. Having previously been denied a visa to visit the US, Gerry Adams was now granted one so he could accept an invitation to attend a peace conference and meet influential Irish–American leaders.[21] The visa came from the top, with influential figures including Democratic Senator Edward Kennedy lobbying President Clinton directly. The US State Department was less enamoured about the idea, while the British government was livid. But Clinton, the arch-pragmatist, reasoned that satisfying the Irish–American lobby was more important than pleasing Major.

The Loyalists were not so sure-footed and were clearly struggling to process what would happen next. At the start of

1994, the UDA released a statement saying it would continue to respond to events militarily, while the Combined Loyalist Military Command, which represented the various strands of Loyalist paramilitary opinion, said it would 'wait and see' what happened before making a final judgement on the declaration. The UDA also released a document calling for Northern Ireland to be repartitioned – with Catholics ethnically cleansed from a redrawn 'Protestant state'. They would be 'expelled, nullified, or interned' if they tried to stay.[22] The DUP politician Sammy Wilson described the proposals as a 'valuable return to reality', congratulating the UDA for 'contemplating what needs to be done to maintain our separate Ulster identity'.[23] In April 1994 there was an appalling attack on a 31-year-old Protestant woman, Margaret Wright, who was mistaken for a Catholic and brutally beaten by a gang of men at a Loyalist band hall in Belfast. She was then shot dead. Two young Loyalist paramilitaries – believed to be responsible – were subsequently shot dead by the UVF.

Five months on from the publication of the declaration, there was no sign that the tit-for-tat killings by the IRA and Loyalists would abate. The IRA booby-trapped the car of Fred Anthony, a Protestant civilian in Lurgan, killing him and injuring his wife and two children. He had been a cleaner at an RUC station. Over the course of 15 and 16 May, the UVF gunned down four Catholic civilians, including two seventeen-year-old boys. The politicians ruminated about how to get the process back on track. Eventually, the British government acceded to Sinn Féin's demand for greater clarity about the declaration, having refused to do so back in January, and responded to a series of twenty questions submitted by the Republicans. Albert Reynolds said that this was a 'comprehensive and positive' response, ever keen to chivvy things along. In fact, Reynolds did something similar himself, writing to the Ulster Democratic Party (the political front office of the UDA), promising that there would be no change in Northern Ireland's status by 'stealth or coercion'.

The summer months were fractious. The tactical alliance between the Unionist parties suffered a 'shattering blow', according to the Ulster Unionist leader, James Molyneaux, after Ian Paisley referred to him as 'Judas Iscariot'.[24] There was lots of briefing and counter-briefing by all sides, some of it in public and a great deal more behind closed doors. As ever, though, the centre of the action was what Sinn Féin and the IRA would decide to do next. Could they be encouraged to seize the opportunity to enter the political mainstream, and would the IRA end its campaign? If it did, would it surrender its arms and how would that even happen? If so, would this look like surrender? Is that exactly what the British wanted, or were they more bothered about simply ending the conflict? If there was a ceasefire, would it be permanent? Would Loyalists follow suit and end their campaign? Would the British leave? These were the kinds of considerations that all sides gamed endlessly over the summer of 1994 and, indeed, over the following years. In early July, the *Sunday Tribune* in Dublin reported that the IRA was considering a ceasefire. A week later, however, nearly 4,500lb of explosives were intercepted at Heysham Port in Lancashire as part of a suspected IRA arms shipment to be used in a new

campaign in Britain. If and until a ceasefire occurred, the organisation was clearly still in war mode. A positive indication
came from the Combined Loyalist Military Command, which
issued a statement saying that Loyalist paramilitaries would
stop their activities if the IRA committed to a ceasefire. Then, at
the end of August 1994, the group did just that. The IRA issued
a statement, which stated: 'Recognising the potential of the current situation ... there will be a complete cessation of military
operations. All our units have been instructed accordingly.'[25] It
was brief and clear, but there was no talk of the ceasefire being
permanent or of any prospect of weapons being surrendered. It
did, however, end with a commitment that the IRA would be
part of the future political process:

> We note that the Downing Street Declaration is not a solution,
> nor was it presented as such by its authors. A solution will only
> be found as a result of inclusive negotiations ... It is our desire
> to significantly contribute to the creation of a climate which will
> encourage this. We urge everyone to approach this new situation
> with energy, determination and patience.

In an instant, the situation was transformed. There was widespread jubilation, not least in Republican West Belfast where
a cavalcade of cars took to the streets beeping their horns and
flying Irish flags. The move saw all kinds of incentives announced
to try to lock in the moment. Money poured in from the
European Union, Washington and the British government to
help lubricate this historic opportunity. Clinton administration

officials now agreed to meet Sinn Féin. The British broadcasting ban was finally rescinded. Border roads that had been closed for decades were opened. RUC patrols were now unaccompanied by soldiers. What patrolling they did was now conducted while wearing soft berets. There was even a story that Ian Paisley had been booted out of Downing Street after he refused to accept John Major's assurances there had been no secret deals with the IRA. By mid-October, the Loyalist paramilitaries also announced a ceasefire that was contingent on the IRA's holding.

The end of the year brought a flurry of changes to the key players who would go on to develop the peace and political process over the next few years. Albert Reynolds's coalition government fell over a scandal involving a judicial appointment and he was replaced as Taoiseach by Fine Gael's John Bruton, who was much more sceptical towards Irish Republicans. The leadership of Reynolds's party, Fianna Fáil, went to Bertie Ahern. Bill Clinton made good on an election promise to send an envoy to Northern Ireland in the shape of former Democrat Senate Majority Leader George Mitchell, a heavyweight appointment that underscored the commitment of his administration to the nascent peace process – and the Irish–American community more widely. In Britain, the Labour opposition, now led by Tony Blair, appointed a new shadow Northern Ireland Secretary, Mo Mowlam. The peace process had begun in earnest and the main cast of characters had now entered stage left.

From here, the pace of the peace process became the problem. How soon should Sinn Féin be normalised so that meaningful negotiations could take place? What were the preconditions that were needed before dealing with them – 'quarantining' as Unionists liked to call it? Was there a risk of not meeting the moment imaginatively if there was no engagement? After all, even Loyalists were saying it was unrealistic to expect paramilitaries to simply give up their guns at this stage. A series of early bilateral meetings took place between Sinn Féin, officials from the Northern Ireland Office and Irish government ministers. John Major at least had an ally in the new Taoiseach, John Bruton. His predecessor, Albert Reynolds, held a meeting straight after the announcement of the IRA ceasefire with Gerry Adams and John Hume, much to the annoyance of British ministers. An implacable opponent of Irish Republicans, Bruton and Major were of similar temperament; ultra-cautious and methodical, and lacking the brio that the moment required. The point of any political process is that things need to keep moving forward. With that in mind, the two governments launched a set of framework documents in February 1995 to give shape to proceedings. Building on the model set out in the Brooke–Mayhew talks from the early 1990s, these covered the 'totality of relationships', how Northern Ireland was to be governed, what arrangements could be put in place to ensure 'north–south' working and the relationship between the island of Ireland and Britain – the so-called east–west dimension: 'Both Governments believe that a new political dispensation ... achieved through agreement and reconciliation and founded on the principle of consent, would achieve that objective and transform relationships in Northern Ireland, in the island of Ireland and between both islands.'[26]

The DUP was characteristically cool on the whole thing. Ian Paisley described the framework documents as a 'one-way street to Dublin', while his deputy, Peter Robinson, claimed that 'Ulster has been served with an eviction notice' from the UK.[27] 'This is not a discussion document,' he said. 'It is a declaration on intent, a joint government programme for Irish unity.'[28] It did not matter that the principle of consent – that Northern Ireland would remain British as long as people living there wanted it to – ran throughout the whole document. Yet again, Unionists sensed betrayal from Westminster. Ten years previously they had seen a Conservative government sign up to the Anglo-Irish Agreement, ushering in an arrangement where the Irish government had an official say on how Northern Ireland was governed. Then they had seen the 'pan-Nationalist front' grow to include their hated foes in Sinn Féin. Now, another Conservative government was building a halfway house with Dublin and expecting them to live in it. By March, even the more moderate Ulster Unionists had come out against the framework documents. Under pressure from the Unionist parties and many on the Conservative backbenchers, who were loath to make things easy on Sinn Féin – even if they were supportive of the overall direction – Major's government started to erect preconditions for Sinn Féin entering substantive talks. Patrick Mayhew outlined a series of demands around the decommissioning of weapons: the IRA must accept decommissioning, agree to a method where this could be verified and have started the act of decommissioning before any meaningful talks could take place. Smacking of surrender, this was anathema to Republicans (and to Loyalists

– it was probably the only issue that the two groups ever agreed upon).

Not everyone was so fastidious. President Clinton invited Gerry Adams to the annual St Patrick's Day reception in the White House and granted him a visa that would also allow him time to court Irish–American backers (for balance, Loyalist representatives were also invited to attend the reception). It was a public snub to the British government and John Major refused to take a call from Clinton for several days. It represented a culture clash between an easy-going American President who was used to cutting deals to get things done, and a grey, uncharismatic British Prime Minister who was twenty points behind in the polls and nursing a small parliamentary majority. It also exposed a more general psychological flaw in the British government's approach to the peace process. It wanted an end to Northern Ireland's Troubles, but it was not getting a victory over the IRA, and the more it was expected to make concessions to people like Gerry Adams, the less it even felt like a draw. His demands for Sinn Féin to be included in ministerial talks and dialogue with the other parties eventually saw John Major relent. In May, Sinn Féin held their first official meeting with a British minister since the Cheyne Walk talks with Willie Whitelaw in 1972. As a mark of how long the Northern Ireland cast of characters had remained on the stage, Martin McGuinness, who was a veteran of that earlier meeting, now led for Sinn Féin, with Mayhew's deputy in the Northern Ireland Office, Michael Ancram, an aristocratic Scottish Catholic, leading for the British. The exchange was formulaic. McGuinness wanted action on disbanding the RUC and releasing IRA prisoners. The British wanted to have assurances about decommissioning. These and other issues would eventually be addressed to everyone's satisfaction, but this was still early days. Further meetings then followed, but both sides were merely circling each other and weighing up the situation. Gerry Adams said that if decommissioning IRA weapons had been a precondition then there would not have been a ceasefire in the first place and that talks with British ministers were not getting anywhere.

John Major had other issues to contend with, namely his own political survival. His government, narrowly re-elected in April 1992, was on a downwards spiral after being ejected from the EU's Exchange Rate Mechanism just a few months later, losing billions of pounds to speculators and forfeiting the Conservatives' credibility for managing the economy. The government had been in political freefall ever since. By now, Major was regarded as weak and incompetent and had become a figure of ridicule in the British media. Especially when judged against the charismatic new Leader of the Opposition, Tony Blair. Major now faced a Cabinet revolt, with his Welsh Secretary, John Redwood, challenging him for leadership of the Conservative Party. Major managed to prevail; however, this merely drew attention to the fact he had as many political enemies behind him as he did in front, while losing a string of parliamentary by-elections had whittled away his small majority.

Even the merest hint of a vacuum was enough to invite problems. The Protestant marching season, difficult enough in a good year, could be relied upon to puncture the cautious optimism that had surrounded the commencement of talks. This year was no exception, with a flare-up at the annual Orange Order march to Drumcree Church in the town of Portadown, County Armagh. The return leg traditionally took the march through a mainly Nationalist area along the Garvaghy Road, where locals were fed up with the Order's triumphalism. Tensions quickly escalated after the RUC told the Order in advance that it had to return along the route it had come. Within twenty-four hours, 1,000 police were trying to hold the line against 10,000 angry Orangemen. Although it had previously been problematic, the tensions surrounding the Orange Order's march were an early consequence of the peace process. Politics and communal tension moved into the sphere of culture: the rights of the Nationalist community to have to put up with sectarian marchers lording it over them, as they saw it, versus the right of the Orange Order to 'walk the Queen's highway' as they had always done. Neither side wanted to budge. It was not long before tension spilled over, with rioting at Drumcree and across Northern Ireland. Neither was it long before Ian Paisley materialised to whip things up, joined by the ambitious Ulster Unionist MP David Trimble. After several days of trouble, a compromise was reached that would see marchers pass down the Garvaghy Road, but without accompanying bands. Paisley and Trimble, both Orangemen and adorned in their sashes, held hands, arms aloft, savouring their victory. On the back of his hard-line stance at Drumcree, Trimble took over from Molyneaux as leader of the Ulster Unionists in the autumn of 1995, following a putsch that saw a 21-year-old party activist stand against the ageing

Molyneaux as a stalking horse. He had lost the grass roots and it was believed that Trimble, bright and abrasive, might do better in fending off Paisley and wringing a better deal from the British government. It was not all plain sailing for Sinn Féin either. Gerry Adams's entire leadership of Sinn Féin was focused on keeping the Republican movement united and avoiding the schisms that had bedevilled it for decades. His 'long game' now needed to speed up to keep pace with a fast-evolving situation, but without losing key figures along the way in what was still a Marxist-inspired guerrilla army. Addressing a rally outside Belfast City Hall, one onlooker shouted at Adams for the IRA to be brought back. 'They haven't gone away, you know,' he replied.[29] This off-the-cuff remark would be used against him repeatedly for implying, as it did, that the Republican movement was being tactical in its approach towards the peace process. Nevertheless, Gerry Adams was a curiosity. Kept off the airwaves for so long, his calm manner in tough broadcast interviews showed that Sinn Féin were no slouches when it came to modern politics. Or to fundraising. Adams paid multiple visits to the US during 1995, where he was a cause célèbre, and raked in nearly $1 million on a single week-long trip in the autumn.

In November, the British government published proposals to divide out the process of decommissioning from the multi-party talks. A so-called twin-track approach. This was endorsed by the Irish government and the parties were invited to enter preparatory talks. On decommissioning, the aim was to establish an independent international team to oversee the process, and as a result the International Body on Arms Decommissioning was established. The suggested chairman was the American envoy to Northern Ireland, George Mitchell. The two governments also had a trump card up their sleeve in the form of Bill Clinton, who paid a visit to Belfast to help sell the process in late November. It was all very well for figures such as Paisley to be rude to British ministers, but the clout of the US President invoked a more respectful response. He visited Unionist and Nationalist areas and then switched on Belfast's Christmas lights. But he also delivered a stark message while visiting a metal plant:

> This twin-track initiative gives the parties a chance to begin preliminary talks in ways in which all views will be represented and all voices will be heard. It also establishes an international body to address the issue of arms decommissioning. I hope the parties will seize this opportunity. Engaging in honest dialogue is not an act of surrender, it is an act of strength and common sense.[30]

The next eighteen months were defined by one issue: the end of the IRA's ceasefire. The pace of the progress that was being made was not rapid enough to keep a critical section of the Republican movement on board. Gerry Adams had been speaking literally when he said that the IRA had not gone away. And he was not bluffing when he said that if decommissioning was a precondition then there would not have been a ceasefire. How do you convert a guerrilla army into a mainstream political movement that gives up its revolutionary demands and embraces political gradualism? Slowly, and with the clear prospect of keeping progress towards achieving historic aims intact. Clearly, many in the Republican movement felt that this was lacking. Then there was the broader political context. British forgetfulness about promises that had been made dovetailed with long Irish memories that recalled how they were never delivered. There was a bridge that needed to be crossed, but it did not yet stretch all the way over to the other bank. Republicans were not going to abandon one tactic when a new, better way forward was not yet guaranteed. The political situation in Westminster was also worsening. Major would have to go to the country and call an election by the following May, but his political fortunes were widely perceived to be holed below the waterline. Was it possible that a Labour government under Tony Blair could provide a better deal? The incessant wrangling about decommissioning and debates over when substantive talks would start hardly helped matters. In January 1997, George Mitchell proposed a series of principles, which would help facilitate all-party talks, as well as fresh elections to a new forum to refresh the various parties' mandates.

However, by early February the point was moot. A large IRA bomb exploded in the Docklands area of London, killing two people, injuring more than 100 people and causing £150 million pounds of damage. The seventeen-month ceasefire was broken and over the next few months there followed a familiar pattern of attacks. Nevertheless, the two governments persevered and announced that talks would commence in June after elections in May. Sinn Féin contested the elections, coming fourth behind the Ulster Unionists, the SDLP and the Democratic Unionists, with a constellation of smaller parties behind them. The talks

process began on Monday 4 June, without Sinn Féin representatives, with Unionists suspicious about Mitchell and everyone
uncertain about where the process would lead. On Saturday
15 June, a massive 3,330lb bomb exploded in Manchester, destroying a huge part of the city centre and injuring 200 people.
It was said to be the second-largest bomb ever exploded in Britain (after the IRA's attack at Bishopsgate). A warning released
ninety minutes beforehand saw 75,000 people evacuated from
the area. Miraculously, no one was killed.

More trouble was brewing at Drumcree for the annual
Orange Order march. Following the previous year's conflict, a
repeat disturbance was widely predicted. Once again, the Order
was instructed by the RUC to return the way it came and avoid
marching through a mainly Nationalist area. Once again, the
Orange Order refused. Paisley and the DUP pulled out of the
talks process in solidarity with the marchers. Trouble broke out
across Northern Ireland, with roads and motorways blocked and
the government forced to send an additional 1,000 soldiers to
support the RUC. Over the course of a week in early July, there
were 758 attacks on the RUC and 662 plastic bullets were fired.
And after dealing with the worst of it, the RUC Chief Constable, Sir Hugh Annesley, relented and allowed the marchers to
proceed down the Garvaghy Road, igniting protests from Nationalists and even the Taoiseach, John Bruton, that he had given
in to Loyalist violence. The following months were marked by
further tension, with Patrick Mayhew announcing a review into
the future management of parades. The talks process resumed
in September, but without Sinn Féin at the table, progress was

clearly going to be minimal, and yet the purpose of carrying on was to try to entice them back in. The IRA's response came in the form of another bombing in October, this time at Thiepval Barracks in Lisburn, County Antrim, the headquarters of the British Army in Northern Ireland. Two large bombs injured thirty-one, with an officer succumbing to his injuries four days later.

On the face of it, things were falling apart, with communal violence, IRA bombings and scratchy politicians achieving little in their deliberations and both governments were unable to inject pace into proceedings. Yet, the key elements of a political process that would go on to bear fruit were in fact coming together. As for the IRA, this was its last tactical move. The strategy of the Republican movement involved crossing that bridge towards exclusively political means. A poll in the Nationalist *Irish News* found 94 per cent of all respondents and three-quarters of Sinn Féin voters wanted a restoration of the IRA ceasefire.[31] Having had a taster of normality, they wanted more of it. The task both for the two governments and Sinn Féin was building the choreography to get there.

*   *   *

There were two key events that were expected in 1997. The first was a fresh IRA ceasefire that would unlock the stalled political talks before yet another moment when something might improve and stabilise in Northern Ireland was lost. The second was the British general election. There was a widespread expectation that Tony Blair's Labour Party would sweep to victory after eighteen unbroken years of Conservative rule. Two-thirds of the Troubles had taken place on their watch and John Major's government had virtually collapsed. Indeed, a run of by-election losses had robbed him of his parliamentary majority, forcing him to turn to David Trimble and his Ulster Unionists for support to pass legislation. Clearly, at such a sensitive time, it was less than ideal that the supposed referee had an allegiance with one of the teams on the pitch. There was a hope that a fresh government with a clear majority and a new mandate could catalyse the peace process, secure a permanent IRA ceasefire and get Sinn Féin back in the talks in order to get a deal over the line.

In March, the talks process was adjourned, subject to the outcome of the election. Speaking at a dinner back in Washington, a frustrated George Mitchell remarked that the 'twin demons' of Northern Ireland were 'violence and intransigence', which led to a 'deadly ritual' where the innocent suffered.[32] These innocuous remarks caused the DUP to demand his resignation as chairman of the decommissioning talks. The general election, held on 1 May, was indeed a watershed moment. Labour stormed to victory for the first time in a generation with a massive 179-seat majority in the House of Commons. A third of Major's Cabinet lost their seats in the Tories' worst defeat since 1906. Tony Blair was Prime Minister and confirmed Mo Mowlam as his Northern Ireland Secretary. The central themes of his New Labour government would be modernisation and pragmatism. 'What matters is what works' was its lodestar. Blair would be an improvement for the better 'as far as Ireland is concerned', remarked Irish Taoiseach John Bruton.[33] Two weeks after he was elected, Blair travelled to Belfast to set out his approach. Sinn Féin could re-enter talks if they agreed to the Mitchell principles on decommissioning and exclusively peaceful means. In the time being, civil servants would continue to meet with them to iron out any problems. He also mentioned that it would be helpful if the Irish government would consider amending Articles 2 and 3 of the Irish Constitution. This issue fell into the lap of a new Taoiseach when Bertie Ahern's Fianna Fáil returned to power following an Irish general election in June 1997.

As if to remind everyone about the stakes, the next month saw two RUC officers shot dead at close range by the IRA in County Armagh. The British and Irish governments announced that they were giving the IRA five weeks to declare an unambiguous ceasefire. After an additional six weeks to assess its veracity, Sinn Féin would be able to re-enter the talks process, which would resume in the middle of September, with a deadline of the following May to try to hammer out an agreement. But first there was the matter of the Orange Order march at Drumcree, which was due to take place on Sunday 6 July. Tony Blair and Bertie Ahern met the week before, with the Taoiseach counselling against letting the march go ahead given the scale of trouble in the past two years and the signal that giving in to Unionist belligerence would send out at a critical time as they tried to coax Sinn Féin back in. Blair disagreed and in the early hours on the Sunday the RUC moved into the area, supported by the British Army, and sealed off both sides of the Garvaghy Road so that the parade could proceed. This meant that

Catholic residents were prevented from leaving their homes and even from going to church, which meant that local priests were forced to hold an open-air Mass surrounded by police, soldiers and armoured vehicles. At 12 p.m., more than 1,000 Orangemen marched past, upholding their right – their birthright as they saw it – to march this route. In the process, dozens of local Catholic families had been evacuated from their homes following a Loyalist bomb threat and thousands of people were even reported to have gone as far as leaving Northern Ireland until things had calmed down, such was the violence that had been experienced in the previous two years. Rioting ensued this time as well, with Nationalists furious that Unionist supremacy and the threat of violence were enough to trample on their rights not to have to face their harassment. By the Wednesday, dozens of protestors and police had been injured, with 117 arrests and the RUC having fired 2,500 plastic bullets. There had been 1,500 petrol bombs thrown and 402 car hijackings. However, there was a sliver of more positive news for the Catholic community when Alban Maginness, a councillor for the SDLP, became the first Nationalist to become Lord Mayor of Belfast.

Fortunately, Drumcree was a hiccup rather than a dealbreaker and a second IRA ceasefire was announced at the end of July. The next day, the Sinn Féin delegation moved into offices in Castle Buildings, on the Stormont estate, where the talks would take place. The DUP immediately left. Erratic as the process was, it was heading in the right direction again. There would never be a lasting settlement without the Republican movement at the heart of it; thirty years of failed political initiatives made that fact plain enough. It would clearly cause some angst and irritation for Unionists to now deal directly with Sinn Féin as political equals, but that was the inevitable price that had to be paid. The IRA ceasefire had lifted the atmosphere and shown that Blair's reforming government could improve the situation in Northern Ireland. The very possibility of progress neutered Unionist quibbles about sitting down with 'the men of violence'. There was simply no room for the foot-stomping of the past, although reminders about the consequences of political failure were still viscerally apparent. A week after the IRA ceasefire, a sixteen-year-old Catholic boy, James Morgan, was found dead, his body dumped in a ditch in County Down. He had been abducted before being tortured and murdered and the suspects were members of the Loyalist Volunteer Force, a violent offshoot of the UVF that was defiantly not willing to embrace reconciliation.

One of the curiosities of the peace process was the divisions that emerged within Unionism–Loyalism. Paisley, the DUP's showboater, was now temperamentally at odds with David Trimble, the Ulster Unionists' prickly academic, who felt the weight of expectations fall on his shoulders. The British government expected a deal, and to get Northern Ireland 'off the books' in terms of it being a perennial problem, and expected Unionism's largest party to work with it to deliver a result. Paisley could flounce around and play to the gallery; however, whether he realised it at the time or not, the audience was shrinking. Loyalists, especially those men who had served time in prison for offences during the Troubles, started to make clear their displeasure at his antics. In August 1997, the *Sunday Times* reported that David Ervine – a one-time UVF commander turned leader of the Progressive Unionist Party, which spoke for the Loyalist paramilitary – had claimed that Paisley had tried to dissuade Loyalists from calling a ceasefire in 1994 and attempted to drive a wedge between the Loyalists and their political representatives. In a classic 'non-denial denial', the DUP claimed Ervine was peddling 'fantasy politics'. In another first, the Ulster Unionist Ken Maginnis took part in a debate with Sinn Féin's Martin McGuinness on the BBC's flagship current affairs programme, *Newsnight*. By the end of the month, a commission had been established on the management of contentious parades. It was in everyone's interests that this was dealt with by an arm's-length process from now on. Sinn Féin was also given the all-clear to re-enter all-party talks after it signed up to the Mitchell principles on decommissioning, although Trimble's Ulster Unionists said they would not physically sit at the same table as anyone from Sinn Féin. When the time came for the Republicans to formally re-enter the talks in a plenary session, Trimble along with members of smaller Loyalist parties decided to boycott the occasion. It was an empty gesture, as they took part just two days later, while the DUP had been clear that it would never sit down with Sinn Féin at any price.

Meanwhile, Gerry Adams was again courting the Irish–American community and attended a fundraiser at which 600 guests paid $500 a head to hear him speak at the Waldorf Astoria Hotel in New York. At the end of September, Ian Paisley addressed 1,000 people at a rally in Belfast's Ulster Hall, entitled 'Ulster's Crisis: Where Now?'. The UUP's David Trimble later

attacked the 'relentless negativity of a minority of Unionists' –
code for Paisley's incessant demonisation of the entire process.[34]
By early October, the position of the DUP was moot. All-party
talks with the two governments were commencing and Paisley
was now on the outside. The structure of the talks would closely
mirror the Brooke–Mayhew process, with three strands covering
arrangements for governing Northern Ireland, the north–south
relationship between Belfast and Dublin and the east–west dy-
namics between Ireland and Britain.

At the end of November, the DUP held its annual conference. Paisley denounced Trimble for committing 'high treason'
by remaining in the talks, and declared George Mitchell was
'working for the total destruction of Northern Ireland'.[35] Unionism was splintering, just as it had in the past, but so was the
Republican movement, as, indeed, it had previously done so.
However, Gerry Adams's long-term, slow-burn pivot away from
armed struggle and towards democratic politics had kept most
people on board or managed to paper over the cracks, in any
event. At the start of December, however, a breakaway Republican group revealed itself. The '32 County Sovereignty Committee' believed that Adams and Sinn Féin had sold out, just as
the previous generation had done in settling for partition. One
of the committee's leading lights, Bernadette Sands McKevitt,
was the sister of Bobby Sands. 'I am not against peace, just this
process,' she said.[36] 'My position is not a maverick or isolated
one. Many people see what is going on but until now have been
afraid to say, "the emperor has no clothes".' Given many of their
own supporters and voters now had 'Troubles fatigue', the Sinn

Féin leadership could ignore their internal critics if the process they were now committed to eventually led to an outcome that advanced their core objective of ending British rule. In December, a Sinn Féin delegation met Tony Blair in Downing Street for talks. The symbolism was telling. These were no longer furtive 'backchannel' communications between intermediaries; this meeting took place in full view of the world's media, offering the most visible representation so far that Sinn Féin was now at the centre of the negotiations on Northern Ireland's future and that if the British Prime Minister could discuss business cordially with the representatives of the IRA then so could everyone else.

The road to the Good Friday Agreement was anything but smooth. Although the two governments, all the major parties (bar the DUP) and even the representatives of Irish Republicanism and Ulster Loyalism were on board, the killings and sectarian violence did not miraculously come to an end. Between July 1997 and the end of January 1998, Loyalists killed thirteen people and Republicans two. There were ninety-three shooting incidents. Where it could be determined, Loyalists had committed fifty-one of them and Republicans twenty-one. There had also been twenty Republican bombings and another six carried out by Loyalists. In addition, there was a growing phenomenon of 'punishment beatings' – with both Republican and Loyalist paramilitaries meting out rough justice to suspected drug dealers and those accused of anti-social behaviour. Such attacks usually involved shooting a victim in the kneecaps and ankles and was preferable to either death or permanent exile from Northern Ireland. The organisation Families Against

Intimidation and Terror estimated that 160 such attacks took place in 1997. In addition, the IRA created a front organisation – Direct Action Against Drugs – to attack and even shoot drug dealers to drive them out of Republican communities.

Early January of 1998 saw Mo Mowlam visit HM Prison Maze to speak with Loyalist prisoners following concerns they were losing faith in the process and that Republicans were winning too many concessions. It was a controversial move for the Secretary of State to make the trip, but vital to persuade them to stay on board, with the blunt-speaking Mowlam winning plaudits for her willingness to go to any lengths necessary to ensure the process succeeded. As the talks resumed in London after the Christmas break, the two governments put forward a heads of agreement paper outlining the shape of any deal, which would include a new Northern Ireland Assembly, north–south cross-border bodies with executive powers and an east–west 'Council of the Isles'. There were also measures on reforming policing, decommissioning paramilitary weapons and the all-important issue of dealing with Republican and Loyalist prisoners. Tony Blair also announced a fresh judicial inquiry into Bloody Sunday under the chairmanship of Lord Saville. It came days before a large march in Derry of crowds numbering 30,000 to commemorate the twenty-sixth anniversary of the massacre. As buses took some of the marchers back to Belfast they were pelted with stones by Loyalists.

Even with the looming prospect of a political deal in the coming weeks, Republican and Loyalist paramilitaries were still active, so much so that the Ulster Democratic Party – the political representatives of the UDA/UFF – were excluded from the talks for breaking the Mitchell principles on non-violence. In February, the same fate befell Sinn Féin after the IRA was accused of killing two suspected drug dealers. From the perspective of the two governments, the decks needed to be cleared as the talks process entered a critical phase and there were enough problems keeping Unionists on board without ceding them the moral high ground of quitting over continuing paramilitary killings. The sanction for Sinn Féin was a perfunctory seventeen-day exclusion from the talks.

Throughout the Troubles there were incidents that, at certain moments, brought everyone together in revulsion at the cruelty of paramilitary violence. On 4 March, gunmen from the hard-line Loyalist Volunteer Force walked into a bar in the town of Poyntzpass, County Armagh. They ordered two men to lie down on the floor and then shot them dead. The men, one a 25-year-old Catholic and the other a 34-year-old Protestant, were friends, living in a mixed community.[37] This was Northern Ireland at its best; desecrated by the bullets and hatred of assassins. Two other men were injured in the attack. The premeditated and ruthless nature of the killings gave everyone pause to appreciate just what was in the balance: more of this or the hope of something different? Catholics and Protestants alike came out to pay their respects at the two men's funerals. Seamus Mallon, the deputy leader of the SDLP and the local constituency MP, was joined by the Ulster Unionist leader, David Trimble, as the two men as representatives of the two largest political parties came to offer their condolences to the families.

The talks now entered their critical phase, with George Mitchell setting a deadline of 9 April to find agreement. Understandably, he struck an upbeat tone. 'I believe strongly that we can and will reach an agreement,' he said.[38] As the pressure started to build, the two Prime Ministers met in Downing Street to ensure they maintained alignment. Despite this, 'large disagreements' remained according to Bertie Ahern. On Monday 6 April, George Mitchell presented a draft agreement to the various parties. 'Lives and deaths are at stake here,' he told them, urging that they break the habit of a lifetime and not leak the proposals.[39] Characteristically, the Ulster Unionists rejected Mitchell's initial draft. Arriving at the talks, Tony Blair told the assembled media outside Castle Buildings that he felt 'the hand of history upon our shoulders'.[40] As Northern Ireland and the wider world waited to see if, finally, a deal that everyone could live with to end the Troubles was possible, the INLA killed a former UVF member in Derry. Even at this stage, with everyone's chips in the pot in the final stages of the most important political negotiation since partition in 1921, there were those who were loath to abandon their old ways.

It was now Maundy Thursday in Easter week, the day when the Last Supper is remembered before the dramatic denouement to the Easter story. The parallels, even at the time, were obvious enough. As final negotiations took place, with the Ulster Unionists in particular checking and rechecking to ensure they had their negotiating teams and grass roots onside, Unionist MP Jeffrey Donaldson walked out of the building, fuelling rumours that the Ulster Unionists were deeply divided over the likely outcome (he would later defect to the DUP). Negotiations stretched on into Good Friday. There was a palpable sense that today would be the day. No one would welcome proceedings dragging into the Easter weekend with the obvious loss of momentum (not least by the participants of the talks heading off to attend church services). The issues were now well-grooved. Not everyone agreed with each part of the deal, but that was unavoidable in a political negotiation. This was politics at its most elemental. You achieved some things that you wanted and learned to live with other things you did not want. The prize on offer was enormous: most obviously, peace in Northern Ireland and an end to thirty years of the Troubles, which had cost the lives of more than 3,500 people. For Nationalists, the prospect of eventual Irish unity was baked into the agreement, with the 'principle of consent' – that there could be no change in Northern Ireland's constitutional position unless a majority agreed to it – no longer just a guarantee for Unionists that there would not be any change, but now a promise that there could be change facilitated by the British. This agreement was a treaty between two sovereign governments and registered with the United Nations. There would be no future British backsliding and Irish Republicans could now have faith in the integrity of the process.

For Unionists, there was the prospect of devolved rule again, with a new assembly and executive, but this time with strict cross-community working to avoid the majoritarian abuses of the old Stormont system. More positively for them, Articles 2 and 3 of the Irish Constitution would be amended to remove the territorial claim, which had been a bugbear for Unionists for decades. For the SDLP leader, John Hume, it was a personal triumph. His decades of advocacy for peace and agreement had finally paid off. His contribution was imprinted on every part of the agreement, but he now shared the limelight with his more irascible deputy, Seamus Mallon, who would go on to become Deputy First Minister to the Ulster Unionists' David Trimble in the cross-party executive. In his inimitable way, Mallon would coin the most apposite remark about the agreement, describing it as 'Sunningdale for slow learners'.[41] What might have happened if that earlier agreement had held in 1973?

Outside, Ian Paisley, attracted to a media throng like a bee to honey, denounced the emerging deal. What he probably did not expect was to be heckled from Loyalists who were genuinely angry at him for his decades of bluster and obstructionism. Their representatives in the Progressive Unionist Party and the Ulster Democratic Party were inside actively participating in the discussions and trying to create something new, while he was playing the same old tune outside. 'We fought for our country while you were living in a big house!' one shouted. 'Go home! Go home!' others chanted. For once, Paisley was lost for words. A British official watching this on the television remarked to George Mitchell that at one time the same loyalists would have thought Paisley a god. 'They went out and killed, thinking they were saving the Union. Now they've turned against him. It's the end of an era.'[42] For the British, the end of the Troubles would be recognised as a masterstroke in statecraft. Tony Blair was often criticised for his ideological evasiveness. What did he genuinely believe? His critics often complained that the answer to this was 'not a lot'. Nevertheless, Blair marshalled his eloquence and charm to magnificent effect, gently cajoling the various parties across the line and securing an historic agreement. At 5.36 p.m., on Good Friday 10 April 1998, George Mitchell made a statement confirming that a deal had been reached. In his understated way, the veteran US politician had proven to be a key ingredient; the ideal facilitator for the talks combining gentle persuasion with the steeliness of a former US Senate Majority Leader. And there it was. A binding agreement was reached between Unionists, Irish Nationalists, Loyalists and Republicans bringing Northern Ireland's Troubles to an end. The Belfast Agreement, as it is sometimes referred to by officials, more commonly known as the 'Good Friday Agreement', had been signed.

CHAPTER 6

MAKING THE BEST OF THINGS

There is more than a measure of mythologising, certainly in Britain, around the idea that the Good Friday Agreement represented the end of the Troubles. Perhaps for Britain it was. Certainly, there were no more IRA bombings in British towns and cities; ergo, no more Troubles. Conflict gave way to an impenetrable array of parties and personalities, with which the average Briton had next to no understanding, rowing with each other about some procedural point or other as the new devolved assembly came into being. But at least they were rowing and not killing each other. For Tony Blair, bringing peace to Northern Ireland was an enduring achievement amid the vicissitudes of a Prime Ministerial career. Even now, for every critic that brings up his record over the Iraq War, someone will counter by mentioning his peace-building work in Northern Ireland. For Mo Mowlam, it was a career high. An enthusiastic Labour conference hall in the autumn of 1998 gave her a long and heartfelt standing ovation for her efforts.[1]

Yet, here, for once, was politics with a happy ending. Perhaps more of a lull, or, to be exact, a pause to take in the enormity of what had just occurred. Three decades of ugly conflict negotiated to a close. Of course, Irish history never ends; and it has a maddening propensity to slide under the door that has just been slammed on it. Twenty-three years later, the post-Good Friday era is still evolving. Even now the situation is a work in progress. There have been many twists and turns over that period, but the sense that the agreement must be protected and adhered to has at least withstood the test of time. Not least because there is no alternative, no other composition that would split the difference between the competing allegiances and desires of Unionists and Nationalists, Loyalists and Republicans so effectively.

The referendums that followed – both in Northern Ireland and the Irish Republic – went smoothly enough, serving to copper-fasten the agreement. A comfortable 71 per cent voted 'Yes' in Northern Ireland to the question: 'Do you support the Agreement reached at the multi-party talks on Northern Ireland and set out in Command Paper 3883?'[2] While 94 per cent of southern Irish voters backed the deal, which included a supplementary question asking if they supported dropping Articles 2 and 3 from the Irish Constitution. The agreement was signed and now sealed by a popular vote and registered with the United Nations. However, the lower figure in Northern Ireland disguised a niggling problem. An estimated 96 per cent of Northern Ireland's Catholics voted in support of the Good Friday Agreement, but just 55 per cent of Protestants did so. Paisley and the DUP campaigned against it, swimming against the current of public optimism, but recognising there was significant doubt among the Unionist community that they could tap into. Peter Robinson, Paisley's deputy – and eventual successor – dismissed the agreement as a 'turbo-charged model of Sunningdale, the Anglo-Irish Agreement with a vengeance – a fully armed version of the Framework document'.[3]

Nevertheless, the Ulster Unionist leader, David Trimble, became First Minister, with the SDLP's deputy leader, Seamus Mallon, becoming Deputy First Minister (in later years, Sinn Féin would subtly change the title to 'deputy First Minister', emphasising parity of esteem with the First Minister). The former Conservative Party chairman and the UK's final governor of Hong Kong, Chris Patten, was asked to lead the Independent Commission on Policing for Northern Ireland that would address the vexed issue of replacing the RUC in order to secure buy-in for policing from Catholics. Legislation to allow the early release of paramilitary prisoners on licence was also passed. Both these measures were extremely unpopular among Unionists, but necessary preconditions for Republicans. They had no faith in the RUC and would not urge their communities to engage with the police until it was reformed out of existence. Similarly, the release of paramilitary prisoners – both Republican and Loyalist – was a red-line demand. Prisoners were often the biggest supporters of the Good Friday Agreement, which confirmed the point that Bobby Sands and the other hunger strikers wanted to have recognised – that their motivations were political. Were it not for the Troubles, very few if any of these men and women would ever have seen the inside of a prison cell.

Even with the agreement in place and unprecedented energy

put into building a new Northern Ireland, the aftershocks of the Troubles were often as visceral and appalling as anything that went before. Despite a new Northern Ireland Parades Commission created to adjudicate contentious marches (even if the Loyal Orders maintained that these were 'marches' not 'parades'), Drumcree was still Drumcree. Just weeks after the signing of the agreement there was once again violence when the Orange Order's contentious journey back down the Garvaghy Road for their 12 July celebration was banned, widespread rioting ensued and ten Catholic churches attacked by Loyalists. And just to show that the horrific violence of the Troubles was not consigned to the past just yet, a pre-meditated arson attack by a Loyalist gang in Ballymoney, County Antrim saw three young brothers aged nine, ten and eleven killed when their home was firebombed by the UVF. The Quinn brothers – Jason, Mark and Richard – lived with their Catholic mother and her Protestant boyfriend in the mainly Loyalist town. In many respects, this family embodied the potential of the Good Friday Agreement; people from both traditions just trying to make an ordinary life in an extra-ordinary place. The murders drew widespread criticism all the way from Tony Blair and Bill Clinton through to the former owner of Chelsea Football Club, Ken Bates, who offered a reward for the prosecution of the boys' killers.

As if there was any need to consider what was at stake, August 1998 provided a terrible reminder. With the conflict effectively over and the Provisional IRA committed to the political process, a 500lb car bomb brought about the single largest loss of life of the entire Troubles. It was planted in Omagh town centre in County Tyrone by dissident Republicans who were opposed to the peace process and the Good Friday Agreement. The bomb went off just after 3 p.m. on a Saturday afternoon. The explosion killed twenty-nine people with a further 220 injured, some grievously so. Vague warning messages were relayed by the bombers and as a result the police inadvertently evacuated people into the path of the blast. The victims were both Catholics and Protestants of all ages, including six children. Again, the political establishment, which now stretched all the way to the White House, were united in condemnation of the barbarity of the Omagh bombing. President Clinton and Tony Blair visited and met relatives of the deceased and injured, the latter describing the bombing as an 'appalling act of savagery and evil'.[4] The SDLP's John Hume called the bombers 'undiluted fascists'.[5] While the Sinn Féin president, Gerry Adams, condemned the dissidents, 'without any equivocation whatsoever'.[6] The Real IRA, the front name of the dissident breakaway group, soon disbanded after being ostracised by the wider Republican movement. In a grim reminder that sectarianism in Northern Ireland had not gone away, even in the face of people united in grief and horror, hardliners in the Orange Order wanted disciplinary action brought against David Trimble and his UUP chairman for attending the funerals of three of the young Catholic victims. The Order's rule that members 'should not countenance by your presence or otherwise any act or ceremony of Popish worship', was apparently immune from the spirit of the moment.[7]

Even with all the heavy lifting done with the signing of the agreement, there were still everyday political tensions to deal with, not least around the way in which paramilitary arms would be decommissioned and how the new executive and government departments would be formed. However, December 1998 saw a rare moment of deserved self-congratulation when John Hume and David Trimble received the Nobel Peace Prize in Oslo. Hume, for his part, was the moral and intellectual inspiration of so much of the peace process and eventual agreement, while Trimble had ensured the Ulster Unionist Party were key members in the process despite the fact that the party was often equivocal about the concessions needed to make the agreement stick. Trimble would continue to endure problems in bridging the divide between the sceptics in his party who were unhappy at the concessions that seemed to be granted to Sinn Féin and the ongoing efforts needed to realise the potential of the agreement. Those initial years after the signing of the agreement still saw the parties shadow-boxing one another with endless stop–start moments as the two governments – joint guarantors of the Good Friday Agreement – tried to coax them into a rapport in the face of not only ideological differences but clashing personalities too.

Tension rose again in March 2000 when Trimble faced a leadership challenge from one of his own MPs, Martin Smyth, who was until recently the Grand Master of the Orange Order and a hardliner who had been opposed to the Good Friday Agreement.[8] The contest was close, with Trimble managing to hold on by 57 per cent of Ulster Unionist Council delegates to Smyth's 43 per cent. Pressure was eventually eased when the IRA announced that they would now 'completely and verifiably' put their weapons beyond use. As a flavour of the burgeoning international involvement in Northern Ireland's political process, the former Finnish President, Martti Ahtisaari, along with the former secretary-general of the African National Congress (and current South African President), Cyril Ramaphosa, were appointed to monitor IRA arms dumps. This decommissioning movement saw the Ulster Unionists back Trimble's approach to entering government with Irish Republicans in the multi-party executive, by a similarly slender margin, 53 to 47 per cent, underlining the problems that he faced in keeping his deeply divided party onside. A legal academic lacking charisma and political guile, Trimble often found himself buffeted by events. Over the next couple of years, he alighted on the tactic of writing post-dated letters of resignation in his frustration at the slow pace of IRA decommissioning. Every time something stalled, the British and Irish governments were on hand to restart talks or to patch things up. In retrospect, this has been a constant feature since 1998, with British ministers chastising any backsliding by the IRA or Loyalists and cajoling the Unionists into staying the course. However, the fundamentals would not change. The Good Friday Agreement was sacrosanct; and it now had to be made to work. It was not a perfect arrangement, but compared to thirty years of conflict it remained instantly preferable.

For Republicans, the transition to exclusive political means in pursuit of their age-old objectives was slow and cautious. The Sinn Féin leadership's 'softly, softly' approach was designed to avoid any further loss of support to dissidents. Bobby Sands's sister, Bernadette Sands McKevitt, remarked that her brother 'did not die for cross-border bodies with executive powers'.⁹ It was a powerful and pointed quip that is often recounted and underscores just how far the Republican movement had travelled. 'Is this what it was all about?' internal critics of the Adams leadership asked. The Republican movement required careful handling, and whatever problems Trimble had in keeping his troops in line, they paled against the difficulties that Gerry Adams faced in turning a heavily armed, Marxist guerrilla army into local councillors and community workers. To be sure, there were bumps in the road. The IRA's reluctance to decommission its weapons dragged on until 2005. There were other diversions, too, notably the robbery of the Northern Bank in central Belfast just before Christmas in 2004. The robbers were said to have netted £24 million in the heist, and although no one has ever been convicted for the robbery, it was widely attributed to the IRA and sucked away political goodwill at a crucial point.

The years following the signing of the agreement would see a sharp decline in killings and paramilitary activity, but there was still a pattern of intra-Loyalist and intra-Republican feuding that scarred society, and sectarianism was still ever-present. A particularly egregious example came in 2001, when Loyalists began blockading the Holy Cross Catholic Primary School in the Ardoyne area of North Belfast. This was a flashpoint community, where the line between Catholics and Protestants had changed over time and as a result the school was on the 'wrong' side of the divide. A confusing row began, with Protestants complaining of intimidation and feeling they could not access local shops on the Catholic side. The school become the focus of their ire. The protests that ensued were ugly and violent and showed to the world how deep and atavistic sectarianism in Northern Ireland could be. Hundreds of Loyalists converged on the school over a period of six months, with clashes often occurring daily. The terrified primary school-aged children and their families were jeered and insulted by Loyalist adults as they tried to make their way to school as missiles, including urine-filled balloons, were being thrown at them. Mainstream Unionist politicians were notable for their lack of condemnation and inaction.

One of the missing aspects of the post-agreement settlement has been the absence of a comprehensive deal on remembering, or coming to terms with, the past four decades of conflict. Sometimes referred to as a 'peace and reconciliation process', after the similar exercise that took place in post-apartheid South Africa, there is still a lack of consensus about how this would work. Would participants be given immunity from prosecution? Would it reignite tensions? Is it better to just move on? The history of Northern Ireland's Troubles is therefore dealt with in a piecemeal fashion, which creates its own problems. If the police have active leads in historical cases they pursue them, but this process is slow and often disjointed, the passage of time in many of the cases making the prospect of convictions – or even just establishing the facts – increasingly difficult as years go by, memories fade and witnesses expire.

One case that has defined the post-agreement era was the publication of Lord Saville's report as a result of his thirteen-year inquiry into the events of 'Bloody Sunday' on 30 January 1972. Originally commissioned by Tony Blair, it fell to David

Cameron to respond to the report's findings. The killing of thirteen unarmed civil rights demonstrators by British paratroopers was 'unjustified and unjustifiable', Cameron told a hushed House of Commons in 2010 as he repudiated the lies concocted by Lord Widgery and the government of his Conservative predecessor, Edward Heath.[10]

There had been a hope that Saville would present his report to Parliament ahead of the 2010 general election to avoid it 'sitting on the shelf' until Parliament reconvened. But it was not to be. A heated meeting had taken place in Derry between Martin McGuinness and Mark Durkan, on behalf of the Bloody Sunday families, with Gordon Brown's Northern Ireland Secretary, Shaun Woodward, who was at pains to reassure the families and their political representatives that this delay was merely parliamentary protocol and not some nefarious device to rob them of the truth for which they had so long campaigned. Indeed, civil servants in the Northern Ireland Office were given to remark that no one even knew what Lord Saville looked like given he guarded his independence and was not in regular contact with officials. The cost and length of time that it took to compile the report came in for criticism by the right-wing media, but the inquiry remained a crucial step in bringing accountability for one of the most notorious events of the entire Troubles; perpetrated by the British state in the full glare of the world's media.

Building trust has been the Holy Grail quest of the post-agreement period. The entire point of the Good Friday Agreement was to institute cross-community executive working.

For Unionists, this would not only mean dealing with the SDLP, but also Sinn Féin. For the Ulster Unionists, this was difficult, not only because the issue of weapons decommissioning was still not resolved, but because there was clearly a large constituency in the Unionist community that did not support the agreement in the first place, nor, indeed, the necessary compromises that came with it. Having been roundly condemned by Loyalists outside the Good Friday Agreement negotiations, Ian Paisley and the DUP bided their time. They would channel the lack of enthusiasm that many Unionist voters had and begin to squeeze Trimble and the Ulster Unionists for the various compromises they had made. By the 2003 Northern Ireland Assembly election, the DUP had supplanted the Ulster Unionists to become the largest party as a slow, yet relentless transition was completed. In the 2005 British general election, Trimble lost his seat in the House of Commons to the DUP and resigned as leader of the Ulster Unionist Party.

A similar process was happening across the political aisle. Sinn Féin had overhauled the SDLP. For so long the good guys – the backbone and moral fibre of Northern Ireland's political system – it was frustrating for them to now play second fiddle to Sinn Féin. The conceptual framework of the Good Friday Agreement – power-sharing, accommodation of different allegiances and identities and all-Ireland institutions – had John Hume's DNA all over it. Yet Hume knew precisely what he was doing by helping bring Sinn Féin in from the margins. Better financed and with more activists, once Republicans threw themselves into politics, they would soon eclipse the SDLP. John Hume defined an age

– and this culminated in him being awarded the Nobel Prize – but having embodied his party for so long it has proven difficult for his successors to carve out a niche in the way that he did. Hume was the leader for twenty-two years, until 2001. In the two decades since, the SDLP has had four leaders, none of whom has managed to change their electoral fortunes. Like the Ulster Unionists, they have had to learn to settle for a reduced billing.

Having replaced Trimble as the pre-eminent figure in political Unionism, Ian Paisley now did exactly what he accused Trimble of doing and went into government with Sinn Féin in 2007 in a carefully choreographed and landmark deal. The very prospect of the hard-line Democratic Unionist Party going into government with Sinn Féin, the representatives of the Provisional IRA, was remarkable enough, but what was entirely unexpected was the cordial and even friendly relationship that developed between Ian Paisley and Martin McGuinness. For so long implacable enemies, they now became known as the 'Chuckle Brothers', for their shared bonhomie. This unusual rapport helped to relaunch devolution. If these two could get along, then anything was possible.

*　*　*

After he came to power in 2010, David Cameron made it clear that he would not be as 'hands on' as Tony Blair and Gordon Brown had been and the parties would need to deal directly with the Northern Ireland Secretary. In an inversion of the New Labour years where the quality of ministers was high, reflecting the priority Blair gave to the process, Cameron's ministers and later those of his successor, Theresa May, were more ephemeral figures. Indeed, between July 2016 and February 2020, there were four individuals appointed to the position of Secretary of State for Northern Ireland. Owen Paterson, Theresa Villiers, James Brokenshire and Karen Bradley came and went. The stop–start nature of the post-Good Friday Agreement institutions has seen two long periods – eight years in all – when the institutions have been suspended. The first, between October 2002 and May 2007, reflected the mutual antagonisms between the Unionist parties and Sinn Féin, partly over the issue of IRA decommissioning, and, more broadly, a basic lack of trust and rapport. The second suspension from January 2017 until January 2020 centred on the fallout from the revelations about the Renewable Heating Incentive (RHI) – an obscure-sounding subsidy to promote the use of wood-burning pellets in commercial premises. Arlene Foster, the current First Minister, had implemented the scheme in her previous role as enterprise minister back in 2012. By 2017, it had come to light that the scheme had a glaring weakness in that there was no control over the amount that claimants could access. 'Burn to earn', as it was dubbed, racked up liabilities that were said to be north of £500 million.[11] Apart from the eye-watering amounts of public money that had been committed, the subsequent row about the incentive's botched implementation exposed a basic problem with the functioning of the executive; with parties that have diametrically opposed beliefs operating in silos, so the scale of the mess surrounding the RHI scheme did not come to light earlier.

There were also a series of notable ironies in this affair. It was Foster's successor as enterprise minister, her DUP colleague Jonathan Bell, who blew the whistle on the scandal. He said that while this would mean the end of his political career, 'God doesn't punish people who tell the truth'.[12] The row also pitted Sinn Féin as custodians of the British public purse against the DUP with its basic lack of financial rectitude. The most significant political fallout came when Martin McGuinness resigned as deputy First Minister, incensed at Foster's defiance in refusing to step aside while the scandal was investigated, but frustrated, too, at the general attitude of the DUP to power-sharing. There was a valedictory tone to McGuinness's resignation letter:

> The equality, mutual respect and all-Ireland approaches enshrined in the Good Friday Agreement have never been fully embraced by the DUP. Apart from the negative attitude to nationalism and to the Irish identity and culture, there has been a shameful disrespect towards many other sections of our community. Women, the LGBT community and ethnic minorities have all felt this prejudice.[13]

It had not been publicly confirmed at that stage but McGuinness was gravely ill with a rare genetic disorder and died shortly afterwards, leaving behind him a massive gap in Northern Ireland's political life. For Sinn Féin, Gerry Adams may well have supplied the theory, but McGuinness brought the force of reputation. The tough young IRA commander at the start of the Troubles who left Derry looking like 'it had been bombed from the air' was, in the words of one British officer, 'excellent officer material'.[14] For those who opposed the political process, he had harsh words, denouncing dissident Republicans as 'traitors' for trying to upend the progress he had painstakingly helped to embed. McGuinness made repeated forays across the cultural divide, shaking hands with the Queen and even attending a state banquet to show Unionists that he was sincere in finding an accommodation with them. For his internal critics he was selling out, but McGuinness was unconcerned. He was always willing to exploit his reputation and desperately wanted power-sharing to succeed, respecting those of different views with a perhaps unexpected generosity of spirit. His life was a micro-cosm of events in Northern Ireland. A journey from belligerence to reconciliation. From nihilism to optimism. In which respect, Martin McGuinness (1970–1994) shows us what happens when politics fails; Martin McGuinness (1994–2017) shows us what is possible when it does not.

Peter Robinson's importance in the power-sharing process lay in his dominance of the DUP. This is what Unionism had been crying out for since Terence O'Neill. Someone who could engage in practical politics with all the necessary deals and con-cessions without worrying too much about his political base. He brought stability and the hope that Northern Ireland could get on with day-to-day business. For so long Paisley's sidekick who stood behind the 'Big Man' at press conferences with his over-sized glasses and dour expression, Robinson was also a shrewd party strategist who masterminded the DUP's usurpation of Trimble's Ulster Unionists. Like McGuinness, he had banked his credibility, and while he was not as daring as the former IRA man, the net result of their double act saw the institutions of the Good Friday Agreement function better than any time before – or since. Robinson was also ruthless, as Ian Paisley eventually learned to his cost. Although Paisley had symbolically led Unionism back into devolved government, in his colleagues' eyes he had now outlived his political usefulness. A year after becoming First Minister, Paisley was despatched in a palace coup. His wife, Eileen, for so long in the background, accused Peter Robinson of politically assassinating her husband 'with words and deeds' and ushering him out of the leadership of the party he had founded.[15] Robinson's response was typically pointed and revealed the tensions that seldom surfaced in the buttoned-up world of DUP politics: 'As someone who faithfully served Dr Paisley for many decades,' he said, 'I will make one final sacrifice by not responding and causing any further damage to his legacy beyond that which he has done himself.'[16] The problem for Arlene Foster, who took over from Robinson in December 2015, is that she lacks the clout that he had built up over decades. She was a defector from the Ulster Unionists for a start, and shares little of the DUP's evangelical Christian fervour. In her acceptance speech on becoming the DUP's leader she rooted her politics in the pragmatic and practical, with a focus on 'ideas and not ideologies'. The people of Northern Ireland 'don't want to hear their politicians squabbling about issues that seem unconnected to their daily lives', she said.[17] It has not often worked out like that for her. Her relationship with her party is often fraught, and there is little rapport that exists with Sinn Féin.

The fallout from the RHI scandal has critically undermined her reputation for competence, while the electoral position of the DUP has continued to slip. The party has only one more seat in the Northern Ireland Assembly than Sinn Féin, while it lost two of its seats in the House of Commons in the 2019 general election – including that of her deputy, Nigel Dodds.

The past five years in Northern Ireland, as they have in Britain, have been dominated by Brexit. However, the issues on the table are different. For starters, Northern Ireland voted to remain in the EU – by 56 per cent to 44 per cent, although, as with the referendum on the Good Friday Agreement, Unionists voted heavily for Brexit, while Nationalists overwhelmingly voted to remain. The DUP's involvement in the Brexit campaign ran to funnelling money from the official Leave campaign to pay for an advertising campaign in a British newspaper that was not even distributed in Northern Ireland.[18] Theresa May, after succeeding David Cameron in 2016, called a general election in 2017 and ended up losing her parliamentary majority. An alliance was formed with the DUP in exchange for a raft of funding measures. Here was Unionism once again at the centre of Westminster power. 'The future's bright, the future's orange!' DUP MP Ian Paisley Jr quipped.[19] In her very first set-piece speech on Brexit, Theresa May breezily proclaimed that nobody wanted to return to the borders of the past, 'so we will make it a priority to deliver a practical solution as soon as we can'. The issue of the Irish border was supposed to be the easy bit. The public would be much more concerned about the divorce settlement that Britain would have to pay the EU, which would run into tens of billions of pounds. There would be a light-touch solution to trade and travel across the border between the two jurisdictions on the island of Ireland, and, by extension, between the UK and the EU. The reality was that the failure to identify a technically viable solution that would adequately police trade across a 310-mile land border would fox British negotiators, who found themselves outflanked time and again by Irish diplomats who were warning that the risk of a hard border would undermine the Good Friday Agreement. Not the agreement per se, but the underpinning assumptions that governed it. An open border had been a happy by-product of peace, and rolling back from that freedom would have consequences, not least the possibility of a renewed Republican campaign to attack any guards or infrastructure. So, why take the risk? As Theresa May's position eroded, unable to negotiate a way forward that would please her internal critics, and with a burgeoning campaign for a second referendum on Brexit, she was replaced in 2019 by her former Foreign Secretary and the central political personality in the Leave campaign, Boris Johnson. Here was someone Unionists could do business with. Johnson had addressed the DUP's annual conference in 2018 warning against any attempt to cleave Northern Ireland away from the rest of the United Kingdom and create a new country called 'UK-NI' that 'is no longer exclusively ruled by London or Stormont – it is in large part to be ruled by Brussels ... now and in the future'.[20] For Unionists, ever watchful for betrayal from British politicians, Boris Johnson's later cynicism was breath-taking, as this is exactly what he later agreed to. His final deal with the EU to secure a

British withdrawal would see him agree to leave Northern Ireland in the single market in terms of goods with checks at ports, in effect creating a border in the Irish Sea. To Unionists, this was tantamount to betrayal and undermined their place in the Union.

Following the fallout from the RHI scheme and the three-year interregnum, the Northern Ireland institutions were resuscitated in January 2020. At the time of writing, they are still in place, but serious pressures remain, not least around Brexit and the border arrangements. Nearly a quarter of a century after the signing of the Good Friday Agreement, Westminster dare not take its eye of its troublesome province.

CHAPTER 7

CENTURY OF DIVISION

So, then, a century of division. It is hard to argue that Northern Ireland has been anything other than a bad idea to begin with that got steadily worse, and resulted in a century that can be separated into distinct periods of fifty, thirty and twenty years; a 50–30–20 century. Five decades in which Unionists carved out a system that elevated their interest over their Catholic neighbours. Then came three decades of bitter violence and carnage – the product of the preceding half-century. The accompanying lack of political imagination or will – from all sides – resulted in more than 3,500 souls perishing. Then came twenty years of stop–start political progress. Incremental development with lots of bumps in the road and setbacks a-plenty. Still, it was preferable to the seventy grim years that went before, although since the signing of the Good Friday Agreement in 1998 there has barely been a decade of devolved joint working between the DUP and Sinn Féin. For detractors, and there are many, this clammy, loveless embrace – a 'forced coalition' – remains a doomed enterprise. Yet, with only a moment's thought about the past 100 years, it is clear that this amounts to the most successful period in Northern Ireland's history. Despite the mutual loathing and lack of generosity – not to mention the periodic breakdowns and absence of trust between the DUP and Sinn Féin – which has led to difficulties in making joint decisions and has crippled the executive at regular intervals, this is the best that Northern Ireland has ever been governed.

To be sure, this is a modest threshold. Without the sectarianism of the first half of Northern Ireland's existence, or the violence of the second phase, just about anything else is preferable. The Good Friday Agreement settlement – the 1998 accord and the subsequent patches which invariably followed – bookended the violence but left the hard task of repairing the damage and building a new rapport between Protestant–Unionist–Loyalists and Catholic–Nationalist–Republicans. Twenty-odd years later, the task is incomplete and regularly requires maintenance from the British and Irish governments; yet it is still progress. Even when major issues have been left unresolved, such as the legacy of the Troubles and what we should remember, condemn, commemorate or conveniently choose to forget. Even now, there is still little by the way of consensus. If anything, the past has an unyielding, undiminished capacity to interfere with the present. To entrench division and halt progress. It remains a fault line, providing both sides with definition and reaffirmation, solidifying hearts and minds. It means that 'normal' politics in Northern Ireland remains as elusive as ever; moreover, there is little chance of this ever much changing. The scratchy, disjointed, antagonistic way in which the Northern Ireland executive has responded to the Covid-19 emergency demonstrates this, with Sinn Féin demanding greater alignment with Dublin's approach and Unionists wanting to copy Westminster. The plain fact is that Northern Ireland does not work. It never has, and, it seems, never will. So, what we have instead is 'normal-for-Northern-Ireland' – and this is still something that is worth having.

The preceding chapters are a brief *tour d'horizon* of many of the key events in this century of conflict. The sheer weight of division – of killings, shootings, bombings, destruction and atrocities – are too numerous and unrelenting to capture in their entirety. Where possible, I have simply tried to reference events that had direct political consequences. In summing up, there is a glaring, unanswered – and all too often unasked – question hanging over this book: What if Northern Ireland had never been created?

Given the pain and division that partition generated, it remains apposite. Was a different history possible? Permit me to offer this historical counter-factual. What would have happened if, for argument's sake, the 1914 Home Rule Bill – which passed its parliamentary stages but was suspended due to the outbreak of the First World War – had been fully enacted? Most obviously, Northern Ireland would never have existed. But what would have replaced it? As many historians argue, pushing forward with Home Rule would have led to civil war. Tens of thousands of armed UVF men would have seen to that. The idea that northern Protestants would have meekly acquiesced to such an outcome is for the birds. Partition might have been a messy compromise, but it was the least-worst option.

It is a familiar-enough argument, but the problem with it is that the new southern Irish state endured a civil war over the terms of partition, and half a century later history caught up with Northern Ireland and it, too, experienced a civil war. It seems there was no scenario where Irish blood was not going to be shed. None of this, I hasten to add, is to make the case that there was a neat, straightforward alternative to the history we have. But the driver for partition – fear of a Loyalist back-lash – was just short-term expediency as David Lloyd George's Liberal government kicked the can down the road with all its might. Would following through with the 1914 Home Rule Bill really have been worse than what was subsequently experienced? Partition and the creation of Northern Ireland was a disaster. It led to the creation of a sour, sectarian state, with discrimination against Catholics locked into the fabric of the place. Moreover, here we are, a century on, still discussing what to do with this troublesome outpost, fumbling around for a settlement that will please all sides. It is hard to see how we got away lightly.

It also created a brittle, mutually suspicious relationship be-tween Britain and the new Irish Free State. The situation un-doubtedly thawed in the run-up to, during and for a few years after the Good Friday Agreement process, particularly during the administrations of Tony Blair and Bertie Ahern. But let us recognise it for what it was: a blip. The relationship before that point, and again after it, was difficult and cool (and in the post-Brexit climate, the mercury has again dipped). But what if, even as late as 1918, Britain had accepted the result of the Irish general election – in which Sinn Féin amassed three-quarters of the seats in Ireland – and taken that as a legitimate democratic mandate for independence? What would relations between Great Britain and a territorially unified, 32-county Ireland have been like?

There would have been division between Irish moderates and radicals about dominion status, that much is clear, but it is unlikely that the Easter Rising of 1916 or anything similar would have occurred. No need for the subsequent War of Independence, either. Perhaps the cast of characters would have been different too. Although the Irish Parliamentary Party's John Redmond died in 1918 and would soon be out of the picture, where would figures like Patrick Pearse or James Connolly, leaders of the Easter Rising, have fitted in? Would someone like Éamon de Valera, another revolutionary turned statesman, simply have gone into mainstream politics from 1914 onwards? Or, for that matter, Michael Collins? Without the British to fight, would the great guerrilla figure who did so much to eject Britain from Ireland during the War of Independence have been so prominent in this alternative historical ramble? Presumably, he would have avoided assassination for his trouble.

It is difficult to consider what effect the First World War would have had in this scenario. Would Ireland have come to Britain's aid? Perhaps the five Irish regiments in the British Army that were disbanded in 1922 at the creation of the Irish Free State would have endured and fought alongside Britain again in the Second World War?[1] By dint of their numbers, Protestants would have undoubtedly played a significant role in a 32-county Ireland. Even in the 1918 general election, in which

Sinn Féin won nearly three-quarters of the seats in Ireland, Unionists won the remaining quarter. The power of the Catholic Church would still have been appreciable but leavened with a massive infusion of Protestants. Perhaps the two traditions would have found a rapport over the following decades, fulfilling Theobald Wolfe Tone's eighteenth-century aim of uniting 'Catholic, Protestant and Dissenter under the common name of the Irishman'.[2] Perhaps we would even have seen a class-based politics of left and right assert itself.

In other words, perhaps Home Rule would have been enough without the need for a full-blown republic. There would have been a call for one, granted, but would it have captured the public mood? Might Ireland have become a mainstay of the Commonwealth? Without the Troubles, perhaps Irish–British relations would have flourished and the transfer of people between these islands would have been even greater than it has been? Maybe 2021 would only just be the point at which Ireland was deciding to go its own way with the relatively benign issue of Brexit providing the rupture, much as it appears to be doing in Scotland. If, indeed, there was such a moment, that departure from the United Kingdom might be amicable and businesslike. Indeed, those Irish Protestants who had found their place in a unified Home Ruled Ireland might be voting for that separation.

An overuse of 'perhaps' and 'could have', granted; and I can only observe that historical hypotheticals tend to generate more talking points than they resolve. However, all of this is relevant in understanding how a different chain of events might have played out. As I said, there were no perfect solutions in that period. Every conceivable decision would have rewarded one group and punished another. No one got everything they wanted and many got nothing at all. But the fact remains that here we are, a century later, and the political ordinance remains volatile. We are not discussing far-away events. They are still contested and still cause real-world problems for us in the third decade of the twenty-first century.

What 1914 certainly represented was the last best opportunity for Britain to avoid the century that followed. Ceding independence to Ireland was always going to be painful and embarrassing, particularly at the height of Britain's imperial prestige. What message would it send out to far-flung liberation movements? But look what happened in any event. Inaction triggered a sequence of events over the next seven years that resulted in Britain being ejected from most of the island of Ireland anyway, creating Northern Ireland as a backfoot compromise. Which outcome was more damaging in the long run? Home Rule represented the triumph of the parliamentary process and democratic persistence. In that respect, it was an honourable retreat for Britain, with parallels to contemporary events. The issue of Irish Home Rule was rather like Brexit. A persistent thorn in the flesh of the Westminster elite. A relentless campaign with a single, clear outcome. A forty-year war of political attrition by its supporters inside and outside Parliament that simply grew and grew until it was achieved.

Alas, Britain chose to do things the hard way. As a result, we have been bequeathed the history with which we are all too familiar. Squandering the initiative in 1914 resulted in the worst possible outcome for all sides. Britain could not hold Ireland and signal its inability to hold on to its empire. The key theme of Britain's post-war imperial decline was founded in the wild countryside of West Cork. The British Empire was not exactly renowned for observing territorial and cultural niceties as it carved up entire continents, creating new states and locking in ethnic and tribal hatreds. That, perhaps, was the point: Ireland was just another colony to manage. It merited no special consideration. Its only strategic importance lay in its proximity: a hinterland for absentee landlords and a possible base of attack.

Unionists did not get what they desired. Northern Ireland was a lifeboat. Irish Unionist Party leader Sir Edward Carson was broken by partition and played no further part in Irish political affairs. Not that the Irish got what they wanted either. They achieved an Irish Free State – the same deal that was on offer in 1914 – but endured a war against the British and a civil war to get there and still lost the north-east of the country. The partition of Ireland was a bad deal for everyone. Here we are, still lumbered with the Irish question. The row about a hard border between Northern Ireland and the Republic of Ireland in the context of securing a post-Brexit trading deal is just the latest example of how the country causes a problem for the rest of the United Kingdom. Even if independence had not happened in 1914, and if the Easter Rising had taken place, the repressive nature of British policy between 1918 and 1922 – replete with the Black and Tans (the mercenaries sent to quell the rebellious Irish) – could have been avoided. As could the creation of a sectarian state for fifty years. And so could the Troubles. This is a recurrent theme of this century of division. Just before things get worse there is a point where more political courage and greater leadership could have forced history onto an alternative track. At every stage there was another path available. One that might have avoided subsequent strife.

*   *   *

So, 100 years on from its creation, what does the centenary of Northern Ireland represent? For Unionists, it is undoubtedly a celebration, not a commemoration. It is a time of rejoicing. They have lasted this long. Despite the indifference and double-dealing of snake-tongued Westminster politicians, the agitation of civil rights protestors and the destructive militancy of the IRA, Northern Ireland is still standing. It has been a struggle that has required constant vigilance, a flinty determination; but the Union is still intact, and so Unionists have prevailed. So, this is not a neutral occasion, less still an inclusive one. The invitation to the centenary party is coloured orange and there is little point pretending otherwise. Not that there is much pretence. Unionism is an ideology founded on communal supremacy and the whole point of the centenary is to assert Northern Ireland's Britishness. There is no all-Ireland dimension. Less still any signals of regret at how things worked out. No reaching out to Catholic–Nationalists to try to build bridges to maximise the prospects of Northern Ireland sustaining itself in the decades ahead. Reflectiveness only leads to self-doubt and therefore in-vites compromise and, inevitably, betrayal. Unionism does not evolve, certainly of its own volition. It changes only when it is forced to adapt, as pressure is applied and it careers headlong into an immovable object with greater mass, which has, invariably, been the British government. The Good Friday Agreement was a case in point. There was a prospect of ending the Troubles and the British and Irish governments gladly took it. Nothing would stand in their way, although it involved painful concessions for Unionists. They would be expected to share power with Nationalists – and Republicans. They had to break bread with 'the men of violence' and watch on as hundreds of Republican (and Loyalist) prisoners walked free from jail. They did not like it, but they were obliged to acquiesce. The Ulster Unionists under David Trimble paid a heavy electoral price for doing so, eclipsed, as they were, by Ian Paisley and the Democratic Unionists for their efforts. Of course, the DUP's acceptance of the Good Friday Agreement settlement – after protesting outside the talks that led to it and berating Trimble for selling out – was little short of shameless; brilliantly so, in fact. So, Unionism has a sort of inert pragmatism that is activated when it is given no choice. Perhaps Westminster learned from the collapse of the Sunningdale Agreement that you must not blink first when dealing with them. If Northern Ireland's is a 50–30–20 century, for Unionists it is 50–50. Fifty fat years during which they shaped the place in their image and interests. From the early 1970s onwards there followed fifty lean years. Unionism has been on the back foot for half a century. Their devolved Parliament was taken from them. Then they were obliged to share power with Catholic–Nationalists. Then the Irish government was given a say in Northern Ireland's affairs. Then came the Downing Street Declaration, framework documents and eventually the Good Friday Agreement that obliged them not only to share power with Catholics, but to sit in government with former representatives of the IRA. At every stage, they have been obliged to cede political territory. To accept compromise. The RUC was effectively scrapped. A long-running row about flying the Union flag above Belfast City Hall was lost. An Irish Language Bill is forthcoming. Gay marriage and abortion have been foisted on them by Westminster. And now the Northern Ireland Protocol. After promising, repeatedly, that there would be 'unfettered' access between Northern Ireland and mainland Britain, Boris Johnson's deal to extricate the United Kingdom from the European Union has delivered a border in the Irish Sea. Amid the severe Covid-19 restrictions, the centenary year, it is fair to say, is not going well – and this is likely to be bookended by the 2021 census, which is widely expected to show that Catholics now outnumber Protestants. This is the very outcome that Northern Ireland, as presently constituted, was designed to avoid exactly 100 years ago.

What about Nationalists and Republicans? Where are they in all this? Perhaps, unsurprisingly, they have defaulted to a position of splendid isolation from the centenary. How could they – from the mildest-mannered SDLP voter, through to the most ardent Republican – possibly validate the discrimination their families and communities faced under the Orange State? There is nothing for them to celebrate about partition. Again, the centenary is not a neutral occasion; it is an exclusively Unionist affair, which means, in turn, it is anti-Nationalist. This is zero-sum politics; if Unionists are up then Nationalists must be down. If Unionists have cause to celebrate then it must have come at the expense of Nationalists. If the boot happened to be on the other foot, the reverse calculation would apply. This is not an academic point; we have been there. We can look back to the commemoration of the 1916 Easter Rising five years ago. There was a particular effort on behalf of the Irish government to make the commemorations – and they were commemorations, not celebrations – holistic and inclusive. The Rising was the foundational moment in establishing Irish sovereignty and removing the British presence from Ireland, yet the events managed to be reflective, not bombastic. There was no chest-puffing or Nationalistic fervour. It was placed in its historical context as part of a wider history, both preceding and succeeding the Rising. There was a focus, too, on the civilian casualties of that revolutionary week. And in a mark of the bona fides that the Easter Rising commemoration was an inclusive affair; there was even room to commemorate the British soldiers who perished. How did Unionism respond to this carefully calibrated approach designed to disappoint many Nationalists and Republicans, I have no doubt, and to cause as little offence to Unionist opinion as possible? By and large, they rebuffed it. The DUP never misses an opportunity to miss an opportunity, but there was a need to make a gesture at least as sincere as the one that Dublin was offering. However, Arlene Foster, forever looking over her shoulder and fearful of the charge of selling out, as every Unionists leader since Terence O'Neill has been, could not muster the grace to meaningfully engage with the occasion.

So how can Unionists engage Catholic–Nationalists around Northern Ireland's centenary? Well, how about an apology for the egregious treatment of them under the Stormont regime? A clear, unambiguous, sincere, unequivocal, full-throated and genuine 'sorry' on behalf of Unionism. It would be a meaningful symbol. A break point, too, writing off the failures of previous Unionist leaders. Disappointingly, perhaps, there has been no such expression of sorrow at the failings of successive Unionist governments for their decades of misrule. It would be refreshing to hear a smart Unionist retort: 'Change the record, we've already conceded our predecessors got it wrong years ago. We live in different times and you can't hang the past over us now.'

Only Unionist politicians have never faced up to their forebears' shortcomings. There have been no mea culpas down the years. You will search in vain for speeches where Unionist moderates repudiate their own side for its woeful misrule. Perhaps David Trimble came closest when referring to Stormont as a 'cold house' for Catholic–Nationalists during his (often thought-provoking) Nobel Prize acceptance speech in 1998.[3] Cold? It was Arctic. Alas, he immediately added that Unionists believed Nationalists would 'burn the house down', somewhat undoing the sentiment and exemplifying the point I am trying to make. Unionists do not appreciate being reminded of all this – and I can understand why. But all political movements modernise and grow by, at least on some level, denouncing their own past. The failure to do that leaves contemporary Unionism pathologically unable to stretch out the hand of, if not friendship, then even that of co-operation towards 'the other'. If you do not jettison your baggage in politics then you end up dragging it around for ever.

Unionists would do well to read Peter Robinson's DUP conference speech from 2011, in which he spelled out – in the clearest terms – that the only way of neutering the appeal of unification to Catholic–Nationalists was to make Unionism acceptable to them: 'There can be no greater guarantee of our long-term security in the Union than the support of a significant part of the Catholic community,' he said. 'Now the conflict has ended we have a window of opportunity to reset the terms of political debate. We have the opportunity to secure our constitutional position beyond the visible horizon.'[4]

We are still waiting.

This lack of regret at how things worked out is particularly remiss when it comes to the Ulster Unionist Party. They governed Northern Ireland from its inception in 1921 right the way through until Stormont was prorogued in 1972 following the massacre on Bloody Sunday. That an apology is warranted from them is surely beyond serious dispute. Were it not for their corruption and appalling hubris, then there would never have been the need for the civil rights movement in the first place, and it is highly unlikely the emergence of the IRA, or any of the other Troubles-related tragedies that followed, would have occurred. Instead of hobbling towards its centenary, perhaps Northern Ireland would be sure of its place in the United Kingdom, having reconciled Catholic–Nationalists along the journey, and would now find itself striding confidently towards its anniversary.

But what about the DUP? While the UUP ran Northern

Ireland as a sectarian fief for half a century, creating and residing over the institutions that would allow inequality to flourish, the DUP was only created in 1971 – the year before direct rule from Whitehall was imposed. So, the DUP's culpability is different. Yet if anything, an apology is even more necessary from the party of Ian Paisley. Indeed, relations between the UUP and DUP have usually been hostile and mutually antagonistic, aside from their buddying up in opposition to the Anglo-Irish Agreement. Paisley never ran anything until he eventually came in from the cold in 2007, yet his destructive influence was pervasive from the mid-1960s onwards. It was a brutal, atavistic, nihilistic contribution; seeking, always, to divide and demonise. Catholics were not just to be kept as second-class citizens through rigging the electoral system, abusing public service allocations and encouraging discrimination in jobs. Under Paisley, the DUP went further than the UUP in encouraging the victimisation of Catholics and, thus, fomenting the Troubles for thirty years. Loyalist violence was encouraged, validated and excused by Paisley and the DUP.

Of course, it would be simplistic to merely assert that Unionists were the black-hatted baddies, while Catholic–Nationalists and Republicans were the righteously white-hatted heroes. But the fact remains: the UUP ran Northern Ireland continuously until the British were compelled to remove the punchbowl, while Paisley's DUP exerted a maniacal influence over the Protestant–Loyalist community, egging on its violence and bringing terror and death for so many Catholic–Nationalists. There was not, until the early 1970s, anything that could meaningfully be described as equivalence from the other side. The IRA was moribund as late as 1969, with no viable democratic vehicle for Catholics before the advent of the SDLP in 1970. Political Unionism held all the cards for fifty years. It shaped Northern Ireland. The point about the civil rights movement was that Catholics lacked any political agency at that point; they were locked into a system that was rigged against them in the land of their forefathers. They were not immigrants fighting for their place in a new society. They were still in the villages and towns of their ancestors, victims of the drawing of an arbitrary border in 1921, and thereafter on the receiving end of state-sponsored oppression and communal violence. These twin antagonisms would congeal in that fateful period between 1967 and 1972. Catholic dissent became organised, first through armed insurrection, as a direct result of the provocation of political Unionism. Of course, it is necessary to make a distinction between 'political' Unionism – the UUP and DUP – and ordinary Unionist people. The latter were and are cursed with poor-quality political representatives, who, for decades, have sought out the lowest common denominator among their community and then indulged it in all its grisly insularity.

There are other apologies that are warranted and timely. There is something unbecoming about singling out killings; creating, as it inevitably does, a hierarchy of victims. All political murder is wrong and, for any family, a dead father is a dead father whatever the circumstances and whatever the beliefs. Grief is grief. So, it is hard to be selective about individual atrocities, but it is clear that some of the Republican paramilitary targeting was overtly sectarian. The massacre of ten workers at Kingsmill in 1975 or the Enniskillen bomb in 1987 targeted people who were Protestants, pure and simple. While the INLA's savage attack at Darkley must rank among the most depraved of the entire Troubles. Indeed, if there is ever a peace and reconciliation process at some stage down the road, it will force Republicans – and others – to come to terms with the destructive things that they did during the Troubles. Would it not show goodwill and a clear intention towards achieving greater reconciliation to take the initiative at this stage? (Of course, the same goes for the Loyalist paramilitaries, who were nakedly sectarian in their choice of targets throughout the Troubles.)

How will the British government commemorate the centenary? Absentee landlord turned referee, turned participant in this bloody century. It would be similarly remiss if there was not some offering of regret at the way things turned out. Amid the low-key royal visits, red, white and blue bunting and tree-planting, there should be a recognition that the gravest failure of all belongs to the British. After all, absentee landlords have an ignominious history in Ireland. The Great Famine of the 1840s came about as a result of, among other things, indifference to the situation on the ground. A failure to react in a timely and proportionate way to spiralling events. Not to leave things to the mercy of chance, or to under-react and then to over-react once you have lost control of the situation. But this is exactly what twentieth-century British leaders have done in Northern Ireland, right into the modern day. It is the prerogative of a writer looking back over the past century to point out the mistakes of successive governments and political leaders and suggest what they might have done instead. So, then, what are the obvious pivots and the inflection points that might have been prevented or even used to catalyse a different approach? The key stages when bad led to worse or where tragedy could have been used to redirect affairs in a more productive direction? The British government had numerous opportunities throughout those benighted decades to avert, limit or put an end to the Troubles.

Moving on from the hypotheticals of what might have happened in those first few decades of the last century, the very real record of successive governments is their repeatedly poor stewardship of Northern Irish issues. It begins as a tale of neglect. Ignoring the place much as the Unionist establishment wanted. Turning a Nelsonian eye on the rampant sectarianism of Orange rule. Denying Members of Parliament the right to ask questions about what was going on there. Allowing the pressure for reform to build and then not acceding to it in a timely way – leaving Unionist reactionaries to brutalise peaceful reformers in the mid- to late 1960s. This under-reaction then led to an over-reaction. The troops sent in to stop a pogrom as Catholics homes are burnt and the Irish government opening field hospitals on the border for those injured by Loyalist terror. Westminster's deployment of soldiers – within the confines of the British state – should have exacted an immediate and comprehensive response from Unionist leaders. There was a window when more decisive action could have averted much of what followed. Just a handful of years from the mid-1960s until the early 1970s set the pattern for the following three decades' worth of chaos. The injustices of the Stormont regime should have been challenged and the demands of the civil rights movement should have been granted without qualification or hesitation. British ministers should have made it abundantly clear that Terence O'Neill was Unionism's last chance. Northern Ireland's very existence was on the table. If the place did not fall into line and start behaving like the rest of Britain, then it could not remain part of it. Clearly, there was pressure exerted by Harold Wilson, James Callaghan and other ministers behind closed doors, but this should have been done publicly. A tougher message from Britain – spelling out the existential penalty that an unreformed Northern Ireland would incur – might have helped liberal Unionists to fend off the Paisleyite ultras. Modernisation was O'Neill's central theme; so, then, why not amplify his message? If Northern Ireland does not change then Northern Ireland will not continue to exist. No half measures or coded language; the place was an embarrassment and reform had to come, whether hard-line Unionists liked it or not.

There would be no further abuses of power. Power-sharing was a basic requirement. Fiddling electoral boundaries would end. Housing would be allocated on need. Discrimination against Catholics over jobs must stop. Sectarianised policing could not continue. Of course, some of this did start to happen following the Cameron Report ('Disturbances in Northern Ireland') into what generated the violence in 1969, but there was still too little pace in the progression of events. There needed to be a conscious shift away from events of the past. A loud, visible change of direction. No false equivalence: Unionism was in the wrong, had behaved appallingly and would have to concede. The first swing of a police baton at Burntollet Bridge should have been enough. Battered and driven off the highways by the RUC and the B-Specials with their Sunday suits covered in blood, the footage of the civil rights marchers on the streets of Derry and Belfast could easily be interchanged with those from Pretoria or Mississippi. The motivation for stopping these protestors was, in any case, identical: stop change and progress through state brutality. But this was a new generation of Catholics who had been to grammar school and university and had an international outlook. This was not a movement hewn out of the same tradition as earlier Catholic protest vehicles. This was the Northern Ireland branch of the successful US protest movement. Did Unionists not get the memo? We shall overcome.

If there had been greater urgency and more certainty, we might have headed off the Troubles. As James Callaghan noted in his autobiography: 'Looking back, I would fix the short period from 1963 to 1966 as the three years when Northern Ireland had its best chance to prevent the bombings and shootings of the 1970s and 1980s. But the chance was lost.'[5] As he pointed out, 'it was not until 1969 that the Ulster Unionists could bring themselves to concede the elementary right of universal adult suffrage'. If they had been more 'far-sighted and generous' and had allowed O'Neill 'to bring forward the reforms that simple justice demanded', the Troubles might have been averted.[6]

In fact, I would go further: it would have helped Unionism to embrace the civil rights agenda; to take the initiative and make the necessary reforms and, perhaps, provide Northern Ireland with a clearer, long-term future. Instead of limping across the finish line, perhaps this centenary year would see North-ern Ireland flourishing. Perhaps the hatred and division of the Stormont years would, by now, have become a distant memory, something that affected earlier generations. With the appalling events of the Troubles largely avoided, Northern Ireland would now be a quiet backwater, having outgrown demands for unifi-cation and a new generation of political leaders, unsullied by the torment of the past, governing in the common interest.

Just as significant a failing was to allow Loyalists to destroy the Sunningdale Agreement in 1974. It was the last, best attempt at a settlement before the Good Friday Agreement. Of course, Seamus Mallon's quip that the Good Friday Agreement was 'Sunningdale for slow learners' was brilliantly accurate. However, by allowing the mob to desecrate it, this guaranteed that all subsequent attempts at a political settlement were doomed to failure. The benchmark had been established. There had to be genuine power-sharing and an all-Ireland dimension. But Unionists – post Prime Minister Brian Faulkner – were having none of it. Rejecting these basic principles meant that the ground was thus tainted and nothing else would grow in it. Abandoning Sunningdale was a massive strategic error. The years that followed were scarred by grotesque violence conducted by the IRA, Loyalists and the British Army. There was no prospect of a political settlement or an end to the carnage until the dialogue between John Hume and Gerry Adams bore fruit in the early 1990s and the seeds of the peace process were planted, which brought us back to a settlement that bore all the hallmarks of Sunningdale from a generation earlier.

What a waste. Not only measured in fruitless decades stretching out with little sign of agreement, but an appalling waste of life. Thousands dead and tens of thousands maimed. Just as a coda to this point, it is worth reflecting on the lifespan of Northern Ireland's political figures. They seem to go on for ever. Gerry Adams, for instance, must appear in more biographies and memoirs of British political figures from the 1970s to the present day than just about anyone else, having first emerged as a key player in the Cheyne Walk talks with Willie Whitelaw in 1972. By and large, the Troubles were fought by young people with their whole lives ahead of them. Those with most to lose lost most: Republicans, Loyalists and British soldiers. This partly explains why progress following the Good Friday Agreement has been sporadic. Many of these people are still active in political life, which has often held back the process of reconciliation. In their defence, many of them have also been the strongest proponents of the agreement and worked behind the scenes to keep the following generation from sliding back towards conflict.

But violence begets violence. The deployment of British soldiers to 'aid the civil power' as Northern Ireland's decrepit system of government struggled to cope with the consequences of its own actions simply heaped the pyre. It was possibly the single worst decision of the Troubles. Soldiers quickly became an extension of the decades-long Unionist abuse of power. A symbol of oppression. The sectarian state was now militarised and directed against the Catholic minority. Civic Nationalism, with its marches and peace songs, gave way to the Republican 'physical force' tradition as Catholic ghettos fought back. The

Irish spirit of rebellion was once again stirred against British troops.

Westminster, oblivious to the failings of Unionist rule, sleep-walked into what became three decades of ceaseless violence within the confines of the British state itself. This was a different Britain back then. One that, itself, was ruled by an *ancien régime* mindset, lost in time as its empire crumbled around it, along with its global reach. One where discrimination and racism were commonplace. Where Irish jokes and mistrust of Catholicism were still widespread. There was sympathy, granted, for Ulster's Catholics, certainly for fellow baby boomers across the Irish Sea. But there was little general sympathy for the querulous Irish and their eternal battle to boot out the British from their land.

So, atrocities came and went. Bloody Sunday – which turbo-charged the IRA – was met with a shameful British cover-up by the then Lord Chief Justice, Lord Widgery. Internment without trial, in which hundreds of ordinary Catholic men were rounded up, was implemented without much dissent in the House of Commons, despite being more akin to the modus operandi of an Eastern European dictatorship. 'Shoot to kill' and the suppression of an entire community were officially sanctioned. Exclusion orders. The Prevention of Terrorism Act. Diplock courts. Supergrass trials. A dirty war and a secret one was initiated in lieu of any political leadership emanating from Westminster.

'The acceptable level of violence', as Reginald Maudling in-elegantly referred to the situation, saw the British state try to contain the outpourings from its failed Northern Ireland policy.

British towns and cities were also sacrificed for this show of machismo. Hundreds of innocent people died upholding a failed containment policy. Yes, at the hands of the IRA, but this did not occur in a vacuum. It happened because there was no political plan for that benighted, marginal part of the United Kingdom. Let us be in no doubt: Unionist misrule created the mess. Unionist misrule gave birth to the IRA. Unionist misrule was the core of the problem. There was never a 'golden age' for Northern Ireland. It was bad from the start, things plateaued out for a few decades and then nosedived. Those austere men of Ulster Unionism created a failed state and could not respond to reasonable demands for its reform. But some bear greater responsibility than others.

When describing Ian Paisley, some things need to be said at the outset. He was a bully and a bigot; viciously anti-Catholic and opposed to co-operation or the granting of equal rights to his hated foes. He was a man out of time who still managed to personify an age, casting a pall over Northern Ireland from the mid-1960s until the turn of the twenty-first century. Fundamentally, however, Ian Paisley was a fascist. I say this not for the shock value or to unnecessarily traduce the late DUP founder. No, the remark is purely descriptive. Paisley deployed his demagogic talent and lurid, sectarian rhetoric to demonise Catholics and scapegoat them for Northern Ireland's ills. His was the politics of division. Of whipping up the mob.[7] That he did so in his characteristically voluminous manner, with his blood-curdling Old Testament rhetoric, merely added to his notoriety. Easy for outsiders to mock, with his hulking presence, Brylcreemed hair and bulging eyes, Paisley's maniacal power over loyalists was genuine.

Jailed twice for public order offences, he and his followers were the mirror opposite of the civil rights movement. They met the call for equality with a defiant cry to maintain inequality. His 'othering' of Catholic–Nationalists from the late 1960s (when there was no IRA to speak of) had a toxic and lethal effect. Addressing a Loyalist rally in 1968, he claimed that Catholic homes had caught fire because they were 'loaded with petrol bombs'.[8] Catholic churches were 'arsenals' and priests 'handed out sub-machine guns to parishioners'. On another occasion, he told a different Loyalist gathering that Catholics 'breed like rabbits and multiply like vermin'. To anyone looking on from outside Northern Ireland, Paisley was a cartoon character – some crazy guy, ranting and raving on the news. The small print hardly mattered – is it any wonder there was a problem over there with people like him stirring it up? A 'reverend' because he established his own church, the tiny, fundamentalist Free Presbyterians, and a 'doctor' courtesy of his honorary PhD from the fundamentalist Bob Jones University of South Carolina (which barred interracial dating until 2000). Paisley was, by any measure, an extremist, and his malevolent influence, dedicated to sowing division and fear, undermined any prospect of normal politics in Northern Ireland for three decades.

He was not particularly bothered about holding office, just in making it as difficult as possible for those who did. Under Paisley, the DUP did everything it could to destroy moderate Unionist leaders and derail attempts at power-sharing with

Catholic–Nationalists. The W. B. Yeats line about how the best people were those who lacked all conviction 'while the worst are full of passionate intensity' could have been written with the intra-Unionist politics of the Troubles in mind. Paisley was loathed by large parts of the Unionist establishment as he cut the ground from beneath them. The passive grandees and pin-striped ex-officer types of the Ulster Unionist Party were simply no match for 'Dr No' and his superlative rabble-rousing. His black-and-white puritanism played well with the gunmen of the Loyalist paramilitaries. For Paisley, Catholics were the enemy within. Disloyal Papist renegades who must be constantly confronted. As we can see from a long line of Unionist politicians – from Carson and Craig a century ago through to the Loyalist paramilitaries who have announced a withdrawal of support for the Good Friday Agreement in protest at the Brexit-inspired border in the Irish Sea – the threat of violence is never far away. Paisley's implicit – and often explicit message – was that the ends justified the means. Although he is easy to dismiss as a kind of pantomime villain, he caused irreparable damage and killed off attempts at sensible, incremental reform time and time again. Terence O'Neill, writing his memoirs as early as 1971, described his 'great personal sorrow' that his attempts to bring about reconciliation were 'wrecked by wicked men' like Ian Paisley.[9]

More recently, the leader of the Progressive Unionist Party, Billy Hutchinson, a convicted UVF killer turned stalwart of the peace process, excoriated Paisley, observing that there were 'plenty of young fellas [who] ended up in Long Kesh [the precursor to HM Prison Maze] who would never have been there if it hadn't been for Paisley's sectarian rhetoric'.[10] Hutchinson recalled berating Martin McGuinness over his fellow 'Chuckle Brother'. McGuinness was apparently defending Paisley's contribution to government, only for Hutchinson to remind the deputy First Minister that Paisley 'was the biggest recruiting sergeant your guys ever had!' Indeed, Hutchinson stated: 'If Paisley had given the same public support to some of the violent actions that he had advocated in private over the years, he would have been the UVF's brigadier.'[11]

As a Protestant cleric, Paisley of course rejected the Catholic notion of transubstantiation – that bread and wine becomes the literal body and blood of Jesus Christ in the Eucharist. He had a similar logic when it came to terror. Paisley hid behind the pretence that when he whipped up hatred against Catholics, consorted with and inspired Loyalist killers, he did not become one of them. As Hutchinson attested, Catholics were killed because of a chain of events that led all the way back to Paisley framing them as the mortal enemy of Loyalists.

In September 2019, BBC Northern Ireland's respected *Spotlight* programme reported the remarks of a former British Army officer who claimed Paisley had helped finance Loyalist bomb attacks in 1969. Major David Hancock recounted how an RUC district inspector told him that Paisley had supplied money for the UVF bombings of water and electricity installations, which they intended to blame on the IRA in a bid to heap pressure on Terence O'Neill's government. Major Hancock was quoted by the programme saying: 'I was good friends with the district inspector down in Kilkeel. He showed me the evidence that they had of the involvement of money from Paisley into what was then called the UVF, where they got the explosives from, how it was carried out, who did it and why.' (It is unlikely this claim will ever be satisfactorily determined one way or the other given the passage of time, and it is only reasonable to point out that his son, the DUP politician Ian Paisley Jr, rejected the BBC's findings.)[12]

And just when Paisley's influence seemed irredeemably baleful, he went and did something useful; noble, even. His temper curbed by old age, or perhaps by the vestigial ambition of a man who had never held political office and needed to satisfy his curiosity, Paisley performed a singular task in bringing his Democratic Unionists, by then the cocks of the Unionist walk, to the table and into government in 2007 with Martin McGuiness and Sinn Féin, to the general betterment of all. 'We don't need Englishmen to rule us. We can do that ourselves,' he is said to have remarked to McGuinness.[13] For this was one of the other ironies of Ian Paisley. Like Sir Edward Carson, he considered himself an Irishman. An Ulsterman, to be precise, and while his fealty to the Crown was certain, he was not British in the conventional, uncomplicated way that people living in England would recognise the term.

Conversion or opportunism, it did not really matter – with the DUP now on the inside, the Troubles were properly over and a real measure of political stability was locked in. But it came at a price. As founder of the Free Presbyterian Church, Paisley had been elected moderator of the church for fifty-seven years in succession. In 2008 he was pressured out. '*Ardens sed virens*' is the motto of his church, which features alongside a motif of the burning bush through which God spoke to Moses. This translates as 'burning yet flourishing'. As Paisley belatedly flourished in politics, his congregation burnt him at the stake. In the end, there were people more unremittingly hard-line than him.

*   *   *

So, this system of government – Stormont – was built without the essential elements of equity and reasonableness to make a Northern Ireland polity sustainable. The lack of basic generosity exhibited by successive Unionist governments, drawing from the poisoned well of a community that felt able to discriminate against Catholics as a birthright, meant that Stormont was always doomed to collapse. The surprising thing is that anyone was surprised. What was ironic, however, was that it was Edward Heath's Conservative government that brought out the dustpan and brush. The horror of Bloody Sunday – not least the television images of the atrocity beamed around the world – meant that Stormont had to go. Unionists could not be trusted to run their own affairs any longer. They were too corrupt. Too mean-spirited. Too incompetent. They had dropped a mess that they had spent five decades cultivating into the in-tray of a British Prime Minister. He acted ruthlessly, despatching his Home Secretary, Reginald Maudling, to Belfast to end this failed experiment in devolution. From a representative of the Conservative and *Unionist* Party, the sentiment was telling. The scale of Unionists' failing was such that one of their own came to shut them down.

British politicians usually get off lightly. Writing this book and ploughing through the turgid memoirs of our political leaders from the 1970s and 1980s, I have been struck by the tone of their remarks about Northern Ireland, events with which they were intimately involved. What is striking is the dissociative tone that is used. Guarded and formal, they relayed the reasonableness of their approach with the inherently unreasonable nature of Northern Ireland's idiosyncratic political class. There are warm words about the place and the people and about the civil servants and military chiefs they worked with, but the parties are usually depicted as the problem. When they reach the part where they describe how their own initiative for restoring local rule proved futile, there is a weary resignation that they did their best and that the warring paddies – of green or orange variety – were simply impossible people to deal with. Two communities, riven by their implacable conviction that the ground beneath their feet should belong in one state or another. I suspect British ministers – professional politicians – felt a significant measure of in-adequacy that they were unable to tame the furies of either side. That is, if they ever really understood them in the first place. (In the case of Theresa May's Secretary of State, Karen Bradley, there is little doubt that she did not, after freely admitting that before arriving in the job she was not aware that 'Nationalists don't vote for Unionist parties and vice versa').[14]

Wilson. Heath. Callaghan. Thatcher. Major. Blair. Northern Ireland's Troubles lasted the length of six premierships be-tween 1968 and 1998. Thirty years. Nine parliaments. Over 3,500 dead. Mostly, the twenty-two Secretaries of State for Northern

Ireland have been unimpressive political figures. Too few of the postholders achieved anything of substance. In that respect, they joined a long and ignominious line of Lord-Lieutenants and Chief Secretaries for Ireland – stretching back to the twelfth century (which makes the modern variant of the role one of the oldest continuous positions in British government). The purpose of the Secretary of State in recent decades has been to pursue Whitehall's unofficial policy towards Northern Ireland: 'try to keep a lid on things'; 'tread water'; 'do not make things worse'. The job has boiled down to co-ordinating the security response and trying, where there was a hint of an opportunity, to move the politics forward. Throughout the 1970s and 1980s, progress in this regard was glacial. The aim, then, was to make it look as though ministers were at least in charge, gaslighting the British public into thinking that the deployment of soldiers, armoured vehicles, gun-toting police, reinforced Land Rovers, razor-wire barricades, army helicopters, checkpoints, roadblocks, detention centres, police fortresses, water cannon and plastic bullets was entirely normal. And it bears repeating that water cannon and plastic bullets have never been deployed anywhere else in Britain.

The periodic shootings and bombings, rioting and kneecappings became everyday occurrences. Anyone outside Northern Ireland would recognise that these were hardly normal experiences for people in any society to contend with. Yet contend with them the poor people of Northern Ireland had to. Following the Good Friday Agreement, the overall quality of the ministers sent to deal with the situation did improve as something closer to normal life blossomed. By this stage, there was a greater need for adroit handling to bed in the delicate settlement that had been so painstakingly agreed.

So, how did the two main parties of government differ in their approach? Superficially, the Conservatives were harsher on the IRA and Labour was tougher on Unionists. The 'bipartisan' approach to handling Northern Ireland that is often referred to has merely meant a lack of imagination on behalf of either side, with both main parties' records tending to tally when weighed and measured. It was the Conservatives that shut down Stormont, held the first face-to-face talks with the IRA, did the heavy lifting on Sunningdale, signed the Anglo-Irish Agreement and opened backdoor channels to the IRA from the 1980s onwards. At Tony Blair's behest, Chris Patten, the former Conservative Cabinet minister and party chairman, led the 1998 review into policing that gutted the RUC and created the Police Service of Northern Ireland in its place, with quotas for the number of Catholic recruits. Granted, the Conservatives are also the party that was in power during the hunger strike, internment and Bloody Sunday, but the records of British governments between the 1970s and the 1990s are broadly interchangeable.

Willie Whitelaw, the first Secretary of State for Northern Ireland, was, in many respects, the most astute. His interventions to help end Billy McKee's hunger strike in 1972 and to invite the IRA delegation over for talks showed imagination and were not without criticism from his own side. (Patrician Conservatives like Whitelaw and Peter Brooke show that basic cordiality can often open sealed doors.) James Prior waded through treacle in the early 1980s after inheriting the job from the hapless Humphrey Atkins, on whose dismal watch the hunger strike had taken place. Prior was responsible for granting the main demands of Republican prisoners and trying to move the situation on with his proposals for 'rolling' devolution. Margaret Thatcher's record remains opaque. She was an implacable opponent of the IRA and showed not an ounce of regret over her policy towards the hunger strike. Michael Foot, the then Labour leader, came to visit her 'asking for concessions to the strikers'. Her response? 'I told Michael Foot that he had shown himself to be a "push-over",' she recorded in her memoirs.[15] She did, however, manage to concede that, while opposing their cause, it was 'possible to admire the courage of Sands and the other hunger strikers who died'.[16] Tellingly, her later U-turn on granting many of the prisoners' key demands merits just a single line in her 914-page autobiography: 'I authorised some further concessions on clothing, association and loss of remission. But the outcome was a significant defeat for the IRA.'[17]

Thatcher's thought process in signing the Anglo-Irish Agreement remains fascinating. Surely she recognised the anguish she would cause to Unionists by formalising a role for Dublin in Northern Ireland's affairs? Yet she did it anyway; facing down the concerted efforts of the Ulster Unionists and Paisley's DUP, enduring their cacophonous opposition to it. She conceded to being taken aback by Unionist hostility, but either her political antennae were not well-calibrated for interpreting the mood in Unionists circles, or she was far more pragmatic than is usually recognised and simply sensed an opportunity to move the situation forward by working more closely with the Irish government to the benefit of Britain. Her autobiography is elliptical about her motivation; however, she did admit that the agreement had not achieved its aim – in her eyes – of locking Dublin and Nationalist sentiment into more concerted action against the IRA.

Speaking in a parliamentary debate six months after the hunger strike, Thatcher remarked: 'Northern Ireland is part of the United Kingdom – as much as my constituency is.'[18] This is usually quoted as her claiming that Northern Ireland was 'as British as Finchley' (the name of her constituency throughout her time in Parliament). The phrase comes up with predictable regularity and is usually employed scornfully to excoriate the gracelessness of her claim, or, more usually, to emphasise how hollow the sentiment was. In effect, Margaret Thatcher's approach to Northern Ireland was as tactical and contradictory as Callaghan's, Wilson's and Heath's. There was an absence of the clear-sighted ideological fervour that characterised her domestic agenda, or, for that matter, her resoluteness when it came to geo-political affairs during the Cold War. In that respect, Thatcherism did not apply to Northern Ireland.

Of course, she mouthed all the usual platitudes, condemning acts of terrorism in the expected manner, but then cut a deal with Dublin. The Anglo-Irish Agreement provided the fulcrum upon which subsequent political developments would be built, culminating in the Good Friday Agreement some fourteen years later. The timeline is instructive. Thatcher signed the agreement just weeks after the IRA attack that saw her nearly murdered at the Conservative Party conference. She may have been the cold, unflinching premier who refused the demands of those on the hunger strike, while allowing the SAS to assassinate an unarmed IRA unit in Gibraltar, but she was also the Prime Minister who quietly acceded to the striker's demands later, while starting a secret dialogue with the Provisional IRA, while publicly protesting there would never be any dialogue with terrorists.

Her approach to the hunger strike of 1981 merits further discussion. What was the government's strategy? It was a tactic that Irish Republicans had used before. Just letting it play out was a counsel of despair (which is what Whitelaw concluded a decade earlier). Indeed, previous form would have told Thatcher that the prisoners had the determination to see it through to its awful, agonising conclusion. Moreover, it was clear that allowing them to do so would have ramifications for both the security situation as well as diminishing the prospect of political development, either with Irish Nationalists in the north or with relations with Dublin. And what was astonishing was that the 'demands' of Republican prisoners were so modest. The right to free assembly inside Europe's most secure prison was neither here nor there. As was the issue of allowing prisoners to wear their own clothes. Did ministers miscalculate in assuming that Bobby Sands could be pressurised or seduced into relenting? Did they believe that no man would die over such a seemingly mundane issue? Even assuming the hearts of right-wing Conservative politicians did not warm towards the hunger strikers and that their welfare was low down on their list of concerns, the practical ramifications of their deaths meant that stopping them from dying was simply smart politics – not least because it made the task of governing Northern Ireland even harder, evidenced by the troop surge that was immediately required.[19] Then there was the international embarrassment. Did Margaret Thatcher look tough? Or just incapable of managing her own backyard? The replacement of Humphrey Atkins with James Prior allowed the hunger strike to end. He simply relented and granted their demands. With an earlier stroke of a ministerial pen, the situation could have been avoided.

So, what about Labour? The party was in power for twelve years between 1964 and 1979, and these were critical times. The prelude to the Troubles as the civil rights movement grew, right the way through to the cusp of the hunger strike. Harold Wilson sent in the troops in 1969. He also introduced the Prevention of Terrorism Act in 1974 that later facilitated the brutal inter-rogations and rushed convictions of the Birmingham Six and Guildford Four. His Secretary of State, Merlyn Rees, removed special category status from prisoners in HM Prison Maze, thus triggering the blanket protest and then the dirty protest. His successor, Roy Mason, was a swaggering brute who was quite open about having little interest in developing a political pro-cess. He was just there to sock it to the IRA. The British Labour Party, as all political parties are, was a broad coalition of interests in those days. There were many Labour MPs deeply sympathetic to the situation that Northern Ireland's Catholics found them-selves in, but the party also represented many working-class Protestant areas where, bluntly, sympathy ran dry. 'The Labour Party owes more to Methodism than to Marxism,' as Wilson once declared.[20] There was most definitely a whiff of anti-Popery in British society in those years, even on the British left.[21] Anyway, the party was more interested in Vietnam protests than civil rights marches in Derry and Belfast. The party's left was usually a safer bet when it came to empathising with, or at least even showing a basic interest in, what went on; but only through the prism of anti-colonialism. This served to dichotomise the argument, with the right of the Conservative Party claiming the cause of Unionists and the Labour left doing much the same for Sinn Féin. It served to ghettoise the whole issue; the centre of gravity in British politics never had much time for Northern Ireland. A similar reluctance to get involved was evident in the British trade union movement. It is hard to see any telling intervention by union leaders during the 1960s and 1970s when they enjoyed massive political influence.

Wilson himself was clearly in favour of Irish unity. His fifteen-year plan for achieving it, devised in the early 1970s, remains the most serious examination of the issue from a British Prime Minister. Moreover, his remarks about Loyalists being the 'spongers on British democracy' following the collapse of Sunningdale remain the harshest rebuke we have seen from a British Prime Minister. Would he have impugned the motivations of British trade unionists, who were capable of similar levels of disruption, in the same manner? Of course not. It was yet another example of 'what goes on in Northern Ireland, stays in Northern Ireland'. He could say anything he liked with no comeback or electoral ramifications. His successor, James Callaghan, displayed little interest in the place. This may seem strange. With his ruddy face and white hair, Callaghan was un-mistakably of Irish stock. He recorded in his memoirs that his Catholic father, a seaman, was refused permission to marry his mother, who was a Protestant. 'My father robustly said that if he had to choose between the Church and my mother, then he would have nothing further to do with the Church.'[22] As a result, Callaghan and his sister were brought up as Baptists. There was a similar lost antecedent with his Chancellor of the Exchequer – and Defence Secretary when the troops were sent in – Denis Healey. He recorded in his memoirs that his grandfather had been a Fenian and his father 'made him rage at the iniquities of the Black and Tans'. Indeed, Healey recounted that during a public meeting while out campaigning in the 1945 general elec-tion, his father got up to ask the party's position on Irish unity. 'I was flabbergasted,' Healey wrote. 'It never struck me that Irish unity could be a matter for political debate in Britain. Twenty years later I discovered I was wrong.'[23] So, then, a Callaghan and a Healey in charge of a Labour government that had little feel for Northern Ireland, nor much real affinity with its beleaguered Catholic minority.

It is easy, then, to see how the British governments of those years under- and over-reacted to events. No one had a strategy or much instinct for the key issues. They were not invested in finding a long-term solution, just in short-term political fire-fighting. It has been the same story for the past century, with every government hoping to forestall any further deterioration in matters before handing over to their successors. Perhaps it helps explain the career prospects of Secretaries of State for

Northern Ireland. For nine of the twenty-two postholders, it was their last job in government. (Francis Pym, the shortest serving postholder, seemed to overlook that he was even Secretary of State, declining to mention it at all in his memoirs.)

What has been the British attitude towards Northern Ireland? Indeed, has the place registered much at all? During the Troubles it was a warzone and occasionally the cause of terror on British streets; but before that, for much of the first fifty years after partition, it was little more than an afterthought. Asked what they thought of Carson, most Brits would assume you meant Frank, not Sir Edward. Outside of cities where there has been a level of spillover from Ireland, like Glasgow and Liverpool, there is little register. The start of the civil rights era in the late 1960s is the first time that most British people would have given any thought to Northern Ireland. And what an introduction. Peaceful protestors beaten off the streets by the Royal Ulster Constabulary's B-Specials. There it was, on the television, in plain view. These were not ordinary decent coppers; they were an armed militia bent on cracking skulls. What had those nice young students and respectable-looking middle-aged marchers done to deserve this? They were singing protest songs and demanding modest concessions like fair voting and even-handed housing policies. They could not have been more reasonable if they had tried, drawing inspiration from the non-violence of Martin Luther King and Mahatma Gandhi.

Of course, events moved rapidly, or deteriorated precipitously, to be more precise. The experience of the British people became grimly familiar. Soldiers sent into a conflict that few ever understood. Shootings and bombings of the most horrendous kind and with a punishing monotony. Eventually, the violence escalated and expanded. Northern Ireland's Troubles headed westward across the Irish Sea. The degree to which British politics and society internalised this turn of events now seems extraordinary. From the early 1970s until the mid-1990s, the Troubles also played out on British streets as the IRA exported its campaign to what newscasters gratingly referred to as 'the mainland'. The British public was eventually dragged in and forced to share the experience. Instead of baulking at the prospect, we just accepted it. The 'ring of steel' around central London. The absence of rubbish bins on train station platforms. The bomb threats and evacuations. The actual bombings and the trickle of thick red blood snaking all the way back to partition.

Most Irish people in Britain were as appalled by the bombings of the IRA as anyone else. Many were caught up in them. Labour's former deputy leader Roy Hattersley, a Member of Parliament in Birmingham, described the reaction in the city's Irish club on the night of the pub bombing in 1974: 'Many of the victims – nineteen dead and 182 injured – were Irish.'[24] A recent attack in nearby Coventry had seen an IRA volunteer killed in a premature explosion. The local council had banned an honour guard for him and there was a delay in flying his body back to Ireland, which eventually took place on the same day as the pub bombings. The Irish in Britain were no less severe than the English in their judgement about the IRA's bombing campaign. 'That night an Irish piper who had been at the Birmingham airport to play a lament for the body ... was thrown through the glass door of the Birmingham Irish Club by Irishmen,' Hattersley recorded. The effects on the community of Irish-born people and their children and grandchildren – far more numerous than the entire population of Northern Ireland – were deep and often raw. Having struggled to establish a foothold in British society through the various waves of immigration since the Great Famine in the 1840s, the Troubles made them targets for scorn. It paid to keep your head down if you had an Irish accent or surname, or red hair, for that matter. Assimilation for a predominantly White minority community was reasonably straightforward, made easier by the tendency for the children of immigrants to want to fit in. Perhaps it was the smart move. The Troubles in Northern Ireland were an often personal and uncomfortable experience for the Irish in Britain too. The co-founder of *The Guinness Book of Records*, the right-wing campaigner Ross McWhirter (who was killed by the IRA in 1975), once suggested that Irish people living in Britain should be compelled to register with the local police and supply photographs of themselves when they wanted to rent a property or check into a hotel.[25] And there cannot have been many households where the cases of the Birmingham Six, the Guildford Four and the Maguire Seven were not only causes célèbres but salutary warnings. The boom in Irish retail culture from the mid-1990s onwards, coinciding with the peace process, altered all that. Irish-themed pubs seemed to spring up everywhere. St Patrick's Day festivals became a de rigueur affectation in our major city centres. It did not matter that Irish tradition was being appropriated, with pipers marching alongside Chinese dragons and the like; it was still evidence of progress. Even when the IRA ceasefire collapsed in 1996 and we saw the bombing of Manchester, the second-largest bomb exploded in Britain since the Second World War, the vibe remained positive (although the van containing the bomb was left near to Paddy's Rat and Carrot, an Irish-themed pub in central Manchester). Yes, the immediate media coverage had a 'hang IRA scum' tone to it, but a couple of weeks later there was a competition to redevelop the bomb-damaged Arndale Centre.

As a country, Britain became inured to the inherent insanity of the problem. The media dutifully reported this episodic horror show. We tutted and carried on. 'Normal for Northern Ireland.' Everyone ran out of superlatives to describe the death and pain brought to so many families. (Some enterprising media studies student will one day reveal that the politicians, army and police had a rotating list of tributes and denunciations to avoid repeating themselves too often.) What was wrong with these people? Did they enjoy slaughtering each other? Or was it simply that conflict was hard-wired into Northern Ireland? It was, fundamentally, a failure of politicians over many decades to take the right, courageous steps when they should have done. Other choices were possible during this century of division. Lloyd George was ultimately content to see Northern Ireland fade away, while at the start of the Second World War, Churchill offered up the prospect of Irish unity if the Irish government would allow Britain to station troops on the island to guard its western flank. As previously explored, Harold Wilson wanted a fifteen-year timetable for unification. Thatcher for ever lashed Northern Ireland to the south by signing the Anglo-Irish Agreement, making it easier for John Major and Tony Blair to later secure the Good Friday Agreement settlement, which provided a blueprint for the peaceful unification of Ireland.

Westminster's mercurial handling of the Irish question is a record of missed signals, squandered opportunities and bad choices. The chance of an honourable compromise, hammered out on the floor of the House of Commons, was wasted. After that, the options only got worse. But there was nothing ineluctable about the creation of Northern Ireland, nor, indeed, the history that it has bequeathed. These 'what if?' moments remain entirely plausible given many were options on the table at the time. You do not need the wisdom of hindsight to see that. A different future, at so many points over the past 100 years, was possible. Having spent the first two-thirds of the past century trying to ignore Northern Ireland, the past twenty-five years have been about gently teeing-up its departure. From the British perspective, the next phase is to wait for a tilt in support for Irish unity in Northern Ireland and a signal that Dublin is ready to step up and take on its historic responsibility. Any British Prime Minister will, at that stage, be supremely enthusiastic about doing whatever is necessary to expedite this process.

Yet, we have the history we have, and each participant in Northern Ireland's story has their own explaining to do for how we arrived at this point. Every side has blood on their hands. No one is exempted. Republicans. Loyalists. Unionist and Nationalist leaders. Westminster and Dublin politicians. Every participant in its troubled and turbulent century has their own moral agency; their own personal responsibility for what they have done and what they have failed to do. Once the killing starts, politics becomes impossible. Minds close and hearts harden. And yet the paradox is that, in such a moment, politics becomes more vital too. Whatever the shortcomings of devolved working in Northern Ireland, it is still infinitely preferable to anything that went before it. Fundamentally, however, Northern Ireland was not built to endure. Over the next few years, that will become all too apparent.

ACKNOWLEDGEMENTS

The violence and suffering that has characterised Northern Ireland's century of division serves as an eternal warning never to pass that way again. It also helps to underline what an enormous achievement the Good Friday Agreement was and is. It has not been a process without difficulty and requires regular maintenance, but it is an enduring reminder that even the most difficult and bitter conflicts can be resolved with perseverance, compromise and goodwill.

I would like to thank my family for their forbearance at my general absent-mindedness to other matters during the production of this book. Writing during the Covid-19 lockdown has involved locking myself away in our small dining room-cum-ersatz library for these past few months, foregoing the small pleasure of scribbling away in a coffee shop, library or even a quiet pub.

The results have immeasurably improved with the services of a great editor in James Lilford and all the team at Biteback. My thanks to them for their insight and patience.

Finally, my thanks to you for reading it. The point of a political book is not to please everyone about everything; that is impossible. Rather, the intention is to add a contribution to the larger conversation that helps to move it along. In that endeavour, I hope I have succeeded.

NOTES

INTRODUCTION

1 '"What a bloody awful country!" the Tory story of Ireland', *Irish Independent*, 18 February 2018.

CHAPTER 1: BUILT TO FAIL

1 David George Boyce, *The Irish Question and British Politics, 1868–1986* (Basingstoke: Macmillan, 1988), p. 51.

2 'Copies of Documents Relating to the Proposals for His Majesty's Government for an Irish Settlement', National Archives, CP 3331, http://filestore.nationalarchives.gov.uk/pdfs/small/cab-24-128-CP-3331.pdf (accessed March 2021).

3 G. B. Kenna, *Facts and Figures of the Belfast Pogrom, 1920–1922* (Dublin: Forgotten Books, 1922).

4 Ibid., p. 27.

5 Ibid., p. 42.

6 Reproduced in the appendices of Kenna, *Facts and Figures of the Belfast Pogrom*, p. 175.

7 John Whyte, 'How much discrimination was there under the Unionist regime, 1921–1968?', Conflict Archive on the Internet (CAIN), Ulster University, https://cain.ulster.ac.uk/issues/discrimination/whyte.htm (accessed March 2021).

8 'Civil Authorities (Special Powers) Act (Northern Ireland), 1922', CAIN, https://cain.ulster.ac.uk/hmso/spa1922.htm (accessed March 2021).

9 'A Protestant Parliament for a Protestant People', *History Ireland*, Vol. 16, Issue 2 (March/April 2008).

10 John Whyte, 'How much discrimination was there under the Unionist regime, 1921–1968?', CAIN.

CHAPTER 2: WE SHALL OVERCOME

1 Terence Marne O'Neill, *The Autobiography of Terence O'Neill: Prime Minister of Northern Ireland 1963–1969* (London: Hart-David, 1972), p. 72.

2 Ibid.

3 Ibid., p. 47.

4 Danny Morrison, '"The Tricolour Riots" – 28 September 1964', *An Phoblacht*, 27 September 2014.

5 'A Chronology of Key Events in Irish History, 1800 to 1967', CAIN, https://cain.ulster.ac.uk/othelem/chron/chr1800-1967.htm (accessed March 2021).

6   'John Bull's Political Scum', *Sunday Times*, 3 July 1966.
7   'So, divided we stand: is this as good as it gets?' *Belfast Telegraph*, 7 January 2013.
8   Hansard, House of Commons debate, 22 April 1969, Vol. 782, CC 262–324.
9   Ibid.
10 'Half-a-century on, we've still to learn lessons of Terence O'Neill', *Belfast Telegraph*, 13 January 2015.
11 'Press Briefing of the Foreign Minister of Ireland', 23 April 1969, United Nations Archives, https://search.archives.un.org/uploads/r/united-nations-archives/9/5/4/954f49dc15cf40b1b-d015aa1645da62141315ff636a12bb83b7d22ecd60d2ec7/S-0884-0010-12-00001.pdf (accessed March 2021).
12 'Violence and Civil Disturbances in Northern Ireland in 1969: Report of Tribunal of Inquiry', April 1972, CAIN, https://cain.ulster.ac.uk/hmso/scarman.htm (accessed March 2021).
13 Roy Hattersley, 'Ian Paisley and me', *The Guardian*, 14 May 2007.
14 Ibid.
15 Terence Marne O'Neill, *The Autobiography of Terence O'Neill*, p. xi.

CHAPTER 3: THE POINT OF NO RETURN
1   Hansard, House of Commons debate, Vol. 827, 29 November 1971.
2   'Internment – A Chronology of Main Events', CAIN, https://cain.ulster.ac.uk/events/intern/chron.htm (accessed March 2021).
3   'Bloody Sunday para said shootings were unjustified', *The Guardian*, 16 October 2002.
4   Hansard, House of Commons debate, 31 January 1972, Vol. 830, CC 32–43.
5   Lewis Baston, *Reggie: The Life of Reginald Maudling* (Stroud: Sutton, 2004).
6   '"Bloody Sunday", 30 January 1972 – A Chronology of Events', CAIN, https://cain.ulster.ac.uk/events/bsunday/chron.htm (accessed March 2021).
7   'Obituary of former Vanguard leader Bill Craig', BBC News, 26 April 2011.
8   Ben Pimlott, *Harold Wilson* (London: William Collins, 2016), p. 593.
9   Ibid., p. 594.
10 Mark Garnett, *Splendid! Splendid!: The Authorized Biography of Willie Whitelaw* (London: Jonathan Cape, 2002), p. 137.
11 Ibid., p. 133.
12 Richard Elder Special, '8 Get Life Terms in London Blasts', *New York Times*, 16 November 1973.
13 'UWC Strike – Text of broadcast made by Harold Wilson, 25 May 1974', CAIN, https://cain.ulster.ac.uk/events/uwc/docs/hw25574.htm (accessed March 2021).
14 'IRA Ceasefire: Secret talks and a truce in 1975', *Independent*, 30 March 1994.
15 Roy Mason, *Paying the Price* (London: Robert Hale, 1999), p. 164.
16 In his memoirs, Mason conceded that his abrasive style and lack of rapport with Gerry Fitt, who thought him 'much too close to the army', had an unintended consequence when Fitt voted to bring down Callaghan's minority government in the famous vote of confidence in 1979.

CHAPTER 4: AND ON IT GOES
1   Mary-Louise Muir, 'Good Vibrations', BBC, 15 September 2011.
2   Hansard, House of Commons debate, 20 November 1980, Vol. 994, CC 7–102.
3   'What happened in the hunger strike', BBC News, 5 May 2006.
4   'Violence – List of People Killed by "Rubber" and "Plastic" Bullets', CAIN, https://cain.ulster.ac.uk/issues/violence/rubberplasticbullet.htm (accessed March 2021).
5   'Northern Ireland Political Review', 23 November – 6 December 1981', CAIN, https://cain.ulster.ac.uk/proni/1981/proni_CENT-1-10-91_1981-12-17.pdf (accessed March 2021).
6   'Interview – Author Danny Morrison', *An Phoblacht*, 14 December 2006.
7   'The Northern Ireland Assembly, November 1982 – June 1986 – A Chronology of Main Events', CAIN, https://cain.ulster.ac.uk/events/assembly1982/chronology.htm (accessed March 2021).

8 'Thatcher Rules Our A Unified Ireland, 1984', RTÉ, https://www.rte.ie/archives/2014/1118/660538-out-out-out/ (accessed March 2021).

9 'A Chronology of the Conflict – 1984', CAIN, https://cain.ulster.ac.uk/othelem/chron/ch84.htm (accessed March 2021).

10 Ed Carty, 'Cardinal hit back at Margaret Thatcher after her "lecture"', *Belfast Telegraph*, 30 December 2011.

11 David Hughes, 'Brighton bombing: *Daily Telegraph* journalist recalls', *Daily Telegraph*, 11 October 2009.

12 '1984: Memories of the Brighton bomb', BBC On This Day, http://news.bbc.co.uk/onthisday/hi/witness/october/12/newsid_3665000/3665388.stm (accessed March 2021).

13 Associated Press, 'Irish Scold Thatcher for Ulster Remarks', *New York Times*, 23 November 1984.

14 'A Chronology of the Conflict – 1985', CAIN, https://cain.ulster.ac.uk/othelem/chron/ch85.htm (accessed March 2021).

15 'A Chronology of the Conflict – 1986', CAIN, https://cain.ulster.ac.uk/othelem/chron/ch86.htm (accessed March 2021).

16 'Robinson said to have "lingered" after Clontibret loyalist incursion', *Irish Times*, 20 November 2015.

17 'Gunmen Slay Catholic Businessman', APNews, 17 September 1986, https://apnews.com/article/7a4da918ac958872f0985cc0290add24 (accessed March 2021).

18 'No DUP apology for Ulster Resistance, despite gun-running leading to murders', *Belfast News Letter*, 13 June 2016.

19 'Speech to European Parliament, 9 December 1986', Margaret Thatcher Foundation, https://www.margaretthatcher.org/document/106534 (accessed March 2021).

20 '"Common Sense: Northern Ireland – An Agreed Process" by Ulster Political Research Group', CAIN, https://cain.ulster.ac.uk/issues/politics/docs/commonsense.htm (accessed March 2021).

21 'A Chronology of the Conflict – 1987', CAIN, https://cain.ulster.ac.uk/othelem/chron/ch87.htm (accessed March 2021).

22 'A Scenario for Peace', Sinn Féin, https://www.sinnfein.ie/contents/15210 (accessed March 2021).

23 Roger Bolton, *Death on the Rock and Other Stories* (London: W. H. Allen, 1990), p. 194.

24 'Hogg compromised over RUC briefing', BBC News, 17 April 2003.

25 Ian Cobain, 'Secrecy and Northern Ireland's Dirty War: the murder of Pat Finucane', *Irish Times*, 19 September 2016.

26 'A Chronology of the Conflict – 1989', CAIN, https://cain.ulster.ac.uk/othelem/chron/ch89.htm (accessed March 2021).

CHAPTER 5: THE END IS IN SIGHT

1 'Timeline: Northern Ireland's road to peace', BBC News, 8 November 1987.

2 'Polls of Opinion and Attitude in Northern Ireland, 1973–2004', CAIN, https://cain.ulster.ac.uk/issues/politics/polls.htm (accessed March 2021).

3 'A Chronology of the Conflict – 1991', CAIN, https://cain.ulster.ac.uk/othelem/chron/ch91.htm (accessed March 2021).

4 Ibid.

5 'Labour TD attacks Rhonda Paisley', *Irish Times*, 31 July 1991, quoted in 'A Chronology of the Conflict – 1991', CAIN, and '"I thought it was a parody": Varadkar reacts to Lord's tweet calling him "typical Indian"', TheJournal.ie, 1 May 2018, https://www.thejournal.ie/leo-varadkar-lord-kilclooney-typical-indian-3988745-May2018/ (accessed March 2021).

6 'Polls of Opinion and Attitude in Northern Ireland, 1973–2004', CAIN.

7 Patrick Mayhew's relatives in County Cork had also been supportive of Ireland's bid for freedom in the early twentieth century.

8 Donald Macintyre, 'Interview/Sir Patrick Mayhew: For the love of the Irish: His exterior

seems classically conventional but what lies beneath the upper crust? Donald Macintyre meets Ulster's new man', *The Independent*, 11 July 1992.

9 'British Military Policy during the End Game of the conflict: Implications for women and the present', Relatives for Justice, http://relativesforjustice.com/wp-content/uploads/2013/10/Collusion-and-the-Targeting-of-Women.pdf (accessed March 2021).

10 'A Chronology of the Conflict – 1993', CAIN, https://cain.ulster.ac.uk/othelem/chron/ch93.htm (accessed March 2021).

11 Ibid.

12 Ibid.

13 Ibid.

14 Ibid.

15 Nick Stadlen, 'The Nick Stadlen interview with Gerry Adams: Part 1', *The Guardian*, 12 September 2007.

16 'John Hume/Gerry Adams Statement, 25th September 1993', Sinn Féin, https://www.sinn-fein.ie/contents/15218 (accessed March 2021).

17 Hansard, House of Commons debate, 21 January 1994, Vol. 235.

18 'A Chronology of the Conflict – 1993', CAIN.

19 Hansard, House of Commons debate, 15 December 1993, Vol. 234.

20 Hansard, House of Commons debate, 2 December 1993.

21 Gerry Adams's trip to the US saw Larry King scoop British and Irish broadcasters to secure the first interview with Adams speaking his own words.

22 'UDA "has drawn up Doomsday plan"', *The Herald*, 17 January 1994.

23 Ian S. Wood, *Crimes of Loyalty: A History of the UDA* (Edinburgh: Edinburgh University Press, 2006), pp. 184–5.

24 'James Molyneaux: Obituary of former UUP leader', BBC News, 9 March 2015.

25 'IRA ceasefire remembered 25 years on', *Irish News*, 30 August 2019.

26 'Full Text of Framework Document', University College Cork, https://www.ucc.ie/academic/law/irishlaw/frameworkdoc/full_g.shtml (accessed March 2021).

27 'Major's vision of Ulster peace', *The Independent*, 22 October 2011.

28 'It's Ulster's Eviction Notice, says DUP Chief', University College Cork, https://www.ucc.ie/academic/law/irishlaw/frameworkdoc/frame03.shtml (accessed March 2021).

29 'Gerry Adams: A past that hasn't gone away', BBC News, 18 October 2019.

30 'Proud traditions coming together: Transcript of President Clinton's speech at the Mackie metal plant in Belfast, Northern Ireland', CNN, 30 November 1995, http://edition.cnn.com/WORLD/9511/clinton_ireland/transcript.html (accessed March 2021).

31 'A Chronology of the Conflict – 1996', CAIN, https://cain.ulster.ac.uk/othelem/chron/ch96.htm (accessed March 2021).

32 'St Andrews Agreement', *Irish Times*, 20 October 2006.

33 'A Chronology of the Conflict – 1997', CAIN, https://cain.ulster.ac.uk/othelem/chron/ch97.htm (accessed March 2021).

34 David McKittrick, 'Ulster: Paisley calls on the faithful to pray for deliverance from talks', *The Independent*, 30 September 1997.

35 'A Chronology of the Conflict – 1997', CAIN.

36 'Interview with Bernadette Sands', *Magill*, 1 February 1998.

37 'UK: Northern Ireland Shooting victim knew he was dying', BBC News, 10 November 1999.

38 'A Chronology of the Conflict – 1998', CAIN, https://cain.ulster.ac.uk/othelem/chron/ch98.htm (accessed March 2021).

39 Ibid.

40 'Tony Blair's key quotes', *The Guardian*, 26 April 2007.

41 Mary Holland, 'A very Good Friday', *The Guardian*, 12 April 1998.

42 Ed Moloney, *Paisley: From Demagogue to Democrat?* (Dublin: Poolbeg Press, 2008), p. 357.

CHAPTER 6: MAKING THE BEST OF THINGS

1   Having developed a brain tumour ahead of taking up her role as Northern Ireland Secretary, Mo Mowlam's final years were dogged by ill-health and she died in 2005 at just fifty-five.

2   'The 1998 Referendums', Northern Ireland Elections, https://www.ark.ac.uk/elections/fref98.htm (accessed March 2021).

3   'Then and now: 10 years on from the Belfast Agreement', CAIN, https://cain.ulster.ac.uk/issues/politics/docs/tuv/tuv090408_then_and_now.pdf (accessed March 2021).

4   'Omagh bombing kills 28', BBC News, 16 August 1998.

5   Theresa Judge, 'Bombers "undiluted fascists", says Hume', *Irish Times*, 17 August 1998.

6   David McKittrick, 'Omagh Bombing: Sinn Féin's shift shown by its words', *The Independent*, 23 October 2011.

7   Deaglán de Bréadún, 'Orange Order moves to reprove Trimble', *Irish Times*, 17 December 1998.

8   David Trimble and Seamus Mallon did not get on – the two men being both prickly and curt – and were said to have had their physical offices as far apart as possible.

9   Suzanne Breen, 'Sister of hunger striker denounces peace process as deception', *Irish Times*, 8 January 1998.

10 'Bloody Sunday: PM David Cameron's full statement', BBC News, 15 June 2010.

11 'RHI scandal: RHI "cash for ash" scandal to cost NI taxpayers £490m', BBC News, 23 December 2016.

12 Chris Sherrard, 'Jonathan Bell: "My political life is over... but God doesn't punish those who tell the truth"', BelfastLive, 16 December 2016, https://www.belfastlive.co.uk/news/belfast-news/jonathan-bell-my-political-life-12329635 (accessed March 20210).

13 Robert Newton, 'Full text of Martin McGuinness's resignation letter', *Irish Times*, 9 January 2017.

14 Emily O'Reilly, 'Disarming Martin McGuiness [ii]', *The Guardian*, 6 February 2000.

15 Henry McDonald, 'Ian Paisley and wife speak out over his ousting as DUP leader', *The Guardian*, 20 January 2014.

16 Gerry Moriarty, 'DUP "saddened" Paisley has damaged his political record', *Irish Times*, 21 January 2014.

17 'Arlene Foster becomes first female leader of DUP', *The Guardian*, 17 December 2015.

18 Pamela Duncan, Liz Carolan, Henry McDonald, Severin Carrell and Rajeev Syal, 'DUP spent £282,000 on Brexit ad that did not run in Northern Ireland', *The Guardian*, 24 February 2017.

19 Benjamin Kentish, 'Conservative–DUP talks: "The future's orange" jokes Ian Paisley Jr as Theresa May meets with Arlene Foster', *The Independent*, 13 June 2017.

20 David Young, 'DUP conference cheered Boris Johnson in Titanic-themed speech on Brexit', *Belfast Telegraph*, 17 October 2019.

CHAPTER 7: CENTURY OF DIVISION

1   The five regiments in the British army were the Royal Irish Regiment, the Connaught Rangers, the Leinster Regiment, the Royal Munster Fusiliers and the Royal Dublin Fusiliers.

2   John Dorney, 'The 1798 Rebellion – a brief overview', The Irish Story, https://www.theirishstory.com/2017/10/28/the-1798-rebellion-a-brief-overview/#.YFInoq_7SUk (accessed March 2021).

3   'Nobel Peace Prize – Acceptance Speech by Mr. David Trimble, 10 December 1998', CAIN, https://cain.ulster.ac.uk/events/peace/docs/nobeldt.htm (accessed March 2021).

4   'Speech by Peter Robinson to DUP Annual Conference (26 November 2011)', CAIN, https://cain.ulster.ac.uk/issues/politics/docs/dup/pr261111.htm (accessed March 2021).

5   James Callaghan, *Time and Chance* (London: Collins, 2006), p. 270.

6   Ibid., p. 271. As an aside, Terence O'Neill merits a single entry, and Northern Ireland just three, in Callaghan's 584-page memoir.

7   'Looks like a prop forward and sounds like Hitler' was the verdict on Paisley provided by one visiting journalist in the late 1960s.

8   'Ian Paisley: In quotes', BBC News, 12 September 2014.

9   Terence Marne O'Neill, *The Autobiography of Terence O'Neill*, p. xiv.

10 Billy Hutchinson and Gareth Mulvenna, *My Life in Loyalism* (Newbridge: Merrion Press, 2020), p. 268.

11 Ibid.

12 Freya McClements, '"No Truth" in claims that Paisley gave cash to UVF for bombings', *Irish Times*, 6 September 2019.

13 Gerry Adams, 'Ian Paisley: Northern Ireland's "no" man who said "yes"', *The Guardian*, 12 September 2014.

14 Rory Carroll, 'Karen Bradley admits ignorance of Northern Ireland politics', *The Guardian*, 7 September 2018.

15 Margaret Thatcher, *The Downing Street Years* (London: Harper Collins, 1995), p. 391.

16 Ibid.

17 Ibid., p. 393. The last point about the government defeating the IRA in this regard is ludicrous given the massive international attention and support the hunger strike generated, propelling Sinn Féin into electoral politics and creating problems for Thatcher from that point on.

18 Hansard, House of Commons debate, 10 November 1981, Vol. 12, CC 421–8.

19 One of the oddities of the British approach to governing Northern Ireland was that the Old Bailey bomber, Dolours Price, was released from HM Prison Armagh midway through the strike on health grounds.

20 Susan Ratcliffe (ed.), *Oxford Essential Quotations*, https://www.oxfordreference.com/view/10.1093/acref/9780191826719.001.0001/q-oro-ed4-00008440 (accessed March 2021).

21 Since it was formed 120 years ago, the Labour Party has only ever had a single Catholic leader, John Robert Clynes.

22 James Callaghan, *Time and Chance*, p. 22.

23 Denis Healey, *The Time of My Life* (London: Michael Joseph, 1990), p. 4.

24 Roy Hattersley, *Fifty Years On: A Prejudiced History of Britain Since the War* (London: Abacus, 1997), p. 247.

25 Steven Moysey, *The Road to Balcombe Street: The IRA Reign of Terror in London* (Abingdon: Routledge, 2019), p. 116.

INDEX